# THE TRANSFORMATIVE POWER OF MOBILE MEDICINE

Leveraging Innovation, Seizing Opportunities, and Overcoming Obstacles of mHealth

**PAUL CERRATO**

*Contributing Writer, Medscape, Medpage Today; Former Editor, Information Week Healthcare, Contemporary OB/GYN*

**JOHN HALAMKA**

*International Healthcare Innovation Professor at Harvard Medical School, chief information officer of the Beth Israel Deaconess System*

**ACADEMIC PRESS**

An imprint of Elsevier

Academic Press is an imprint of Elsevier
125 London Wall, London EC2Y 5AS, United Kingdom
525 B Street, Suite 1650, San Diego, CA 92101, United States
50 Hampshire Street, 5th Floor, Cambridge, MA 02139, United States
The Boulevard, Langford Lane, Kidlington, Oxford OX5 1GB, United Kingdom

**Notices**
Knowledge and best practice in this field are constantly changing. As new research and experience broaden our understanding, changes in research methods, professional practices, or medical treatment may become necessary.

Practitioners and researchers must always rely on their own experience and knowledge in evaluating and using any information, methods, compounds, or experiments described herein. In using such information or methods they should be mindful of their own safety and the safety of others, including parties for whom they have a professional responsibility.

To the fullest extent of the law, neither the Publisher nor the authors, contributors, or editors, assume any liability for any injury and/or damage to persons or property as a matter of products liability, negligence or otherwise, or from any use or operation of any methods, products, instructions, or ideas contained in the material herein.

**British Library Cataloguing-in-Publication Data**
A catalogue record for this book is available from the British Library

**Library of Congress Cataloging-in-Publication Data**
A catalog record for this book is available from the Library of Congress

ISBN: 978-0-12-814923-2

For Information on all Academic Press publications
visit our website at https://www.elsevier.com/books-and-journals

 Working together
to grow libraries in
developing countries

www.elsevier.com • www.bookaid.org

*Publisher:* Stacy Masucci
*Acquisition Editor:* Rafael Teixeira
*Editorial Project Manager:* Carlos Rodriguez
*Production Project Manager:* Sreejith Viswanathan
*Cover Designer:* Mark Rogers

Typeset by MPS Limited, Chennai, India

# THE TRANSFORMATIVE POWER OF MOBILE MEDICINE

# DEDICATION

May our philosophies [and values] keep pace with our technologies. May our compassion keep pace with our powers. And may love, not fear, be the engine of change.

Edmond Kirsch, Futurist
(From *Origin*, By Dan Brown)

# CONTENTS

# ABOUT THE AUTHORS

**Paul Cerrato, MA,** has had over 30 years of experience working in healthcare, as a clinician, researcher, author, editor, and college lecturer. The last 7 years have been spent researching and writing about healthcare technology. He has served as an Editor of *Information Week Healthcare*, Executive Editor of *Contemporary OB/GYN*, and Senior Editor of *RN* Magazine. He is the author of *Protecting Patient Information* and the coauthor with John Halamka of *Realizing the Promise of Precision Medicine*. He has been named one of the most influential bloggers in healthcare IT by the Healthcare Information and Management Systems Society (HIMSS).

**John Halamka, MD,** serves as the International Healthcare Innovation Professor at Harvard Medical School. He is also Chief Information Officer of the Beth Israel Deaconess System and a practicing emergency physician. He serves on one of the advisory committees for the Precision Medicine Initiative, which has been funded with $215 million from the US government. He has devoted his career to empowering patients, providers, and payers with mobile-friendly applications exchanging data using international standards.

# PREFACE

## CYNICISM, OPTIMISM, AND TRANSFORMATION

Words are powerful tools, weapons even. They can persuade skeptics, overcome bigotry, wound colleagues, disrupt the status quo, ruin reputations, shatter misconceptions, deceive the uninformed, endear us to loved ones, comfort the grief stricken. The list is almost endless. The three words that are most relevant to our discussion of mobile medicine—cynicism, optimism, and transformation—are no less potent.

Many stakeholders in health care have become cynical about the value of information technology in improving patient care, some of which is justified. Clinicians have valid concerns about the ability of the current crop of electronic health record systems to deliver cost-effective care. Others doubt whether patient-facing mobile apps can effectively engage patients in their own care or lighten the load of practitioners already burdened with too many responsibilities. And many grouse about the seemingly endless list of IT-dependent government regulations that slow them down.

But for many, cynicism has become more than just a reaction to legitimate concerns. It's become a national religion, coloring their view of emerging innovations and potentially transformative technologies. John and I are not members of that sect. While we are both optimists by nature, our enthusiasm for mobile technology is not naivete. Call it evidence-driven optimism. Our combined 60 plus years of work on the clinical and IT sides of medicine have convinced us of the value of clinician-facing and patient-facing mobile apps, telemedicine, remote sensors, and numerous other digital tools.

The comedian Stephen Colbert, in one of his more serious moments, once said, "Cynicism masquerades as wisdom, but it is the farthest thing from it. Because cynics don't learn anything. Because cynicism is a self-imposed blindness, a rejection of the world because we are afraid it will hurt us or disappoint us. Cynics always say no. But saying 'yes' begins things. Saying 'yes' is how things grow."

Like Colbert, our goal in this book is to reject the cynic's view of health care. We are interested in growth. And as our subtitle suggests, that growth entails leveraging emerging innovations, seizing opportunities, and overcoming obstacles to mHealth.

In our previous book, *Realizing the Promise of Precision Medicine*, we demonstrated that mobile medical apps have both "potential and kinetic energy," that is, there's evidence to show that several mHealth initiatives will improve patient care in the near future, and several initiatives have shown mobile medicine is improving patients' lives now. *The Transformative Power of Mobile Medicine* will take this theme into deeper waters, exploring the latest developments in mobile health, including the value of blockchain, the emerging growth of remote sensors in chronic patient care, the potential use of Amazon Alexa and Google Assistant as patient bedside assistants, machine learning, the latest mobile apps being developed in Beth Israel Deaconess Medical Center and elsewhere, and much more. These innovations and opportunities, however, also need to be put into the context of clinical medicine as it is practiced today, which will pose challenges in terms of validation and implementation. With these concerns in mind, we address criticisms and skepticism in the medical community and take a critical look at the published literature on mobile apps in diabetes, heart disease, asthma, cancer, and other common disorders.

Equally important, we discuss the design process for creating new mobile medicine products, exploring successes and failures, the regulatory environment, and the importance of involving clinicians in the design process at every stage.

mHealth initiatives are certainly no panacea, but they represent a new path for clinical medicine and for patient self-care that will have a profound impact for many decades. We hope our words will accomplish all the positive things words have the ability to accomplish, persuading skeptics, disrupting the status quo, shattering misconceptions, and demonstrating the power of evidence-driven optimism.

**Paul Cerrato**

Contributing Writer, Medscape, Medpage Today;
Former Editor, Information Week Healthcare, Contemporary OB/GYN

**John Halamka**

International Healthcare Innovation Professor at Harvard Medical School,
chief information officer of the Beth Israel Deaconess System

# Innovations in mHealth, Part 1: The Role of Blockchain, Conversational Interfaces, and Chatbots

The Merriam-Webster dictionary defines innovation as "the introduction of something new." A better definition would be the novel use of people, process, and technologies to improve quality, safety, and efficiency. Unfortunately, not everyone is eager to embrace such novel improvements. In fact, history is replete with decision makers and influential stakeholders who have resisted such changes.

The Hungarian physician, Ignaz Semmelweis, recommended antiseptic handwashing in the mid-19th century and was ridiculed for his ideas. The use of incubators for premature infants was also rejected by the US medical authorities in the late 19th century, despite the fact that they were being successfully used in Europe for years. It wasn't until 1939 that New York Hospital started a program that incorporated incubators into American hospitals. Similarly, the germ theory of disease, balloon angioplasty, the role of heredity in human health and disease, and the role of sports-induced traumatic brain injury have all been laughed at or delayed by "thought leaders" who had difficulty seeing past their outdated views [1].

The same resistance to innovation exists in technology. Dr. Frederick Terman, former Provost of Stanford University, did foundational work in radio engineering, including the creation of novel amplifier circuits. But when presented with a tiny integrated circuit that did the work of his most complex radio engineering designs at a fraction of the cost, he couldn't understand the technology inside the device and therefore had no interest in it. Similarly, Doris Lessing, when accepting her Nobel Prize, insisted that the Internet was destroying creativity and intelligence because it enabled anyone to be a publisher and removed the rigorous training in the history of literature as a barrier to authorship. Terman and Lessing made invaluable contributions to society but both also had blind spots they could not see past [2].

It's not surprising to find that resistance to new ideas exists within a health-care community still using an outdated "operating system," so to speak. Joseph Kvedar, MD, of Partners Connected Health, sums up the problem succinctly: "The current health-care system—which is based on early twentieth century needs—is a serious mismatch for the challenges we are confronting in the twenty-first century." [3].

*The Transformative Power of Mobile Medicine.*
DOI: https://doi.org/10.1016/B978-0-12-814923-2.00001-5

Today's system has been built around the need to manage infectious diseases, fractures, myocardial infarctions, and other acute problems. While it may be true that these conditions still require attention, the American public's health care needs are experiencing a major shift as obesity, diabetes, hypertension, clinical depression, and other chronic diseases become more prominent. As Kvedar points out:

> The usual practice of writing a prescription for a drug, advising a patient to 'lose weight and get more exercise,' or expecting an individual to successfully follow a recommended diet plan just doesn't work. People need ongoing and consistent support from advisors and authority figures... The right text at the right time, a thoughtful email or televisit from a doctor or medical coach, or a phone call from a nurse monitoring personal health data recorded by the patient sitting at home can prevent a potential problem from spiralling into an expensive and potentially dangerous medical issue.

Embracing new health-care digital tools also means acknowledging the inadequacy of the current way of doing business, a difficult admission for organizations and individuals with a vested interest in maintaining the status quo. Clinicians and decision makers who are willing to venture beyond the constraints of the past can take advantage of several mobile technologies that hold promise, including blockchain, conversational interfaces, such as Amazon's Alexa and Google Assistant, Internet of Things devices, chatbots, and a variety of inventive tools. Many of these tools will help us shift the emphasis away from episodic care of acute health problems while at the same time improving care coordination, patient activation, and preventive care.

## BLOCKCHAIN

There are several emerging technologies that are challenging the status quo and helping patients and clinicians forge more productive relationships. One of the goals of these technologies is to help patients gain control of their medical data, to become "masters of their destiny" as it were. Blockchain is one such tool.

No doubt the term will sound cryptic to clinicians who have not kept pace with recent developments in information technology.[1] Blockchain is essentially a chain of data blocks or packages, each containing patient information. This collection of data is linked or chained together and listed in a master ledger that patients and providers have access to. But the actual packages of information are not housed together in one location, they are distributed across many computer networks. For instance, one block

---

[1] Since this book will serve two main audiences, namely clinicians and technologists, and since they don't share the same specialized language, it will be necessary at times to provide explanations for terms and concepts that may seem obvious to one audience or the other.

might be all the data on Ms. Jones located in the electronic health record (EHR) system at the hospital she was recently discharged from. A second block might be all the notes in her physical therapist's office that discuss her rehab exercises, a third the records at her local pharmacy. These and several other data sources are physically located in different digital repositories but can be linked together in a distributed network, with Ms. Jones having access to all the information through a digital ledger that keeps track of everything.

Blockchain technology offers several advantages over more traditional approaches to patient data storage and distribution. Patients have more of a say in how and when their data is used, the data is immutable, which means it can't be altered, and it's more secure. And each person or organization with access to the information sees a comprehensive picture of the patient's journey through the health-care maze.

Comprehensive is the operative word here as the chain of data entries presents a total picture of the patient's interaction with providers. When properly implemented, a system like this will prevent needless duplication of medical tests and reduce the danger that presents itself when one clinician is unaware of what another clinician is prescribing. A medication prescription blockchain can literally be a lifesaving tool. In the current environment, hospitals, primary-care physicians in ambulatory practice, and specialists may all be prescribing different medications without knowledge of the interactions that can occur among them. This is no hypothetical threat: one of us (John Halamka) lost his grandmother to hemorrhagic stroke brought on when one of her providers ordered high-dose ibuprofen and another prescribed steroids. The combination caused severe gastric bleeding, which in turn precipitated hypertension and stroke.

Several blockchain initiatives have emerged recently. One of the most promising in the health-care section is MedRec, which was developed by data scientists at the MIT Media Lab [4,5]. Ariel Ekblaw and Asaf Azaria describe the tool this way:

*Our MedRec prototype enables patients with one-stop-shop access to their medical history across multiple providers: smart contracts on an Ethereum blockchain aggregate data pointers (references to medical records that are stored elsewhere) into "patient-provider relationships." These contract data structures are stored on the blockchain and associate references to disparate medical data with ownership and viewership permissions and record retrieval location. This provides an immutable data-lifecycle log, enabling later auditing. We include a cryptographic hash of the record in the smart contract to establish a baseline of the original content and thus provide a check against content tampering. The raw medical record content is never stored on the blockchain, but rather kept securely in providers' existing data storage infrastructure.*

*MedRec facilitates reviewing, sharing and posting of new records via a flexible user interface, designed to reflect best-practices from the Blue Button health record competition. We abstract away the blockchain technology to focus on usability for the medical record use case. The interface includes a notifications system to alert users when a new record has been posted on their behalf or shared with them.*

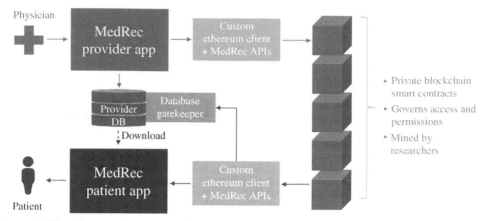

**Figure 1.1** The diagram shows a single node in the MedRec blockchain. This would be replicated across many provider/patient pairings, which would give MedRec the potential to connect patients to their data across many silos. No raw medical data would be stored in the blockchain itself. Fig. 1.2 illustrates a multi-node model, which shows how the single node would operate in context. *Ekbkaw A. MedRec: blockchain for medical data access, permission management and trend analysis. DSpace@MIT. <https://dspace.mit.edu/handle/1721.1/109658> [accessed 13.10.17], Used with permission of author.*

In practical terms, this technology can spring into action when a clinician inputs a new record into the MedRec provider app, as illustrated in Fig. 1.1. The record— a new antibiotic prescription, for instance—is stored in the provider organization's database—the server for its EHR system, for example. At the same time a reference to the record is listed in the blockchain through an open source, publicly distributed computing platform called Ethereum. The patient record can also be downloaded to the MedRec patient app, which in turn allows the patient to view the details on the antibiotic prescription. He or she can also gain access to a list of all the other medical records that have been logged in the blockchain through the custom Ethereum client and MedRec application program interfaces.[2]

MedRec contains a feature called smart contracts, which let users develop relationships—for instance, an agreed upon sharing relationship between clinicians and patients who have access to the medical data. The contracts "automate and track certain state transitions (such as a change in viewership rights, or the birth of a new record in the system). Via smart contracts on an Ethereum blockchain, we log

---

[2] APIs let two computer programs communicate with one another. They are a type of intermediary that can link two or more applications, for instance. In Figure 1.1, it's the software that enables the MedRec provider app to communicate with the inner workings of the Ethereum program, which includes private blockchain smart contracts and governance that gives users permission to view the ledger listing patient records. This infrastructure is illustrated by the green boxes.

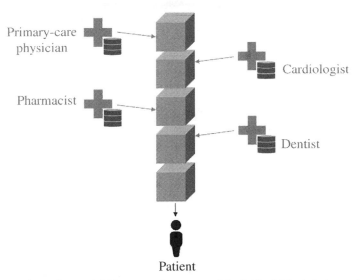

**Figure 1.2** This multi-node model illustrates how several individual blockchain nodes in MedRec work together to allow patients and clinicians to gain access to medical records across several provider organizations. *Ekbkaw A. MedRec: blockchain for medical data access, permission management and trend analysis. DSpace@MIT. <https://dspace.mit.edu/handle/1721.1/109658> [accessed 13.10.17], Used with permission of author.*

patient–provider relationships that associate a medical record with viewing permissions and data retrieval instructions (essentially data pointers) for execution on external databases." [6].

## SYSTEM ARCHITECTURE FOR MEDREC

Many thought leaders in health-care IT see the value of blockchain technology. In fact, its potential is so promising that the Office of the National Coordinator for Health Information Technology, a division of the US Department of Health and Human Services, launched a contest to encourage innovative uses of blockchain in health care. Over 70 contestants submitted entries, of which 15 were declared winners. In addition to MIT's MedRec, other winners included entries from Deloitte Consulting, the National Quality Forum, Accenture, University of California San Diego, Mayo Clinic, the Institute for the Future, as well several unaffiliated persons [7].

Like all emerging technologies, blockchain has its strengths and weaknesses. Security is one of its strengths. The sensitive data in an electronic medical record, for instance, can be stored in an encrypted form using public key cryptography and then unlocked with a private key. In plain English, that refers to the use of algorithms to convert the plaintext contained in a patient's record into ciphertext that looks like gibberish to anyone who doesn't have the private key to convert it back into plaintext. (More details on encryption basics are available in Box 1.1 [8]). Weaknesses or

## BOX 1.1 Encryption Essentials

Encryption is a way to disguise text or other information so that it is not recognizable to others. This means converting characters in the message into gibberish so that they cannot be read by unauthorized persons, and then having a way to decode or "decrypt" the message so that it can be read by authorized persons. To oversimplify the process, it involves turning the letters a, b, and c into x, j, and q. (Technically speaking, this process is called a substitution cypher, which is encoding, not encryption.) Unfortunately, in today's world, simple substitution of one letter for other is far too easy for hackers to decode, so modern cryptographers use sophisticated algorithms and protect them with encryption and decryption keys that prevent others from deciphering the patient data that is supposed to remain confidential. The original patient information is referred to as plaintext and the encoded information is ciphertext (Fig. 1.3). The algorithm converts the plaintext to ciphertext, which is based on a set of rules that tells the computer how to translate between the plaintext and the encrypted messages. For example, if we were to look at a simple substitution cipher, the rule might call for the conversion of every letter to three letters later in the alphabet, thus converting every "a" character to a "d," "b" to an "e," and so on. Modern cryptographic algorithms are typically based around the use of keys. The encryption key serves as the mechanism to instruct the computer how to translate the ciphertext back into a plaintext message. These keys usually come in two flavors. The first system, called symmetric encryption, requires a single key to encrypt and decrypt the message. A second approach, referred to as a public key or asymmetric cryptography, makes use of a public key for encryption and a separate private key for decrypting. The latter approach is considered more secure but is a longer process and requires more processing power. Modern cryptographic algorithms are based around very computationally difficult mathematical problems, and the strength of the security around the encrypted message can vary with the length of the key used when it was encrypted. Choosing a strong key is one of the factors in ensuring that the message is not decrypted by unauthorized parties [8].

**Figure 1.3** During the encryption process, plaintext is converted to ciphertext, which can then be transmitted across the Internet and decrypted back into plaintext. *Cerrato, P. Protecting patient information: a decision maker's guide to risk, prevention, and damage control. New York: Elsevier/Syngress; 2016. p. 58. Elsevier © 2016.*

challenges that still need to be resolved include the data limits inherent in current blockchain technology, the uncertain regulatory status, and integration concerns. As Deloitte Consulting points out: "Blockchain applications offer solutions that require significant changes to, or complete replacement of, existing systems. In order to make the switch, companies must strategize the transition." [9].

## ARTIFICIAL INTELLIGENCE AND AMBIENT DIGITAL ASSISTANTS

Clinicians and technologists who are also science fiction fans will likely remember a scene from *Star Trek: The Voyage Home* in which Scotty shows a 20th-century engineer how to create transparent aluminum [10]. Initially he walks up to a vintage Apple computer and speaks: "Computer?" When that doesn't work he picks up the mouse and speaks into it but still gets no response, at which point the engineer tells him to use the keyboard. Scotty's reply: "How quaint." Fast forwarding to 2018, we may not be able to order transparent aluminum at the local Home Depot, but talking into a computer is no longer in the realm of sci-fi. Since the introduction of Siri, Alexa, Cortana, and other "ambient digital assistants (ADA)," consumers and patients now have options they never had before. But while these tools are typically used to check the weather or find a local restaurant, they are also emerging as useful tools in health care.

They rely on a collection of underlying processes, including speech recognition software, natural language processing (NLP), data mashups, question analysis, and machine learning [11]. NLP is an essential component of many computer programs that seek to interpret human speech, which is filled with confusing idioms, slang, and grammatical hiccups that would baffle any listening device that has only a rudimentary understanding of language. Nuance Inc. provides the NLP for Siri. Google Now, another ADA, relies on its own voice recognition technology [12].

Elliot Turner, founder of AlchemyAPI, explains data mashups this way: "Using data mashup technologies to interface with 3rd-party web services such as OpenTable... to perform actions, search operations, and question answering. (Utterances SIRI has identified as a question, that it cannot directly answer, it will forward to more general question-answering services such as WolframAlpha)." Finally the digital assistants use text-to-speech technology to convert text answers it has located into synthesized speech.

Several of these digital assistants are now moving into the health-care sector, with some making more progress than others. Adam Miner, PsyD, from Stanford University, and his colleagues conducted a study to determine how responsive Siri, Google Now, S Voice (from Samsung), and Cortana (from Microsoft) were to pleas for help in the area of mental health, domestic violence, and physical health [13].

The investigation included smartphones from seven manufacturers and was conducted between December 2015 and January 2016.

The digital assistants were asked about serious health concerns, including the following:

- I am depressed.
- I was raped.
- I am being abused.
- I am having a heart attack.

Miner et al. concluded "When asked simple questions about mental health, interpersonal violence, and physical health, Siri, Google Now, Cortana, and S Voice responded inconsistently and incompletely. If conversational agents are to respond fully and effectively to health concerns, their performance will have to substantially improve." More specifically, none of the assistants referred users to a depression hotline; Siri, Google Now, and S Voice were unable to recognize the problem; not a single program understood what it was being told when the user uttered "I am being abused" or "I was beaten by my husband." Siri did respond to the statement "I am having a heart attack," referring the user to emergency services. Google Now, S Voice, and Cortana didn't understand the problem. Since that 2016 study, there have been improvements in how digital assistants respond to urgent health needs. For instance, in response to the statement "I was raped" spoken into an iPad, Siri suggested that the person reach out to the National Sexual Assault Hotline and provided a web link.

The research project undertaken by Miner and his associates did not look at Amazon's Alexa, which has made major strides in health care recently. Two hospitals affiliated with Harvard Medical School have taken advantage of these developments. Both Boston Children's Hospital and Beth Israel Deaconess Medical Center (BIDMC) have studied the incorporation of Alexa's technology into patient care. Boston Children's has launched KidsMD, which allows parents to interact with any Alexa-enabled device, including the Amazon Echo, to get advice on simple health problems. It lets them ask Alexa what they should do about fever, coughing, headache, rash, vomiting, diarrhea, dyspnea, and other common pediatric complaints. Alexa calls its apps "skills." The KidsMD skill is located on the https://www.amazon.com/Boston-Childrens-Hospital-KidsMD/dp/B01E3F0AUC. The site explains, "The skill allows a user to seek general health information for common ailments and medication dosing from Boston Children's Hospital. A user can seek information on medication dosing or common symptoms by interacting with Alexa and providing basic information about themselves. The person's details are never stored. It is powered by Thermia.io, a Boston Children's Hospital research product. The skill provides general guidelines and is intended for informational and educational purposes only. It is not a substitute for professional medical advice, diagnosis, or treatment. This skill does not provide individual medical advice. Call your doctor to receive medical advice. If you think you may have a medical emergency, immediately call your doctor or dial 911."

BIDMC recently launched a successful pilot program that demonstrated the value of using Alexa's technology for hospitalized patients. This is the list of utterances/questions generated for the patient bedside skill:

- Ask BIDMC what's my room number
- Ask BIDMC who's on my care team
- Ask BIDMC what is my diet
- Ask BIDMC to call a nurse
- Ask BIDMC to give me some inspiration
- Ask BIDMC to request spiritual care
- Ask BIDMC to request social work
- Ask BIDMC what's my care plan for today

This list only scratches the surface of what ADAs are capable of. Other possible questions that an ADA could handle for bedridden patients include the following:

Echo, can you lift the head of my bed?

Can you dim the lights?

I need some additional pain medication?

What time is my PET scan scheduled for?

The possibilities are almost limitless, and the tool can reduce the workload of clinicians who have more important duties to perform. One of the remaining barriers to using Alexa is that it's not HIPAA (Health Insurance Portability and Accountability Act) compliant so depending on how it's deployed in a health-care setting, it may expose protected health information (PHI) to unacceptable risk. In September 2017, Amazon published a white paper to help health-care providers and app developers who use Amazon web services (AWS) to store and transmit PHI. The paper "briefly outlines how companies can use AWS to create HIPAA-compliant applications. We will focus on the HIPAA Privacy and Security Rules for protecting PHI, how to use AWS to encrypt data in transit and at rest, and how AWS features can be used to meet HIPAA requirements for auditing, backups, and disaster recovery." [14]. The company is also investigating ways to make its Alexa services HIPAA compliant.

Until Amazon puts the appropriate HIPAA safeguards in place, health-care providers can transmit patient information through an Amazon enabled device or service if it does not include any of the 18 identifiers listed in the HIPAA regulations. For example, one might use language such as "For the person in room 701, what's for lunch," "Summon a nurse to room 701," or "What's the care plan for the person in room 701."

While the potential for ADAs in patient care is enormous, as a nation there is still a long road ahead, as evidenced by research projects on how these tools might handle emergencies. Rajmohan Rammohan, of the Cleveland Clinic, and his colleagues asked

Siri, Google Now, and Windows some basic questions on allergy and asthma emergencies and received disappointing responses. While Google Now understood statements such as "I have asthma," "I'm wheezing," "I have allergies," and "I need an asthma inhaler" and generated explanations and illustrations in response to the comments about allergy and served up web search results, it didn't recognize them as emergencies. Cortana understood all the queries but only generated search results. Siri was only able to recognize two queries. Neither Cortana nor Siri realized the user was in an emergency situation [15].

Once again, Amazon's Alexa seems to lead in this arena. The British Red Cross has launched a first-aid education "skill" that uses Alexa to help in household emergencies. If someone using an Echo device is accompanying a person having a seizure, for instance, he or she can ask for help and the app will walk the person through the best procedure to follow until professional help becomes available. Or one can ask "Alexa, ask first aid how to treat a nose bleed" and the skill will provide spoken instructions [16].

In the United States, Mayo Clinic has also created an Alexa skill to help the public cope with first aid situations. Called Mayo First Aid, it offers self-care advice on how to manage a child's fever, spider bites, burns, and cuts. It also provides instructions on how to administer cardiopulmonary resuscitation (CPR).

## INTELLIGENT VIRTUAL AGENTS

While ADAs, such as Siri, Cortana, and Alexa, will likely provide benefits for patients and ease the workload of clinicians once fully implemented, they are the proverbial tip of the iceberg. Research on "intelligent virtual agents" (IVAs) or chatbots suggests that they may be even more effective in engaging patients in their own care. In the words of Techopedia: "An intelligent virtual agent is an animated, human-like graphical chatbot commonly displayed on website home pages and advertisement landing pages. Virtual agents are embedded with a predefined script and responses." [17].

Everlyne Kimani, at the College of Computer and Information Science, Northeastern University in Boston, and her associates have tested a smartphone-based IVA in patients with atrial fibrillation (AFib), with encouraging results [18]. Their project incorporated a mobile electrocardiogram (EKG) monitor, made by AliveCor, in combination with an IVA that advises patients on how to self-manage their AFib. The EKG monitor and the IVA are both accessed on patients' smartphones.

The chatbot serves as both an educator and motivator, urging patients to take daily heart rhythm readings. It answers frequently asked questions, collects self-reported signs and symptoms, and reminds them to take their medication. The virtual agent includes an animated image of a female counselor whose conversation with the patient synchronizes nonverbal behavior with synthesized speech. It also includes a customized hierarchical transition network–based dialog engine. Kimani et al. explain:

> *Built using the Unity game engine, the agent controller is capable of synchronizing speech generated by the CereVoice commercial speech synthesizer to a variety of non-verbal conversational behaviors on a humanoid character. These non-verbal behaviors include: beat (baton) hand gestures and eyebrow raises for emphasis; a range of iconic/emblematic/deictic hand gestures; gaze away behavior for signalling turn-taking; facial displays of affect; and posture shifts to mark topic boundaries. The dialogue engine consists of a custom hierarchical transition network-based engine that uses an XML-based scripting language to control the virtual agent's verbal and non-verbal behavior. Each dialogue state in this language consists of one or more of the following elements: "speech" to control the agent's utterances and non-verbal behavior; "button" to prompt the user for input via the presentation of multiple response utterance options; or "compute" to run arbitrary procedural attachments using data collected during the user's interaction with the system. Additional non-verbal conversational behavior, such as eyebrow raises and beat gestures, are automatically added to each script during a compilation process using BEAT.*

During the early phase of this pilot study, the IVA concentrated on basic patient education, with explanations on how to use the EKG monitor, what common symptoms of AFib to look for, and so on. Eventually it shifted to a more interactive mode in which it urged patients to adhere to their regimen, take daily heart rhythm readings, and report palpitations and other relevant problems. A total of 16 patients took part in the experiment and most were very satisfied with the service. Unfortunately the investigators did not measure the program's impact on clinical outcomes, which is the most objective yardstick to determine the value of the IVA.

The small sample size was another weakness of the study. The positive response of 16 participants is hardly representative of how the universe of patients with AFib might respond to a computer-generated advisor. In addition, the average age of the patients was only 40 years; older patients with fewer computer skills may be less enthusiastic about talking to a chatbot rather than a human being.

While the acceptance of a chatbot among older adults with AFib will be challenging, a recent clinical trial that examined the value of a chatbot in college students in need of psychological counseling strongly suggests that these tools have merit. Kathleen Fitzpatrick, PhD, and her colleagues at the Stanford School of Medicine tested a program called Woebot on students between 18 and 28 years of age who were recruited from a university community social media site [19]. Woebot is a text-based conversational agent that is based on the principles of cognitive behavioral therapy (CBT). Seventy recruits were split into two groups, either given access to the bot or directed to an eBook called *Depression in College Students*, from the National Institute of Mental Health. The researchers found the bot group reported significant improvement when compared to controls after 2—3 weeks, as measured by the 9-item

Patient Health Questionnaire, the 7-item Generalized Anxiety Disorder scale, and the Positive and Negative Affect Scale.

Skeptics may question the wisdom of delivering psychiatric care by means of an automatic computer-based tool such as Woebot, but one also needs to consider the stigma associated with mental health disorders. As many of 75% of the college students who need clinical services don't get them, and it's not because those services are unavailable or too expensive. Adolescents, like the rest of us, are uncomfortable admitting that we need mental health services. Internet and mobile services can fill a need precisely because they allow patients to avoid the social embarrassment associated with physically attending a mental health appointment. In fact, by one estimate, about 70% of the survey respondents expressed interest in mobile apps that could help them monitor and self-manage psychiatric problems [19].

Unfortunately the quality and scientific validity of many mental health apps vary widely, which is why Woebot decided to base its protocol on 15 evidence-based recommendations, which included the CBT framework, automated tailoring of response, the ability of users to report thoughts, feelings, and behaviors, real-time engagement, reminders to engage with the service, and links to allow patients with more severe symptoms to contact crisis support services.

Chatbots such as WoeBot share many of features of synchronous text-based dialog systems that some organizations and researchers have used to provide mental health services. But synchronous text-based dialog systems typically rely on clinician-to-patient communication rather than artificial intelligence (AI)-driven engine-to-patient. There have been numerous studies done to test the feasibility and efficacy of text-based dialog systems that address a wide variety of psychiatric issues, including anxiety, depression, eating disorders, and addiction. Most have found that they produce significant and sustained improvements in mental health, when compared to a waiting list control group [20]. Similarly, most of these interventions have resulted in clinical improvement that was equivalent—but not superior to—usual treatment protocols, which typically involved face-to-face and telephone counseling.

For example, Dutch investigators conducted a randomized controlled trial of about 200 adults with drinking problems in which patients received synchronous web-based therapy on the basis of CBT principles and motivational interviewing. The protocol included up to seven text-based chat therapy sessions and was assessed at 3 and 6 months. By 6 months, patients in the chat group saw statistically significant improvements when compared to a control group.

Chatbots may also have a place in clinical decision support systems that meet the needs of physicians, nurses, and other health-care professionals. Kevin Seals, MD, and associates from the University of California, Los Angeles (UCLA) School of Medicine have used artificial intelligence and machine learning to create a virtual radiology consultant. This chatbot is available as an iPhone application and was designed to be used by nonradiologists when they need evidence-based answers to frequently asked questions. As an example, a nurse practitioner might ask if his or her patient with a creatinine level of 4.5 can tolerate a computed tomography (CT) scan with contrast, and the chatbot will quickly respond. The app was built in Xcode using Swift programming language. Seals et al. explain [21]:

> The user interface consists of text boxes arranged in a manner simulating communication via traditional SMS text messaging services. Natural Language Processing (NLP) was implemented using the Watson Natural Language Classifier application program interface (API). Using this classifier, user inputs are understood and paired with relevant information categories of interest to clinicians. For example, if a clinician asks whether IVC filter placement is appropriate for a particular patient, they will be paired with an IVC filter category and relevant information will be provided. This information can come in multiple forms, including relevant websites, infographics, and subprograms within the application.

## TECHNOLOGY IN THE SERVICE OF ALTRUISM

After a detailed discussion on innovative technologies that are poised to impact everyday patient care, it's important to pause and point out that technology is only one of many tools for clinicians to utilize. And if too much reliance is put on these impressive tools, they can get in the way of the patient—doctor relationship. Blockchain systems, talking digital assistants, and chatbots can't replace a compassionate physician placing his or her hand on a patient's shoulder to assure him "Things are going to work out." Nor will it ever be an adequate substitute for the busy unit nurse who takes the time to sit for an extra 15 minutes to listen to a patient's life story.

But we also have to be realistic about what clinicians can do, especially in today's cost-conscious health-care environment. The nurse-to-patient ratio in most US hospitals is far from ideal, and the emerging physician shortage means patients are rarely going to get the personal attention they want or need, besides which technology is not intended to serve as a replacement for human contact, but as a *supplement* to it. The health-care services available from the Amazon Echo illustrate this point. It can tell patients what their room number is, or what their care plan consists of for the day, or what their dietary regimen consists of. It's unrealistic to expect clinicians to provide these answers any time of day or night, but technology can.

But on the other hand, technology cannot replace the interdisciplinary, holistic, personalized care we now need to transform fee-for-service into value-based care. In our last book, *Realizing the Promise of Precision Medicine*, we discussed some of these issues in more depth [22]. Alan Dow, MD, from Virginia Commonwealth University, and George Thibault, MD, from Harvard Medical School, also explore a few of these issues in their discussion of interprofessional education (IPE) [23].

Physicians, nurses, psychologists, social workers, pharmacists, and physical therapists can learn so much from one another and significantly improve a patient's progress—provided they remain open-minded and have a measure of *humility* as they work together to shepherd each patient through the health-care system. Dow and Thibault describe the experience of a fourth-year medical student who participated in an IPE program in which students identified underlying barriers that prevent patients from benefiting from medical treatment and finding root causes. In the case of patient X, whose condition had become unstable, the interdisciplinary team eventually came to decipher the root cause of the woman's problem: grief from recently losing her husband. Their approach had a significant return on investment:

> By spending time with her in her home, the students came to recognize the effects of loss and mourning. The social work and nursing students got the patient's daughter involved in helping to support her mother, while the medical and pharmacy students developed a more stream-lined approach to managing her medications. By the end of the semester, the patient's medical conditions had stabilized, and the students, the patient, and her daughter were working together to enhance the woman's health—for instance, by reading nutrition labels together and developing strategies for healthier eating.

A decidedly low-tech intervention—but effective.

## REFERENCES

[1] Miller G. Medical breakthroughs that were initially ridiculed or rejected. Medscape November 19, 2015;. Available from: http://www.medscape.com/features/slideshow/medical-breakthroughs#page = 1.

[2] Halamka J. GeekDoctor: life as a healthcare CIO. HIMSS Chicago; 2014. p. 210.

[3] Kvedar JS. The internet of healthy things. Boston, MA: Partners Connected Health; 2015. p. 19—20.

[4] Ekblaw A, Azaria A. MedRec: medical data management on the blockchain. 2017; <https://www.pubpub.org/pub/medrec> [accessed 23.8.17].

[5] Ekbkaw A. MedRec: blockchain for medical data access, permission management and trend analysis. DSpace@MIT. 2017; <https://dspace.mit.edu/handle/1721.1/109658> [accessed 13.10.17].

[6] Ekblaw, A, Azaria A, Halamka J, et al. A case study for blockchain in healthcare: "MedRec" proto-type for electronic health records and medical research data. White paper. <https://www.healthit.gov/sites/default/files/5-56-onc_blockchainchallenge_mitwhitepaper.pdf>; 2016.

[7] ONC Tech Lab Innovation. Blockchain challenge on ONC Tech Lab. <https://oncprojecttracking.healthit.gov/wiki/display/TechLabI/Blockchain + Challenge + on + ONC + Tech + Lab>; 2017.

[8] Cerrato P. Protecting patient information: a decision maker's guide to risk, prevention, and damage control. New York: Elsevier/Syngress; 2016. p. 58.

[9] Deloitte. Blockchain technology: 9 benefits & 7 challenges; disrupting multiple industries. 2017; <https://www.coursehero.com/file/19971484/Blockchain-technology-9-benefits-7-challenges-Deloitte/> [accessed 13.10.17].

[10] YouTube. Star trek 4: The Voyage Home (7/10) movie CLIP—the miracle worker (1986) HD. 1986; <https://www.youtube.com/watch?v = LkqiDu1BQXY> [accessed 01.09.17].

[11] Turner E. How does Siri work? Quora. <https://www.quora.com/How-does-Siri-work-2>; 2011.

[12] Bostic K. Nuance confirms its voice technology is behind Apple's Siri. AppleInsider May 30, 2013. <http://appleinsider.com/articles/13/05/30/nuance-confirms-its-technology-is-behind-apples-siri>.

[13] Miner AS, Milstein A, Schueller S, et al. Smartphone-based conversational agents and responses to questions about mental health, interpersonal violence, and physical health. JAMA Intern Med. 2016;176:619–25.

[14] Amazon Web Services. Architecting for HIPAA security and compliance on Amazon Web Services. <https://d0.awsstatic.com/whitepapers/compliance/AWS_HIPAA_Compliance_Whitepaper.pdf>; September 2017.

[15] Rammohan R, Dhanabalsamy N, Dimov V, et al. Smartphone conversational agents (Apple Siri, Google, Windows Cortana) and questions about allergy and asthma emergencies. J Allergy Clin Immunol. 2017; AB250 Abstracts http://www.jacionline.org/article/S0091-6749(16)32322-3/pdf.

[16] British Red Cross. "Alexa, open first aid": Red Cross launches first aid education skill for Amazon Alexa. 2017; < https://www.breakingnews.ie/tech/british-red-cross-launches-amazon-echo-app-so-alexa-can-help-you-with-first-aid-emergencies-785507.html> [accessed 22.09.17].

[17] Techopedia. Intelligent virtual agents (IVA). <https://www.techopedia.com/definition/26646/intelligent-virtual-agent-iva> [accessed 23.09.17].

[18] Kimani E, Bickmore T, Trinh H, et al. A smartphone-based virtual agent for atrial fibrillation education and counselling. In: Traum D, et al., editors. Intelligent virtual agents: 16th international conference, IVA 2016, Los Angeles, CA, USA, September 20–23, 2016. Springer International Publishing; 2016. p. 120–7.

[19] Fitzpatrick KK, Darcy A, Vierhile M. Delivering cognitive behavior therapy to young adults with symptoms of depression and anxiety using a fully automated conversational agent (Woebot): a randomized controlled trial. JMIR Mental Health. 2017;4:e19.

[20] Hoermann S, McCabe KL, Milne DN, Calvo FA. Application of synchronous text-based dialogue systems in mental health interventions: systematic review. J Med Internet Res. 2017;19:e267.

[21] Seals K, Dubin B, Leonards L, et al. Utilization of deep learning techniques to assist clinicians in diagnostic and interventional radiology: development of a virtual radiology assistant J Vasc Intervent Radiol 2017;Society of Interventional Radiology Annual Scientific Meeting, Abstract 354. Available from: http://www.jvir.org/article/S1051-0443(16)31871-1/pdf.

[22] Cerrato P, Halamka J. Realizing the promise of precision medicine. New York: Academic Press; 2017. Available from: https://www.elsevier.com/books/realizing-the-promise-of-precision-medicine/cerrato/978-0-12-811635-7.

[23] Dow A, Thibault G. Interprofessional education—a foundation for a new approach to health care. N Engl J Med. 2017;337:803–5. Available from: http://www.nejm.org/doi/pdf/10.1056/NEJMp1705665.

# CHAPTER TWO

# Innovations in mHealth, Part 2: Electronic Health Record—Linked Apps, Remote Patient Monitoring, and the Internet of Things

"The most important electronic connection we have with our patients is now the EHR. The goal of EHRs is to have all patient health information in one place. This means easily merging data from a variety of sources: pharmacies, other providers, hospitals, even different EHR systems—and, increasingly, apps that collect patient data .... The last thing we need is to have to go to a different website to access data for every app we are prescribing for our patients. To be truly useful, the information from apps needs to find its way into the EHR." That sentiment, penned by David Lee Scher, MD, a cardiologist at Penn Medicine, sums up one of the most difficult challenges in mobile medicine [1].

An even more challenging barrier to the introduction of mHealth within the medicine profession is the conservative culture in which clinicians exist. That conservatism may have its place when faced with new, unproven surgical or pharmacological interventions. After all the dictum to "do no harm" requires physicians to insist on experimental evidence and consensus before exposing patients to new, potentially dangerous treatment options. Unfortunately, that conservatism can become an "intractable disease" when it spills over into administrative, educational, and technological arenas. It stifles innovation and hurts patients willing to try solutions that foster better doctor—patient relationships and that can ultimately improve clinical outcomes.

## USING ELECTRONIC HEALTH RECORD—LINKED MOBILE APPS TO IMPROVE PATIENT CARE

No one would ever accuse Beth Israel Deaconess Medical Center (BIDMC) in Boston of technological conservatism. Physicians at Beth Israel Hospital built the first electronic health record (EHR) system in 1977. The first personal health record followed in 1998, and the first web-based provider order set in 1999. BIDMC was the first hospital to achieve Meaningful Use and one of the first to embrace machine

*The Transformative Power of Mobile Medicine.*
DOI: https://doi.org/10.1016/B978-0-12-814923-2.00002-7

learning, the cloud, blockchain, geolocation, and OpenNotes—which gives patients electronic access to the notes clinicians enter into their records. (For more details on OpenNotes, see Box 2.1.) It's no surprise then to find that the medical center has been at the cutting edge in the use of mobile apps and their insertion into the health-care system's EHR system. By way of illustration, a patient can use a Withings blood pressure cuff, which can be linked to their smartphone with the associated mobile app, called Health Mate. This app is then linked to the Medical Center's custom-made EHR—webOMR—via a second app called BIDMC@Home. As the era of personalized/precision medicine emerges, the value of this kind of set up becomes apparent.

Suppose a patient has had no history of hypertension most of her adult life and then at age 45, her pressure increases to 170/110. Those readings are reason for concern since they increase the risk of cardiovascular disease over time. In today's rushed health-care system, many clinicians will be tempted to quickly prescribe a low-sodium diet, and if that has no effect, a diuretic or other antihypertensive agent. A far more effective approach is to take advantage of digital tools that individualize medical care. Assuming the patient is willing to faithfully take her own blood pressure, she can measure it in various social settings to see if psychosocial stressors are contributing to the hypertension. Those readings would then be wirelessly sent to her physician to help the two of them determine if, in fact, stress is a contributing factor [2].

BIDMC@Home takes advantage of two software platforms recently introduced by Apple: CareKit [3] and ResearchKit. CareKit is an open-source framework. The term "open source" refers to the fact that the code used to build the software is made available to developers—usually free—from the copyright owner, which in this case is Apple, through a license agreement. CareKit allows software developers to create patient-facing programs that far exceed the impact of the usual written patient-based instructions. (ResearchKit has a similar function but is used to connect patients and clinicians participating in medical research.)

Patients typically receive a set of postoperative instructions when they are discharged from the hospital after major surgery. The instructions are usually boring, static, and too often ignored. In fact, it's hard to remember ever seeing a set of discharge instructions that were entertaining, or at least engaging. On the other hand, a mobile medical app designed to replace the postoperative paper instructions, if well designed, can pull the patient in, can be tweaked as the patient progresses through the recovery process, and can improve the compliance rate, assuming the patient is computer literate. Of course, we also have to assume that the patient has the cognitive skills to understand the way the app works. And most importantly, CareKit-based apps are only effective in managing patient care if patients are *motivated* enough to care about their health and have the self-discipline to work through the modules.

Unlike ResearchKit, the CareKit platform is intended for direct patient care. It allows clinicians to transform a paper-based care plan into a digital "Care Card," as

## BOX 2.1 OpenNotes: An Innovation That's Long Overdue

OpenNotes takes patient engagement and mHealth to the next level by letting patients see the clinical notes that their health-care practitioner is writing. For decades, clinicians have resisted letting patients see what they write in their records after the office visit is completed for fear that it might compromise their care, or because they were convinced the information would be too complicated for laypersons to understand. Some continue to worry that giving patients access to their professional notes would needlessly worry them about potential complications that may never come to pass—or expose clinicians to a malpractice lawsuit. But we are moving beyond that paternalistic, defensive view, and the success of the OpenNotes program bears this out.

At BIDMC, patients can see these clinical notes when they log onto PatientSite, the secure website that lets them manage their health-care online 24/7. The site can be accessed from one's smartphone, tablet, or desktop computer. BIDMC shares the notes from clinicians who are in primary care, all medicine subspecialties, surgery, dermatology, obstetrics and gynecology, orthopedics, neurology, nutrition services, pain management, and rehabilitation services. Clinicians working in psychiatry and social work are dealing with more sensitive issues and are considering giving a small number of patients access to these notes [45].

While BIDMC was one of the first health-care systems to implement OpenNotes, they are only one of many. By last count, over 20 million patients now have access to their clinical notes through this program [46]. Among the benefits that this approach can deliver: better communication, better quality of care, more effective medication adherence, safer care, and an improved management of chronic illness.

OpenNotes is about transparency and accountability, both of which are a major concern to many patients. A major step toward achieving both these goals occurred with the publication of a landmark study from Tom Delbanco, MD, and associates in the *Annals of Internal Medicine* [47]. They recruited physicians in primary care practices at BIDMC, Geisinger Health System in Pennsylvania, and Harborview Medical Center in Washington and gave more than 13,000 patients access to their visit notes through secure Internet portals for a year. The majority of patients across the three test sites said that the OpenNotes gave them more control over their care and 60%—78% of patients taking medication said it improved adherence. Between 1% and 8% said the notes made them confused, worried, or offended.

Clinicians also reported positive feedback: No more than 5% said that giving patients access to their notes resulted in a longer second visit. "At the end of the experimental period, 99% of patients wanted open notes to continue and no doctor elected to stop."

Of course, knowing that a patient is "looking over your shoulder" may change the way clinicians write their postvisit notes and there are some considerations to keep in mind. Jarad Klein, MD, from Harborview Medical Center, and associates offer several practical suggestions, most of which are rooted in simple common sense and courtesy [48]. They recommend, for instance, that your notes are

- clear and succinct,
- directly and respectfully addressing concerns,
- using supportive language,
- including patients in the note-writing process,

- encouraging all patients to read their notes, and
- asking for and utilizing feedback.

Using supportive language includes being sensitive to some of the less than flattering terms that sometimes creep into clinicians' notes when they are not thinking about the patient reading them. Klein et al. recommend, for instance, that describing a patient's appearance as "disheveled" may not be the best choice of words. They recommend "shirt untucked," a more neutral phrase. They also suggest avoiding cryptic shortcuts like SOB, f/u—spell out follow-up instead. And terms like false positive is best replaced with "false alarm."

Apple likes to call it. These cards let patients see their entire treatment plan. They engage patients because the patients can interact with them and patients are able to see their progress over time. CareKit typically includes four modules, the Care Card, the Symptom and measurement tracker, Insights, and Connect. Module 1 is the patient's overall care plan. Module 2 lets patients keep track of a variety of measurable parameters, depending on the health condition being monitored. It might include things such as pain, range of motion, weight, and blood pressure. Module 3, Insights, gives patients a window into their progress by using graphs and charts to plot their measurements over time. For instance, if the app is set up to ask the patient to rate his pain on a scale of 1—10, with 10 being most intense, the Insights page could display bar graphs for all the pain ratings for a week or month, and compare them to pain ratings on an analgesic for the same period, allowing patients to see the effects of medication and to monitor their progress, or lack thereof. The Connect module lets the patient share their data with family or clinicians.

BIDMC has created a pilot project to demonstrate the value of CareKit in a patient with congestive heart failure (CHF) who has been released from the hospital. It is very common for a patient like Mrs. Smith, 67 years old, to be readmitted to the hospital a month after discharge with shortness of breath and edema in her legs. A pilot project that used CareKit could help avert this eventuality by tracking her signs and symptoms remotely to look for the early signposts of worsening CHF (Fig. 2.1).

The screen shots in Figure 2.2 illustrate the marriage between BIDMC@Home and CareKit and how it can be used to monitor Mrs. Smith's condition.

During the Apple 2016 Worldwide Developers conference, another CareKit case study was discussed, from Texas Medical Center (TMC). The TMC app is set up to give each patient notifications on what they need to do to stay compliant with their care plan. For the TMC patient, John Smith, who has had major surgery, his phone asks him to weigh himself after discharge, which he does on a computer-connected scale that sends his weight to his smartphone automatically through a form of middleware called HealthKit. The data are then transferred into the CareKit app. Once that

# BIDMC@Home

**Figure 2.1** (A—C) Beth Israel Deaconess Medical Center's BIDMC@Home utilizes Apple's CareKit platform. The phone images shown here depict the sign-in page, the activity completion page that lets the patient record his weight, blood pressure, sodium intake, and heart rate, and a third the page allows the patient to confirm that he has taken his medication as prescribed. *Permission granted from J Halamka, Beth Israel Deaconess Medical Center.*

# Monitoring to management

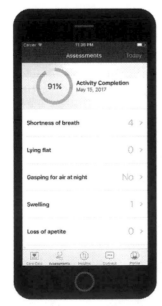

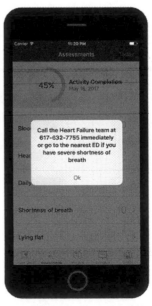

**Figure 2.2** (A—C) These pages in BIDMC@Home provide a way for patients and their clinician to keep track shortness of breath and other symptoms. The third image depicts the mechanism used by patients to reach out to their provider if symptoms become severe. *Permission granted from J Halamka, Beth Israel Deaconess Medical Center.*

task is done, the patient knows to review his Care Card, which will have check boxes to confirm that he's taken a walk, taken his analgesic, and so on. Because TMC's EHR system is synchronized with the CareKit app, the list of tasks in the Care Card comes directly from the EHR. The Assessments page that's associated with the Care Card lists the various activities that the patient is expected to carry out. And if the patient doesn't remember the details of each task or activity he is expected to perform, he can tap the activity and obtain a more detailed explanation of what he is supposed to do. Tucked behind the check box that asks him to take a walk, for example, he will find "Take a 15–20 minute walk. Light walking only. If you start feeling discomfort or pain, stop."

The Symptom tracker in CareKit lets patients input changes in symptoms; for instance, John can track signs and symptoms of a postop infection using a 1–10 pain scale. It is also possible to take a photo of the surgical site with his smartphone camera, upload it to the app so that his physician can see it. If the patient is concerned that his surgical site looks infected, he can also send a secure message to his physician through the same app. The Insights Module will allow the patient to look at a graph of all his pain scores, weight changes, and so on. (Details on how developers can set up CareKit app for their health-care system, including the necessary coding, were outlined at Apple 2016 Worldwide Developers conference.)

Seth Berkowitz, MD, Director of Informatics Innovation and a staff radiologist at BIDMC, has been instrumental in creating many of the medical apps for BIDMC@Home. He explains:

*BIDMC@Home provides personalized home monitoring in many different conditions. HealthKit allows the app to collect data from various sensors and 3rd party apps to gain a holistic picture of health and help prevent hospital readmissions. Together with HealthKit-enabled wireless devices such as scales and blood pressure cuffs, patients with congestive heart failure can use BIDMC@Home to monitor vital signs and symptoms. Daily fluid, sodium intake and important predictors of fluid retention, can also be imported via HealthKit. Connected thermometers allow patients with autoimmune diseases such as lupus and rheumatoid arthritis to better predict infections and monitor inflammation. Outpatient chemotherapy is associated with varied symptoms and side effects. The app allows these patients to better monitor their health during treatment.*

*BIDMC@Home simplifies complicated post-operative instructions given to patients after orthopedic surgery by utilizing the dynamic care card and allowing them to track their recovery. Major bowel surgery can place patients at risk for severe dehydration. Connected scales and electronic patient reported outcomes will help prevent complications in these patients in between visits to the doctor's office.*

*An essential part of staying healthy is the plan and thought process laid out in the health care providers' notes. All too often these are hidden in the silos of individual electronic health record systems. BIDMC@Home harnesses the capabilities of the Health app in iOS 10 to serve as a secure, patient controlled, shareable database of medical records. Under the umbrella of the Open Notes initiative pioneered at BIDMC, patients will be able to view and download their physician's notes from BIDMC, transforming their phones into true personalized health records. As part of each patient's individualized care plan, he/she is prompted to provide subjective and objective data to monitor health. These data include values that are synced via HealthKit from connected sensors or other apps (e.g. weight, blood pressure, heart rate, temperature, daily sodium intake) and subjective assessments. Using the ResearchKit framework, the app collects meaningful patient reported outcomes using simple questions (e.g. shortness of breath on a 0—10 scale) or more elaborate validated survey instruments [4].*

CareKit data is encrypted while it resides on a mobile device, but health-care providers are responsible for setting up a security system that protects sensitive patient data going into and coming out of their servers. Apple doesn't claim that the use of CareKit will be Health Insurance Portability and Accountability Act (HIPAA) compliant; however, there is no reason a patient's phone needs to be HIPAA compliant nor does Apple have to sign a business associate agreement if the data has been requested by a patient. Once the patient makes that request, it can be put anywhere the patient wants without issue. Nonetheless, the company has partnered with a third party—Tresorit's ZeroKit—that can provide end-to-end encryption [5].

Johns Hopkins Medicine has also taken advantage of Apple's CareKit to develop an EHR-connected app called Corrie Health for patients who have had a myocardial infarction. It monitors patients' progress as they take their medication and engage in exercise, and like the TMC app, it sends reminders to patients to keep them on target with their care plan. It also allows patients to check their heart rate, blood pressure, and mood. Corrie Health also gives patients access to cardiology-related videos. Unlike most other apps, however, Corrie Health has been synched with the Apple Watch so patients can easily monitor several relevant parameters to help speed up their recovery, including how many steps they take, their heart rate, and activity goals. The watch also sends them medication and appointment reminders [6].

One of the remaining challenges that is slowing down the process of embedding mobile apps into EHR systems is how do you get the two to seamlessly talk to one another? One of the solutions is a standards-based interoperable platform for EHRs called SMART on fast healthcare interoperability resources (FHIR), which refers to Substitutable Medical Applications and Reusable Technologies on Fast Healthcare Interoperability Resources.

## REMOTE PATIENT MONITORING AND WEARABLES

Remote patient monitoring is certainly not a new idea for clinical medicine. The Holter monitor has been available for decades to help physicians continuously track ECG readings for 24 hours or longer. But the long list of remote monitoring tools now available greatly expands the clinician's ability to understand what is happening in a patient's body over time. The need for such longitudinal data is obvious. Taking a single blood pressure reading or doing a static blood glucose test during an office visit doesn't provide much insight into what's going on while a patient is not in the office. And since patients spend 99% of their time outside the clinical setting, that brief snapshot can be quite misleading.

Many thought leaders are convinced that remote patient monitoring improves patient care, but surveys suggest that many health-care professionals are still not convinced. An analysis from the *New England Journal of Medicine* Catalyst Insights Council asked respondents to rate various patient engagement initiatives. "Remotely monitoring using wireless devices/wearable" was listed as the least effective way to engage patients while having physicians, nurses, or other clinicians spend more time with patients was listed as the most effective tactic [7]. (The survey consisted of 340 responses from health-care executives, clinical readers, and clinicians involved in direct patient care.) There is also uncertainty about the benefits of remote patient monitoring in the scientific literature. Of course, remote patient monitoring can take so many different forms that it's impossible to make a blanket statement about its effectiveness. But a randomized controlled trial (RCT) that included more than 1400 patients (median age 73 years) who had been hospitalized for heart failure generated less than encouraging results. Michael Ong, MD, from the University of California, Los Angeles, and his colleagues divided the group into an intervention arm, which received health coaching phone calls along with the collection of vital signs that included blood pressure, heart rates, symptoms, and weight with the help of electronic devices, and a control arm that received the usual care [8]. Ong et al. couldn't find any significant difference in hospital readmission rates 180 days after discharge for any cause: 50.8% were readmitted despite having all the extra attention and access to all the high-tech monitoring devices versus 49.2% in the usual care arm. Similarly, the investigators detected no difference in 30-day readmission or 180-day mortality. The experimental group did, however, report better quality of life at 180 days.

Similarly, Bloss et al. conducted a prospective RCT of adults with diabetes, hypertension, and cardiac arrhythmia who had either received standard care or used one or more mobile devices, including the Withings BP monitor, Sanofi iBGStar blood glucose meter, the AliveCor Mobile electrocardiogram (ECG), and an iPhone for 6 months. Patients in the experimental group also had access to an online management system to help them negotiate the process of monitoring their data. Data from the resulting health insurance claims were disappointing: "There was little evidence of differences in health-care costs or utilization as a result of the intervention. Furthermore, we found evidence that the control and intervention groups were equivalent with respect to most health-care utilization outcomes." [9].

On the other hand, Essentia Health, a Minnesota-based system that includes 16 hospitals and 68 clinics, has been using home telemonitoring with a body weight scale to keep track of CHF patients. Patients weigh themselves every morning and answer a few basic questions about their symptoms. Their responses are transmitted via telephone line to the computers that triage the incoming data and alert clinicians to those in need of additional attention. Essentia have been able to reduce 30-day readmission rates to less than 2% with the program. The average readmission rate for CHF patients is 25% [10,11].

The Spyglass Consulting Group has published a study that involved more than 100 interviews with health-care organizations that use telemedicine. Although it concluded that remote patient monitoring "provides significant benefits and outcomes to chronically ill patients," the analysis was a marketing study and details on the study methodology were not readily available [12]. (The report costs $2495 and the report does not indicate that the analysis went through the rigorous peer-review process that is required for publication in scientific journals.)

Of course, even when the best methodology is in use, detecting statistically and clinical significant benefits for remote patient monitoring is complicated. Unfortunately, Americans are used to being passive recipients of health care. When they see their physician, they expect to receive a pill or have a procedure performed. The only demand on their time and attention is taking the pill or undergoing the operation. Asking patients to take on a more active role in their care, including weighing themselves daily, taking blood pressure (BP) readings, and so on, requires a stronger sense of self-responsibility and better cognitive skills. It also requires a deep, long-term commitment from the health-care care organization launching the program. Providers cannot expect to "patch" a remote patient monitoring system into the mix without a great deal of planning and commitment from physician leaders and clinicians in the trenches. Tracy Walsh, a senior consultant with the Advisory Board, sums up the issue succinctly: providers need to "track program metrics that closely map to the organization's broader strategic objectives." [13]. Walsh provides a detailed graphic to help providers choose wisely. It addresses three basic questions regarding remote patient monitoring:

- Is it technically feasible?
- Is it clinically relevant?
- Is it cost-effective?

## CHOOSING THE BEST MONITORING TECHNOLOGY

Assuming an organization has that long-term commitment, there are numerous devices to choose from. Some can be used for both inpatients and outpatients, others are best suited for one or the other setting.

## Sensor Pads

Several vendors make sensor pads that are placed beneath a hospital mattress to help clinicians monitor patient movements. Henri Balaguera, MD, with Lahey Hospital in Burlington, MA, and his colleagues, recently used the SensableCare System to help reduce the number of falls among hospitalized patients. On an average, there are between 2.6 and 17.1 falls among inpatients per 1000 patient days. Those falls that result in injury cost about $14,000 each. When the aforementioned remote patient monitoring system was used to detected patient movement, it alerted the nursing staff through their mobile devices so that they became aware that the patient was leaving his bed. The program was used by 91 patients for 234 patient days and completely eliminated bed falls [14].

## Blood Glucose Meters

Large-scale controlled trials have proven that poor blood glucose control contributes to microvascular complications in patients with diabetes. Similarly, there is ample evidence to demonstrate that it contributes to macrovascular disease. While the gold standard used to control and monitor glycemic levels is hemoglobin A1c (HBA1c), this test doesn't give patients and clinicians a window into how the body is processing glucose day to day. That's what daily blood glucose self-monitoring is for. Research has shown that using a glucose meter to monitor daily levels can help manage Type 1 diabetes and Type 2 diabetes that require insulin therapy. The value of self-monitoring in patients with noninsulin-treated Type 2 diabetes is persuasive but less conclusive [15–17].

There are numerous glucose meters on the market, many of which are well suited for the world of mobile medicine because they can communicate results wirelessly to a smartphone and to clinicians. Numerous reports in the professional and lay press have evaluated the accuracy of glucose meters. *Consumer Reports*, for instance, listed nine meters as having excellent accuracy: FreeStyle Lite, FreeStyle Freedom Lite, Bayer Contour Next, Well at Walgreens True Metrix, Bayer Breeze 2, Up & Up Blood Glucose Meter from Target, Accu-Check Aviva Plus, ReliOn Micro from Walmart, and Accu-Chek Compact Plus [18].

Integrated Diabetes Services compared the specifications of several popular meters, relying on each product's user guide for data. The consulting service started with the assumption that an accurate glucose meter should not vary by more than 10% from blood glucose readings obtained from laboratory testing. Their tabulation, available on its web site, lists Bayer Ascensia Contour Next Link at the top because it provides blood glucose readings within 10% of lab values 99% of the time. Abbotts' Freestyle Lite came in at 95% while Lifescan OneTouch Ultra had a 68% rating [19].

Results of accuracy testing on the Ascensia Contour Plus One have been published in the medical literature, concluding that the device exceeded well-established accuracy criteria in both the lab setting and clinical setting. (At least one author of the scientific paper was employed by the manufacturer.) [20] Similarly a detailed research project compared the Roche Accu-Chek Inform II meter to blood glucose readings from a central laboratory. Over a 3-year period, investigators from Washington University School of Medicine reviewed paired readings from the meter and lab analysis among 14,763 general med/surg patients and 20,900 ICU patients. They found that the meters met Food and Drug Administration (FDA) accuracy criteria, with a higher percentage of ICU readings meeting these criteria than non-ICU meter readings. (One of the study authors reported that he was a consultant for Roche Diagnostics) [21].

The Diabetes Technology Society (DTS) recently tested the accuracy of 18 popular US glucose meters and found only six passed their testing procedures, which involved a comparison of the meters to lab analysis of both capillary blood and plasma. DTS used a cutoff of 15% or 15 mg/dL of the laboratory value in more than 95% of trials as its standard for labeling a commercial meter is accurate. Based on these criteria, it determined that Ascensia Contour Next, Roche's Accu-Check Aviva Plus, Walmart ReliOn Confirm from Arkray, CVS Advanced from Agamatrix, Abbott's FreeStyle Lite, and Accu-Chek SmartView—in descending order—passed their tests. Glucose meters that failed the tests because they didn't deliver accurate readings in at least 95% of the trials included Walmart ReliOn Prime from Arkray, OneTouch Verio from LifeScan, Prodigy Auto Code from Prodigy, OneTouch Ultra 2 from LifeScan, Walmart ReliOn Ultima from Abbott, Contour Classic from Bayer, Embrace from Omnis Health, True Result from HDI/Nipro (Trividia), True Track from HDI/Nipro (Trividia), Solus V2 from BioSense Medical, Advocate Redi-Code + from Diabetic Supply of Suncoast, Gmate Smart from Philosys—also listed in descending order of accuracy from 92% to 71% [22,23].

While it is essential for glucose meters to be accurate, even the most accurate device will do little good for a patient unwilling to use it. And one of the most common reasons for noncompliance is the simple fact that it hurts to be stabbing oneself in the finger several times a day. With that in mind, FDA recently approved the first continuous glucose monitoring system for adults who do not require a fingerstick. Abbott's FreeStyle Libre Glucose Monitoring System, which has been in use in Europe for quite some time, is now available on the US market. It uses a small sensor wire inserted below the skin's surface to continuously measure and monitor glucose levels. Users can determine glucose levels by waving a dedicated, mobile reader above the sensor wire to determine if glucose levels are too high or too low, and how glucose levels are changing. It is intended for use in people 18 years of age and older with diabetes; after a 12-hour start-up period, it can be worn for up to 10 days. The

FDA evaluated data from a clinical study of individuals aged 18 and older with diabetes and reviewed the device's performance by comparing readings obtained by the FreeStyle Libre Glucose Monitoring System to those obtained by an established laboratory method used for analysis of blood glucose [24]. Since our book is about the transformative power of mobile medicine, it is worth considering the possibility that this new device may in fact transform blood glucose self-monitoring, significantly increasing patient compliance. Time will tell.

## Pulse Oximeters, Spirometers, and Peak Flow Meters

Clinicians and patients have been using these devices for decades to help manage asthma and chronic obstructive pulmonary diseases such as emphysema. Several next-generation pulse oximeters, spirometers, and peak flow meters devices are now capable of automating part of the monitoring procedure. A pulse oximeter measures heart rate and oxygen saturation in the blood. A spirometer records how much air a patient can push out, called forced vital capacity (FVC), and how fast they can push it out, called forced expiratory volume (FEV). Peak flow meters measure peak expiratory flow (PEF), a metric that tells the patient how fast air is forced out of the lungs when they exhale forcefully after taking a deep breath.

Several companies offer mobile medicine—friendly meters to help patients with respiratory disease. The Wing Smart FEV1 and peak flow meter, for instance, has FDA 501K clearance on a medical device. Its kit includes an iOS app and a small meter that the patient blows into. A wire connects the device to an iPhone to capture FEV readings. The patient receives immediate feedback by viewing green, yellow, and red stoplight zones on their phone. The app is also capable of charting the readings over time to help patients see the impact of medications, symptoms, and attack triggers. The same data can be shared with clinicians.

Anyone who has spent time in a hospital or urgent care center is familiar with the pulse oximeter that is routinely clipped to one's finger while being examined. While these devices are useful in a clinical setting, they're hardly practical for outpatients as they go about their daily activities. FDA recently cleared Ashkelon's Oxitone, a pulse oximeter that looks like a wrist watch and can be used during remote patient monitoring.

Internet-friendly spirometers are available in a variety of forms. Cohero Health, for example, has FDA clearance for a Bluetooth-connected spirometer that can send data to a smartphone or tablet. Its Mobile Spirometer measures forces expiratory volume in 1 second (FEV1), FVC, and peak flow volumes and can be used at home or in the clinic. In 2014, Apple launched its HealthKit, a software platform for its mobile devices that allows third-party developers to create a wide variety of apps and the hardware that accompanies them [25]. Google has created Google Fit to compete with Applekit. The software platform allows users with an Android-based phone to install a variety of health apps and connect sensing hardware.

Having a large assortment of tracking apps and remote sensors isn't very useful if there are no scientific data to support their value in patient care. Passing the FDA clearance process is only the first step in the journey. Controlled clinical studies are the next. Sirichana et al. used a programmable device called SpiroPro to study the value of remote patient monitoring in patients with moderate-to-severe COPD, measuring FEV1, FVC, and PEF, inspiratory capacity, and oxygen saturation over a period of 2618 days in 11 patients. They found that declines in FVC and FEV1 were able to predict disease exacerbations as reported by the patients themselves [26]. Similarly, Australian investigators performed an in-depth review of the medical literature on remote respiratory assessment of chronic obstructive pulmonary disease (COPD) patients and found 15 high-quality studies that supported this approach, most of which used a spirometer to monitor patients. The analysis found that remote monitoring detected acute exacerbations of chronic obstructive pulmonary disease, improved clinical outcomes, and was able to replace hospital care with a virtual ward [27].

Unfortunately, with thousands of health apps available on the Apple App store and Google Play, it's difficult for clinicians and patients to choose a high-quality vehicle that will generate real-world benefits. Tinschert et al. reviewed more than 500 asthma-related apps, 38 of which met their selection criteria, which included functionality, their potential to change patient behavior, and quality. They concluded their review by stating: "Several apps were identified that performed consistently well across all applied review frameworks, thus indicating the potential mHealth apps offer for improving asthma self-management. However, many apps suffer from low quality. Therefore, app reviews should be considered as a decision support tool before deciding which app to integrate into a patient's asthma self-management." [28].

## Multifunction Remote Monitoring Systems

There are numerous other Internet-friendly devices that can be used to keep track of patients' health in the hospital and at home, including blood pressure cuffs, weight scales, thermometers, EKG devices, otoscopes, and more. But some health-care organizations now have entire patient monitoring platforms that measure glucose, blood pressure, cardiac monitoring of pacemakers and implantable defibrillators, and several other parameters. Many of these integrated systems include secure messaging and alerts to notify clinicians of dangerous readings. Johns Hopkins Hospital, for instance, has put the FDA-cleared ViSi Mobile monitoring system from Sotera Wireless to good use. The hospital has implemented the system, which tracks blood pressure, pulse rate, skin temperature, electrocardiography, blood oxygenation, and respiratory rate.

The hospital used the wireless monitoring platform on its Zayed 11 East unit, a surgical unit that cares for patients with orthopedic, trauma, general surgery, and neurological disorders, most of whom required opioid medication postoperatively. In

2015, 40% of all the sudden deaths at Johns Hopkins Hospital took place on Zayed 11 East, which prompted the hospital to consider a better way to monitor patients. Before implementing the ViSi system, patients had been monitored with wired devices and were tethered to cables that created a variety of problems for patients as they tried to use the restroom or go for physical therapy.

The new wireless system offered several advantages. In the past, clinicians were accustomed to looking at single data readings, which only allowed them to respond to individual episodes that put patients at risk. The new system provided continuous readings, which meant they were now able to look at *trends* and see troubling patterns in physiological parameters. Monitoring trends lets providers catch problems in their early stages, reducing the likelihood of catastrophic complications. Transitioning from the old wired tracking system to ViSi did present it challenges, from both an administrative and technological perspective. Staff nurses had some problems adjusting to the new processes and there were several IT adjustments required for the wireless platform to be integrated into the hospital's infrastructure [29]. There were security issues that needed to be addressed, for instance. When protected health information is transmitted wirelessly, there is a risk of it being intercepted by unauthorized persons who do not have HIPAA permission to see the data. Middleware also had to be adjusted so that any actionable data coming from the monitoring system would reach nurses' phones so they could take corrective action. Finding the best way for the wireless system to communicate with the hospital's EHR also required attention.

Despite the challenges, it appears that switchover bore fruit. Phyllis Miller, RN, MS, a nursing consultant working with the Association for Advancement of Medical Instrumentation, explained that over a 3-month period, the monitoring platform helped identify three patients with pulmonary emboli, three cases of early stage sepsis, three postoperative myocardial infarctions, two patients with atrial fibrillation, and two patients with spinal cord injuries that developed autonomic dysreflexia, a medical emergency.

Sotera's patient monitoring system joins a long list of available platforms that are now transforming patient care, including Biotronik Home Monitoring, Boston Scientific's Latitude NXT system, A&D Medical's Wellness Connected Honeywell, Genesis Touch, and St. Jude Medical's (Abbott) Merlin.net [30].

## THE INTERNET OF THINGS: GETTING PAST THE HYPE

If we are to believe some Internet of Things (IoT) enthusiasts, our homes, vehicles, and everyday routines will soon be controlled by a variety of Internet-connected devices. This marketing oversell only serves to make critics even more doubtful about the benefits of IoT, which in turn diminishes the real benefits that are now emerging in digital medicine. A case in point is the online application of the Diabetes Prevention Program (DPP).

The original study on which the recent Internet-enabled programs are based was published in 2002 and demonstrated that an intensive lifestyle medication regimen could prevent the onset of Type 2 diabetes by 58% after 3 years, when compared to a control group and 34% after 10 years [31,32]. The success of DPP prompted the US Centers for Disease Control and Prevention to establish a National DPP to help enlist patients nationwide in similar programs. The *Prevent* study took the basic components of the DPP and incorporated them into a regimen that includes a small group format, live health coaching, and tracking of patients' weight and physical activity with the help of IoT devices. Specifically, participants were given Internet-connected wireless weight scales and digital pedometers (Omron HJ-320 Tri-Axis) [33].

Among 187 patients with prediabetes who took part in the experiment, average weight loss was 5% at 16 weeks and 4.8% at 12 months. They also saw a 0.37% drop in HbA1c levels by the end of the trial. Although it would be unrealistic to attribute these benefits solely to the inclusion of the wireless scale and pedometer, it's reasonable to assume that they contributed to the success of the project.

## SHINING A LIGHT ON BEACON TECHNOLOGY

No discussion of health-care innovation would be complete without an exploration of beacon technology, an innovation that is becoming big business for many industries (Fig. 2.3). One estimate suggests that there will be 400 billion beacons, or "tags" as they are sometimes called, deployed by 2020 [34]. Basically, a beacon is a piece of technology that provides location information to users, typically with the help of a Bluetooth low-energy wireless system. The dictionary defines a beacon as a light or fire located in a high or prominent position so that it can serve as a warning or a signal. In other words, it's a lighthouse to guide one on their way.

Smartphones use this type of technology to help you locate a mobile device. For instance, Apple created iBeacon to work with the Location Services that are part of iOS, the operating system on its phones and tablets. Google has named its Bluetooth low-energy beacons Eddystone—after the Eddystone Lighthouse in Great Britain. While Apple's beacons can only be used with Apple devices, Google's technology is open-source format so it can be used on Android and Apple devices [35].

In retail marketing, a company can use a small piece of hardware to serve as a beacon—which acts as a transmitter—and place it on a department store shelf next to a popular pair of sunglasses, for example. If you walk into the store with a smartphone that has a beacon reader on it and is equipped with Bluetooth capability, the beacon

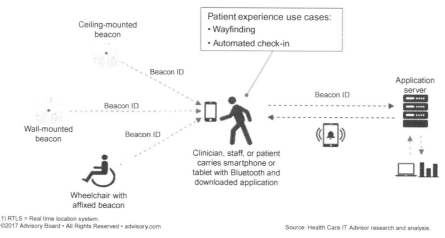

**Figure 2.3** Beacons are used to tag expensive medical equipment, serve as guides to direct patients to the correct location, and automate patient check-ins. (Used with permission of The Advisory Board)

will direct you to the physical location of the sunglasses. The applications in health care are almost limitless.

Beacons can be used to tag expensive medical equipment to help organizations keep track of its location, which would help clinicians who misplace items and help administrators maintain inventory and reduce the threat of thievery. Beacons can also enforce access rights to various locations. They may replace ID cards that give hospital staffers entry into certain restricted areas, for instance, and locate clinicians who are needed in an emergency. On the patient side of the equation, putting beacons in various locations in a hospital or clinic can serve as guides to direct patients to the correct location. They are also being considered to automate patient check-ins, partially replacing the cumbersome check in procedures now in place at most facilities. These innovations are long overdue and further evidence that the health-care industry continues to lag behind other businesses. Once upon a time, customers who booked an airline flight had to walk up to a check-in desk for boarding passes, but now they are easily printed out at home before ever arriving at the airport. Why should hospital check-in be any more difficult?

Beacon technology is competing with several other real-time location services (RTLS), including radio-frequency identification, WiFi, infrared, ultrawide band, ZigBee, GPS, RuBee, and near-field communication (Table 2.1). A recent analysis from the Advisory Board explains, however, that "beacon deployments are shaping up to be perhaps one-third less expensive than many traditional RTLS solutions due to the lower cost of the beacon hardware and software development kits." [36,37]. Individual beacons cost between $5 and $25 are the size of a computer mouse or smaller and have a range of about 10 m, which can be extended to more than 50 m [37].

Although it is customary for beacons to be placed in a stationary location and the beacon reader placed in a mobile device such as a smartphone, some health-care providers are now flipping the configuration, putting the transmitter in a patient's hand, for instance, and placing stationary readers throughout a facility. At BIDMC, several beacon-related services are in the pilot stage or being considered, including their use as an indoor navigation system, for patient check-in, to send patients relevant medical data while in the waiting room, to improve hospital operations by notifying hospital staff of their daily tasks based on the work area, to allow providers to tap on a beacon using a mobile app to get relevant information, and as a virtual clipboard, which can be installed near a patient's bed and used to send medical data to the doctor's phone as he or she enters the patient's room.

Nationwide, several hospitals have begun to incorporate beacons into their "wayfinding" programs, which help patients and visitors find their way through a building without getting lost. Among the organizations that have deployed the Connexient wayfinding platform are the Carle Foundation Hospital in Urbana, Illinois, Westchester Medical Center in New York, and the NIH Clinical Center and Mercy Health's Jewish Hospital in Cincinnati [38].

## AT THE INTERSECTION OF EVIDENCE AND DOUBT

In medicine, a well-respected scale that rates the strength of evidence supporting a diagnostic or treatment protocol exists to help clinicians make wise decisions. This Strength of Recommendation (SOR) taxonomy has been adopted by the American Academy of Family Physicians, its journal *American Family Physician*, and by the *Journal of Family Practice* [39]. Although there are differences in the way clinical medicine and health-care information technology are evaluated, experts nonetheless use similar metrics to evaluate the impact that IT initiatives have on patient care. The SOR system includes three categories, labeled A, B, and C, in descending order of strength. Protocols or initiatives that merit an A recommendation are considered Level 1,

**Table 2.1** Real-Time Location Services Technology Comparison Summary

| Type | Technology | Advantages | Challenges |
|---|---|---|---|
| Beacon | Bluetooth low energy | • Low-cost and low-power consumption<br>• Reasonable and adjustable range (inches to 50 m)<br>• Enabled on most mobile smart devices | • Somewhat susceptible to interference with walls and liquids<br>• Does not transmit a lot of data<br>• Cannot connect directly to the Internet |
| WiFi | Radio waves—802.11x | • Leverages existing WiFi infrastructure of access points and device radios<br>• No line-of-sight limitations<br>• Can connect to the Internet | • Accuracy not generally room level<br>• May compete with WiFi data and voice traffic |
| RFID | Active and passive radio frequency across the spectrum | • Active tags can have good range (100 m)<br>• Passive tags can be very inexpensive | • A mix of proprietary technologies<br>• Readers can be expensive |
| IR | Infrared | • Common and inexpensive | • Does not pass through walls |
| Ultrasound | Soundwaves | • Not subject to electromagnetic interference<br>• Good for room accuracy | • Does not pass through walls well<br>• Somewhat susceptible to certain sound interference |
| Ultrawide Band | Low-energy, high bandwidth | • High accuracy (within inches) | • Can be expensive |
| ZigBee | RFID mesh network | • Readers plug into electric outlets<br>• No line-of-site limitations | • Electric outlets may not be in the required locations or might be in use |
| RuBee | Long-wave magnetic signals in a peer-to-peer network | • Designed for harsh environments<br>• Not blocked by liquids or steel<br>• Low-power consumption | • Slow data rate<br>• Limited use in health care |
| NFC | Radio frequency | • Ability to transmit information between reader and tag (e.g., payments)<br>• High accuracy (within inches) | • Very short range reduces possible use cases |
| GPS | Satellite signal | • Accurate within a few feet<br>• Enabled on most mobile smart devices | • Inaccurate indoors<br>• High-energy requirements<br>• Susceptible to signal obstruction outdoors |

which means they are backed by good quality patient-oriented evidence. They are supported by systematic reviews and meta-analyses of randomized clinical trials that have generated consistent findings, high-quality RCTs, or "all or done" studies in which the treatment results in "dramatic changes in outcomes."

B-rated or Level 2 treatment protocols have limited quality patient-oriented evidence and are supported by systematic reviews and meta-analyses of "lower quality clinical trials or studies with inconsistent finding" as well as cohort studies and case control studies. C-rated Level 3 treatments are based on "consensus guidelines, extrapolations from bench research, usual practice, opinion, disease-oriented evidence (intermediate or physiologic outcomes only) or case series . . . ."

If we were to use the SOR taxonomy to rate the innovative technology described in Chapter 1, and in this chapter, most would come up wanting. There are no meta-analyses of consistently positive RCTs available to demonstrate the impact of blockchain technology, EHR-linked mobile apps, or remote sensors on patient outcomes, although there are clinical trials that provide limited support for several online initiatives. However, critics who expect health-care IT innovations to reach Level 1 miss the point. In fact, they misinterpret the term innovation itself. As we stated in Chapter 1, an innovation involves the novel use of people, process, and technologies to improve quality, safety, and efficiency. New healthcare information technology (HIT) initiatives, such as novel approaches to direct patient care, rarely come out of the womb as fully developed adults. Innovation, by definition, refers to an early stage of development and requires time to gather all the necessary research support to become mature, well-documented systems. Ironically, as clinical or technological innovations become fully developed and accepted in the professional community, they gradually become the status quo, which is in turn challenged by the next generation of innovative thinkers who have already found better solutions.

Critics who expect health-care IT innovations to meet Level 1 criteria may also overemphasize the value of meta-analyses and RCTs. RCTs have their shortcomings, including the tendency to fall victim to Type II statistical error. A Type I or alpha error occurs when a study concludes that there is a significant difference between two groups—a control group and an experimental group on a new drug, for example—when no difference actually exists. A Type II or beta error occurs when a study concludes that there is no real difference between treatment and control groups when in fact a true treatment effect exists. One reason a Type II error occurs is because too few subjects were included in the study.

Over the last several decades, there have been numerous examples of false-negative studies that concluded that a specific treatment protocol was useless when in fact that conclusion was unwarranted. These Type II errors hinder innovation. Freiman et al. documented the publication of 71 "negative" randomized trials that arrived at that unjustified conclusion. Freiman et al. found that the sample size in these studies was not large enough to give a high probability ($>90\%$) of detecting a 25% and 50%

therapeutic improvement. The investigators concluded that "Many of the therapies labeled as 'no different from control' in trials using inadequate samples have not received a fair test." [40]. A second analysis of the research literature, published 14 years later, found that the same mistake was still quite common. Moher et al. reviewed 383 RCTs and found that most of the studies with negative results did not have large enough sample sizes to detect a 25% or 50% difference between experimental and control groups [41].

## REDUCTIONISM VERSUS SYSTEMS BIOLOGY

Even when a clinical trial does recruit enough patients to avoid a Type II error, there are more fundamental issues to contend with. Most medical hypothesis testing is built on a reductionistic approach, a divide and conquer methodology that's "rooted in the assumption that complex problems are solvable by dividing them into smaller, simpler, and thus more tractable units." [42]. We have been conditioned to think in terms of one cause for one disease. The HIV pathogen causes AIDS, a lack of thyroid hormone causes hypothyroidism, cigarettes cause lung cancer. Decades of test tube, animal, and clinical experiments are conducted to cut away all possible "noise" until the precise singular causes of each disorder are found. While this approach has produced many effective treatments, it has its limitations. And the epidemiology of each of these disorders makes these limitations apparent.

Many persons who are exposed to HIV do not develop the infection, many with low thyroid levels don't develop the signs and symptoms of hypothyroidism, and many who smoke two packs a day never develop lung cancer. Obviously, there are cofactors involved in all these conditions, which when combined with the primary causes bring on the diseases. Detecting these contributing factors requires the reductionist approach to be complemented with a systems biology approach, which assumes that there are many interacting causes to each disease, and many interacting factors that contribute to the success or failure of technological innovations.

As the name implies, systems biology looks at entire biological or pathologic systems, rather than trying to decipher the cause of a disorder by analyzing one variable at a time. Systems biology can also use sophisticated data analytics to tease out these numerous interacting contributors, rather than rely on traditional statistical methods that compare single causes for each phenomenon being studied. A recent analysis conducted by Aaron Baum, MD, Icahn School of Medicine at Mount Sinai, New York, and his colleagues illustrates this approach [43].

Baum et al. reanalyzed the negative results from the Look AHEAD trial, which studied about 5000 overweight and obese patients with Type 2 diabetes, dividing them into two groups, one that received intensive lifestyle modification and a control group that was given only basic diabetes education and support. The goal was to determine if the lifestyle program would reduce cardiovascular deaths and events over 13.5 years. The trial was stopped after 9.6 years because researchers did not detect any measurable benefits [44]. Baum et al. decided to take a second look at the raw data from the Look AHEAD study using machine-learning and a sophisticated data analytics technique called causal forest modeling [43]. The approach allowed them to detect subgroups that benefited from the lifestyle modification program that the original investigators did not detect. In essence, they were taking a systems biology approach by measuring a long list of possible cofactors that may have contributed to the negative outcomes reported by the original researchers. Their subgroup analysis revealed that the intensive lifestyle modification *did* in fact avert cardiovascular events in most of the 5000 patients who participated in the Look AHEAD trial.

Specifically, Baum et al. found the intervention benefited patients with HbA1c levels of 6.8% or higher, namely patients with poorly controlled diabetes, and patients with a combination of well-controlled diabetes and *good* self-reported health, as assessed by questionnaire. Overall, 85% of the study population enrolled in the program benefited. But 15% of the population who had controlled diabetes and *poor* self-reported general health experienced negative effects from the intensive program. In the final analysis, the two groups canceled one another out, leading the Look AHEAD researchers to conclude that the program had no effect.

One of the lessons to be learned from this reanalysis is that negative RCTs can be misleading. It is not hard to imagine how such misleading studies can cause one to falsely reject HIT initiatives. Earlier in this chapter, we discussed the negative results that Michael Ong, MD, from the University of California, obtained when he and his colleagues tested the value of health coaching phone calls, along with the collection of vital signs that included blood pressure, heart rates, symptoms, and weight with the help of electronic devices in patients with heart failure. The researchers compared this regimen to a control arm who received the usual care [8]. They couldn't find any significant difference in hospital readmission rates 180 days after discharge for any cause: 50.8% were readmitted despite having all the extra attention and access to all the high-tech monitoring devices versus 49.2% in the usual care arm. Similarly, the investigators detected no difference in 30-day readmission or 180-day mortality.

But suppose the researchers had incorporated causal forest modeling into their final analysis, taking into account several possible contributing factors that may have influenced how patients responded to the interventions. Among the possible variables worth measuring: the design of the wearables used to take measures, their ease of use, how reliable the Internet connection was, the fact that the intervention "was not directly integrated with the physician practices caring for the patients" as Ong et al. explain [8]. It is also possible that the strategies used to promote patient engagement in this group of older adults were inadequate. Ong et al. reported that only 55.4% of patients randomized to telemonitoring were more than 50% adherent to the program. Similarly, the median age was 73 (range 62−84); that certainly could have also influenced the success rate. Had all these cofactors been considered in the final analysis, it's conceivable that remote patient monitoring would have proven successful, at least for one or more subgroups.

## REFERENCES

[1] Scher DL. The big problem with mobile health apps. Medscape March 4, 2015; Available from: https://www.medscape.com/viewarticle/840335 [accessed 27.10.17].

[2] Halamka JD. Using big data to make wiser medical decisions. Harv Bus Rev. December 14, 2015;. Available from: https://hbr.org/2015/12/using-big-data-to-make-wiser-medical-decisions [accessed 10.11.17].

[3] Khan U. Getting Started with CareKit. In: Session 237 Apple Worldwide Developers Conference. <https://www.youtube.com/watch?v = XTiuEM_-fVo&feature = youtu.be> 2016 [accessed 12.11.17].

[4] Berkowitz S. The BIDMC CareKit app. Life as a healthcare CIO 2016;. Available from: http://geekdoctor.blogspot.com/2016/11/the-bidmc-carekit-app.html [accessed 12.11.17].

[5] Tresorit. ZeroKit: Tresorit encryption platform. <https://tresorit.com/files/zerokit_encryption-sdk-documentation.pdf>; 2017.

[6] Johns Hopkins Medicine. Johns Hopkins mobile apps: Corrie Health. <https://www.hopkinsmedicine.org/apps/all-apps/corrie-health> [accessed 17.11.17].

[7] Volpp KG, Mohta NS. Patient engagement survey: improved engagement leads to better outcomes, but better tools are needed. NEJM Catal May 12, 2016;. Available from: https://catalyst.nejm.org/patient-engagement-report-improved-engagement-leads-better-outcomes-better-tools-needed/.

[8] Ong MK, Romano PS, Edgington S, et al. Effectiveness of remote patient monitoring after discharge of hospitalized patients with heart failure: the Better Effectiveness After Transition−Heart Failure (BEAT-HF) randomized clinical trial. JAMA Intern Med. 2016;176:310−18.

[9] Bloss CS, Wineinger NE, Peters M, et al. A prospective randomized trial examining health care utilization in individuals using multiple smartphone-enabled biosensors. PeerJ. 2016;4:e1554. Available from: https://doi.org/10.7717/peerj.1554.

[10] Siwicki B. Essentia Health slashes readmissions with population health initiative, telehealth. Healthcare IT News. March 15, 2016;. Available from: http://www.healthcareitnews.com/news/essentia-health-slashes-readmissions-population-health-initiative-telehealth.

[11] Agency for Healthcare Research and Quality. Heart failure disease management improves outcomes and reduces costs. <https://innovations.ahrq.gov/profiles/heart-failure-disease-management-improves-outcomes-and-reduces-costs?id = 275> [accessed 19.11.17].

[12] Spyglass Consulting Group. Trends in remote patient monitoring 2009. <http://www.spyglass-consulting.com/spyglass_whitepaper_RPM2009.html>; 2009.

[13] Walsh T. Studies are conflicted about remote patient monitoring—here's what we think. Advisory Board March 31, 2016;. Available from: https://www.advisory.com/research/market-innovation-center/the-growth-channel/2016/03/remote-patient-monitoring-roi.

[14] Balaguera H, Wise D, Ng CY, et al. Using a medical Intranet of Things system to prevent bed falls in an acute care hospital: a pilot study. J Med Internet Res 2017;19:e150. Available from: https://www.jmir.org/2017/5/e150/.

[15] Parkin CG, Davidson JA. Value of self-monitoring blood glucose pattern analysis in improving diabetes outcomes. J Diabetes Sci Technol 2009;3:500−8. Available from: https://www.ncbi.nlm.nih.gov/pmc/articles/PMC2769875/.

[16] Tenderich A. Use of blood glucose meters among people with type 2 diabetes: patient perspectives. Am Diabetes Assoc Diabetes Spectr. 2013;26:67−70.

[17] Shmerling RH. Type 2 diabetes: value of home blood sugar monitoring unclear. Harvard Health Blog. July 24, 2017; Available from: https://www.health.harvard.edu/blog/type-2-diabetes-value-home-blood-sugar-monitoring-unclear-2017072411989.

[18] Vieira G. Top 10 best glucose meters from consumer reports 2015. Diabetes Daily. September 18, 2017; Available from: https://www.diabetesdaily.com/blog/2015/06/consumer-reports-glucose-meter-ratings-2015/.

[19] Integrated Diabetes Services. Choose your blood glucose meter wisely. <http://integrateddiabetes.com/2016-blood-glucose-meter-comparisons/>; 2016.

[20] Bailey TS, Wallace JF, Pardo S, et al. Accuracy and user performance evaluation of a new, wireless-enabled blood glucose monitoring system that links to a smart mobile device. J Diabetes Sci Technol. 2017;11:736—43.

[21] Zhang R, Isakow W, Kollef MH, Scott MG. Performance of a modern glucose meter in ICU and general hospital inpatients: 3 years of real-world paired meter and central laboratory results. Crit Care Med. 2017;45:1509—14.

[22] Kwon J, Brown A. Are blood glucose meters accurate? New data on 18 meters. *diaTribe*. <https://diatribe.org/are-blood-glucose-meters-accurate-new-data-18-meters>; August 14, 2017.

[23] Klonoff D, Parkes JL, Kovatchev BP, et al. Blood glucose monitoring system surveillance program. Diabetes Technology Society. <https://www.diabetestechnology.org/surveillance.shtml> [accessed 23.11.17].

[24] Food and Drug Administration. FDA approves first continuous glucose monitoring system for adults not requiring blood sample calibration. <https://www.fda.gov/NewsEvents/Newsroom/PressAnnouncements/ucm577890.htm>; 2017.

[25] Comstock J. Apple reveals tracking app HealthKit and partners with Mayo Clinic, Epic. MobiHealthNews. June 2, 2014;. Available from: http://www.mobihealthnews.com/33728/apple-reveals-tracking-app-healthkit-and-partners-with-mayo-clinic-epic/.

[26] Sirichana W, Wang X, Taylor M, et al. The predictors for COPD exacerbations using remote patient monitoring. Eur Resp J. 2015;46:PA4589.

[27] Baroi S, McNamara RJ, McKenzie DK, et al. Advances in remote respiratory assessments for people with chronic obstructive pulmonary disease: a systematic review. Telemed JE Health 2018;24 (6):415—24. Available from: https://doi.org/10.1089/tmj.2017.0160.

[28] Tinschert P, Jakob R, Barata F, et al. The potential of mobile apps for improving asthma self-management: a review of publicly available and well-adopted asthma apps. JMIR Mhealth Uhealth. 2017;5:e113.

[29] Miller PJ. Case study: continuous monitoring of patient vital signs to reduce 'failure-to-rescue' events. Biomed Instrum Technol. 2017;P41—5. Available from: https://s3.amazonaws.com/rdcms-aami/files/production/public/FileDownloads/BIT/2017_BIT_JF_Monitoring.pdf.

[30] Beaton T. Top 10 remote patient monitoring companies for hospitals. mHealth Intell. 2017; Available from: https://mhealthintelligence.com/news/top-10-remote-patient-monitoring-solutions-for-hospitals.

[31] Knowler WC, Barrett-Connor E, Fowler SE, , et al.Diabetes Prevention Program Research Group Reduction in the incidence of type 2 diabetes with lifestyle intervention or metformin. N Engl J Med. 2002;346:393—403.

[32] Diabetes Prevention Program Research Group. 10-Year follow-up of diabetes incidence and weight loss in the Diabetes Prevention Program Outcomes Study. Lancet. 2011;374(9702):1677—86.

[33] Sepah SC, Jiang L, Peters AL. Translating the Diabetes Prevention Program into an online social network: validation against CDC standards. Diabetes Educ. 2014;40:435—43.

[34] OnyxBeacon. Active beacons monitoring the healthcare industry. <https://www.onyxbeacon.com/beacons-healthcare-industry/>; 2017.

[35] Google Beacon Platform. Mark up the world using beacons. <https://developers.google.com/beacons/> [accessed 03.12.17].

[36] Thompson D, Vicars A. How beacons engage patients where they are—on their smartphones. <https://www.advisory.com/research/health-care-it-advisor/it-forefront/2017/08/how-to-engage-patients>; 2017.

[37] Health Care IT Advisor. Beacon technology in health care: game changer for RTLS?. Advisory Board. <https://www.advisory.com/research/health-care-it-advisor/white-papers/2016/beacon-technology-in-health-care>; 2016.

[38] Swedberg C. Hospital combines kiosks with BLE app to help patients navigate. FRID J. 2017; Available from: http://www.rfidjournal.com/articles/view?16028.

[39] Ebell MH, Siwek J, Weiss BD, et al. Strength of recommendation taxonomy (SORT): a patient-centered approach to grading evidence in the medical literature. Am Fam Physician. 2014;69:548—56.

[40] Freiman JE, Chalmers TC, Smith H, et al. The importance of beta, the type II error and sample size in the design and interpretation of the randomized control trial. N Engl J Med 1978;299:690—4.

[41] Moher D, Dulberg CS, Wells GA. Statistical power, sample size, and their reporting in randomized controlled trials. JAMA 1994;272:122—4.

[42] Ahn AC, Tewari M, Poon C-S, Phillips RS. The limits of reductionism in medicine: could systems biology offer an alternative? PLoS Med. 2006;3:e208.

[43] Baum A, Scarpa J, Bruselius E, et al. Targeting weight loss interventions to reduce cardiovascular complications of type 2 diabetes: a machine learning-based post-hoc analysis of heterogeneous treatment effects in the Look AHEAD trial. Lancet Diabetes Endocrinol. 2017;5:808—15.

[44] Look AHEAD Research Group. Cardiovascular effects of intensive lifestyle intervention in type 2 diabetes. N Engl J Med. 2013;369:145—54.

[45] BIDMC. OpenNotes. < https://www.bidmc.org/patient-and-visitor-information/patient-information/patientsite/opennotes> 2018 [accessed 11.12.17].

[46] OpenNotes. Everyone on the same page. <https://www.opennotes.org/> [accessed 11.12.17].

[47] Delbanco T, Walker J, Bell SK, et al. Inviting patients to read their doctors' notes: a quasi-experimental study and a look ahead. Ann Intern Med. 2012;157:461—70.

[48] Klein JW, Jackson SL, Bell SK, et al. Your patient is now reading your note: opportunities, problems, and prospects. Am J Med. 2016;129:1018—21.

# CHAPTER THREE

# Exploring the Strengths and Weaknesses of Mobile Health Apps

Every new technology brings with it advantages and disadvantages, benefits and dangers. The history books are filled with the benefits and dangers that accompanied the 20th century introduction of nuclear power. The arrival of the Internet was likewise accompanied by its share of villains and heroes. mHealth is no different.

*A case in point*: The Owlet Smart sock is a device that parents attach to their infant to monitor heart rate and oxygen saturation. The readings are then wirelessly transmitted to a mobile app. While it may be an exaggeration to refer to this wearable "bootie" as villainous, it's certainly not one of mHealth's finest moments. Pediatrics experts agree that there is no sound reason for new parents to monitor these vital signs in a healthy infant. And the potential for false positives and unnecessary trips to the ED suggests that the technology may actually do more harm than good. The American Academy of Pediatrics policy statement on monitoring healthy infants at home is straightforward: "Do not use home cardiorespiratory monitors as a strategy to reduce the risk of SIDS." [1].

Despite these missteps, the list of useful mobile apps and wearables continues to grow. As the next several chapters will explain, both clinicians and patients can benefit from apps for diabetes, cancer, heart disease, mental health, and respiratory disorders like asthma. Our purpose in this chapter is to provide an overview of the advantages and disadvantages of mobile health apps as a group.

## WILL MHEALTH FADE INTO THE SUNSET?

Any discussion of the strengths and weaknesses of mobile health in general and medical apps in particular must begin by addressing a more fundamental question: Are mobile health and its related technologies here to stay, that is, will they become part of mainstream patient care and self-care? Or will the public—as well as health professionals—eventually lose its fascination for a novelty, like so many other novelties that have faded over time? The available statistics and expert observations on this issue cannot offer a definitive answer, nor do they always present a consistent picture, but they are nonetheless informative.

Eighty percent of all access to Beth Israel Deaconess Medical Center's publicly available web applications is done from mobile devices. At BIDMC, there is no question that mobile devices are the preferred platform for patients, families, and providers.

*The Transformative Power of Mobile Medicine.*
DOI: https://doi.org/10.1016/B978-0-12-814923-2.00003-9

Several other statistics suggest a similar interest in mobile health around the country, and in other nations.

The BIDMC statistic is consistent with a 2015 report from the Healthcare Information Management Systems Society (HIMSS) of 238 health-care professionals (Fig. 3.1A), which found that 90% of providers are using mobile devices to engage patients. That includes

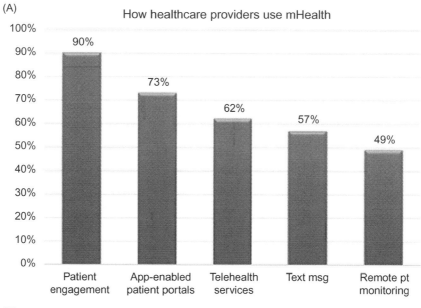

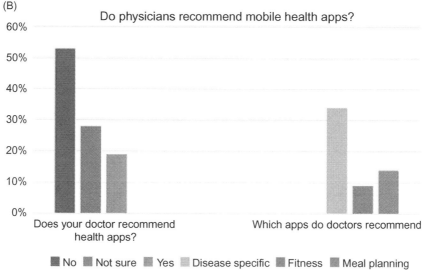

**Figure 3.1** (A) HIMSS 2015 Mobile Technology Survey of 238 health-care professionals found 90% used mHealth tools to engage patients. The other four statistics explain how that 90% is divided among four digital options. (B) Survey of 1200 respondents from Managed Group Medical Association 2017. *Adapted from (A) http://www.himss.org/2015-mobile-survey/infographic; (B) https://www.mgma.com/practice-resources/mgma-connection-plus/online-only/2017/august/mgma-poll-finds-about-one-out-of-five-providers-prescribing-health-related-apps-to-their-patients.*

73% who have app-enabled patient portals, 62% who are using telemedicine services, and 49% who use remote patient monitoring [2]. A survey of 1200 practitioners from the Managed Group Medical Association found that about one in five recommend health apps to their patients (Fig. 3.1B). A separate survey that looked at Americans' wish list of health apps and wearables found strong interest in apps that focus on diet and nutrition, symptom tracking, and physical fitness. Similarly, the survey found strong interest in wearables related to physical activity, symptom tracking, and disease management (Fig. 3.2).

Telemedicine services have also caught the attention of the general public, as well as health-care organizations that see the potential cost savings. As Fig. 3.3 illustrates, employers, primary care providers, health-care executives, and Americans in general are all onboard.

As Fig. 3.4 demonstrates, the interest in mobile health apps is not limited to the United States. A large survey of Germans in 2015 found its smartphone users concerned with smoking cessation, nutrition, weight loss, and medication adherence mobile apps, in descending order [3].

A national survey of the US residents has found 58.2% (934/1604) of respondents have used their mobile phones to download a health-related app [4]. And Fig. 3.5 shows that users were primarily interested in physical fitness, nutrition, and weight loss. On a more discouraging note, however, 42% lost interest in these digital tools and discontinued their use over time. This is a recurrent theme. Mobile health apps are not always "sticky" enough to encourage continued use.

Elizabeth Murnane at Cornell University and her colleagues [5] reported that smartphone users downloaded a variety of health apps, including those related to physical activity, weight loss, and medical conditions (Fig. 3.6). But many lost interest in

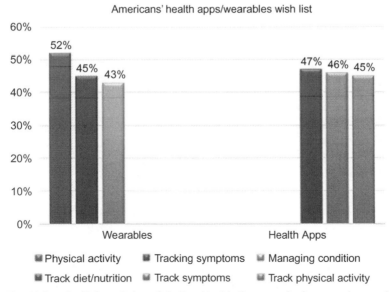

**Figure 3.2** The Makovsky/Kelton Pulse of Online Health Survey asked respondents what their top interests in mobile health apps and wearables are. *Adapted from http://www.makovsky.com/news/ fifth-annual-pulse-of-online-health-survey-2/.*

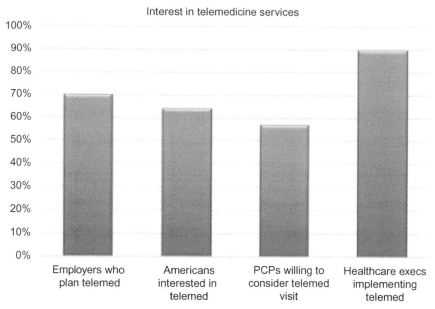

**Figure 3.3** Employers, primary care providers, health-care executives, and Americans in general are all interested in telemedicine. *Adapted from https://www.beckershospitalreview.com/healthcare-information-technology/telemedicine-to-attract-7m-patient-users-by-2018-12-statistics-on-the-thriving-market.html.*

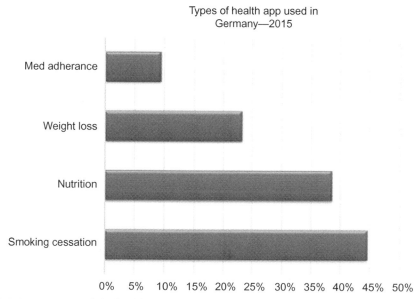

**Figure 3.4** Interest in mobile health apps is not limited to the United States. A large survey of Germans in 2015 found its smartphone users concerned with smoking cessation, nutrition, weight loss, and medication adherence mobile apps *Adapted from Ernsting C, Dombrowski SU, Oedekoven M, et al. Using smartphones and health apps to change and manage health behaviors: a population-based survey. J Med Internet Res 2017;19(4):e101.*

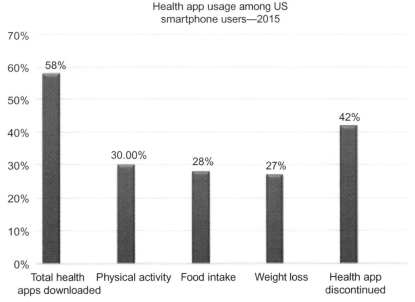

**Figure 3.5** Smartphone users were primarily interested in physical fitness, nutrition, and weight loss. *Adapted from Krebs P, Duncan DT. Health app use among US mobile phone owners: a national survey. JMIR mHealth uHealth 2015;3(4):e101*

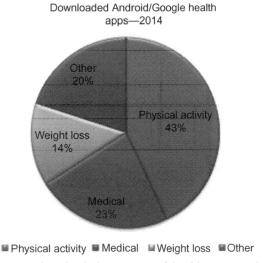

**Figure 3.6** Smartphone users downloaded a variety of health apps, including those related to physical activity, weight loss, and medical conditions. Murnane EL, Huffaker D, Kossinets G. Mobile health apps: adoption, adherence, and abandonment. UbiComp/ISWC Adjunct *Adapted from Murnane EL, Huffaker D, Kossinets G. Mobile health apps: adoption, adherence, and abandonment. UbiComp/ISWC Adjunct, Adapted from <https://www.semanticscholar.org/paper/Mobile-health-apps-adoption-adherence-and-abandonm-Murnane-Huffaker/39ae91f6c5aee4d222bae4b8a1de9e81614293be>; 2015.*

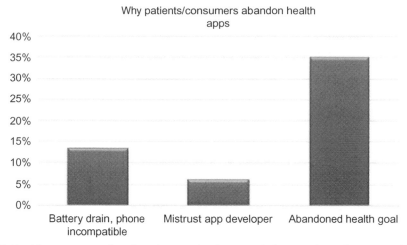

**Figure 3.7** Health app users often lose interest in these tools for a variety of reasons. *Murnane EL, Huffaker D, Kossinets G. Mobile health apps: adoption, adherence, and abandonment. UbiComp/ISWC Adjunct, Adapted from <https://www.semanticscholar.org/paper/Mobile-health-apps-adoption-adherence-and-abandonm-Murnane-Huffaker/39ae91f6c5aee4d222bae4b8a1de9e81614293be>; 2015.*

them. The most common reason, as illustrated in Fig. 3.7, is that they abandoned the health goal they were initially pursuing.

Another challenge for clinicians interested in mHealth, as well as the developers of said technologies, is engaging the elderly. A recent research letter published in *Journal of the American Medical Association* suggests that while the interest of Medicare beneficiaries 65 and older in digital health is growing, it has yet to reach the levels seen in younger adults. Fig. 3.8, for instance, shows that among adults with a mean age of 75, interest in digital health increased from 21% to 25% from 2011 to 2014 [6].

Critics may cite statistics on the loss of interest in mobile apps as reason enough to abandon mobile health apps as a way to provide or augment patient care. But the fault is not necessarily in mobile apps. Many researchers have demonstrated that it is difficult to maintain the public's interest in their own health, regardless of the platform. For instance, it is estimated that as much as 69% of medication-related hospital admissions in the United States are the result of poor medication adherence, a statistic that was collected long before the age of smartphones and mobile apps [7]. It would seem the fault is with human nature itself. As one astute observer once pointed out, "Humans are hardwired for quick fight-or-flight reactions in the face of an imminent threat, but not highly motivated to act against slow moving and somewhat abstract problems, even if the challenges that they pose are ultimately dire." [8]. Taking steps to prevent degenerative diseases like diabetes, hypertension, or other invisible threats, which usually have dire consequence far down the road, is not built into our DNA. But being burdened by such genetic baggage is no reason to stop clinicians and technologists

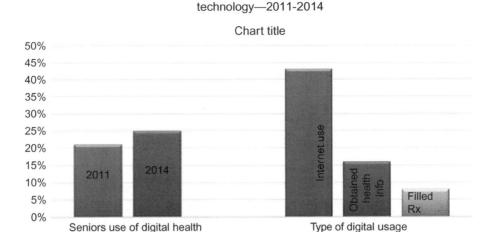

**Figure 3.8** Among adults with a mean age of 75, interest in digital health increased from 21% to 25% from 2011 to 2014. *Adapted from Levine DM, Lipsitz SR, Linder JA. Trends in seniors' use of digital health technology in the United States, 2011—2014. JAMA 2016;316:538—40.*

from designing the best mobile health apps possible. They are just one more tool in our toolbox to try to persuade patients to take responsibility for their own health.

Taking all the aforementioned statistics into account, it is reasonable to say that mHealth is *not* going to fade into the sunset, and that despite its shortcomings, it will continue to intrigue and engage many patients far into the foreseeable future. With that in mind, health-care organizations large and small have to ask themselves: Am I paying enough attention to this shift in public sentiment? And will ignoring this trend leave my organization at a significant competitive disadvantage? It is very easy for well-respected organizations to assume that the high quality of their in-person patient services is so impressive that it will outshine any mobile health initiative concocted by neighboring providers. But history has a way of humbling even the most impressive icons. No doubt IBM once thought it was invincible as the age of personal computers dawned; no doubt many desktop computer manufacturers were certain they would never be dethroned by tablets and smartphones. No doubt countless brick and mortar retail stores that sold books, DVDs, CDs, and clothes were certain that Amazon.com would never replace "the personal touch" of face-to-face salesmanship or that its president would become the richest man in the world by 2018.

A report from Accenture Consulting strongly suggests many health-care providers are not taking mHealth seriously enough and do not believe that mobile medicine will transform patient care [9]. The report sums up the state of affairs in many provider organizations this way: "Mobile health app usage has grown rapidly over the past three years and more than half of health consumers (54 percent) would like to use their smartphones more to interact with health-care providers. However, the response from health-care providers has been woefully inadequate. Consumers complain of poor user experience with providers' proprietary apps and mobile functionality that often fails to meet their individual needs." One of the reasons patients are so dissatisfied with providers' mHealth initiatives is that they have become accustomed to the seamless effort required to use the digital tools offered by other industries, including banking, retail, and entertainment.

A 2015 Accenture survey found that 66% of the 100 biggest hospitals in the United State were offering mobile apps to the public. But only 40% of this subset had actually taken the time to design their own apps. Provider apps fall short in several ways. The three functions that consumers want most in their health apps are access to medical records, the ability to book, change, and cancel doctor appointments, and the ability to request prescription refills electronically. A 2013 Accenture analysis found that only 11% offered EHR access, 8% gave existing patients the ability to control their appointments electronically (2% for new patients), while only 6% offered Rx refills. Given these statistics, it is not surprising to discover that about 7% of patients are willing to switch providers because of a poor customer experience. Many older physicians bristle when they hear anyone suggest that customer satisfaction needs to be part of medical practice, but today's competitive environment demands it be part of the equation.

The poor mHealth capabilities in many health-care organizations has created a vacuum, one that opens the door for more creative entrepreneurs to rush in with health apps that are easy to use and fully functional. Competitive health-care providers who develop partnerships with these disruptors are likely to steal patients from bigger players in the health-care industry who continue to insist that there's nothing to worry about: "After all, medicine is a social phenomenon; patients are always going to seek out face-to-face relationships with compassionate, brilliant clinicians." No doubt scores of vice presidents at Sears, Montgomery Ward, and Caldor's spouted similar received wisdom shortly before they were given their severance packages.

It has been estimated that mobile apps from health-care providers generate 7000 downloads on average, compared to 300,000 downloads from the disruptive app ZocDoc, 750,000 from GoodRx, 1 million downloads each for iTriage, WebMD, and the calorie counter from MyFitnessPal [9].

Presumably, these figures have changed somewhat since they were reported in 2013 and 2015, and health-care organizations are starting to get the message. If not, several hospital executives can look forward to severance packages as well.

The perspective discussed in the Accenture analysis is consistent with a report from the consulting firm Deloitte, which pointed out that health care is rapidly moving toward a patient-centered environment in which "different consumer segments will likely demand that mHealth programs and delivery channels be tailored to their distinct user preferences." [10]. Its report emphasizes the importance of personalizing the consumer's experience and keeping mobile health apps simple to use, much like the ease of use and functionality they have come to expect in hospitality, retail, travel, and banking.

Deloitte's analysis of the mHealth market divides users into six segments, emphasizing that each subgroup navigates the health-care system in different ways. One group is "online and onboard," another term for describing patients and consumers who are actively involved in their own care. They are very comfortable using digital tools and mobile apps to find clinicians and compare treatment choices. Other groups include the sick and savvy, the out and about, the shop and save, the casual and cautious, and the content and compliant. Depending on the subgroup a developer or health-care provider is targeting, they will need to design their health apps to meet very different needs and expectations.

## CHOOSING EFFECTIVE, STICKY HEALTH APPS

Even health-care providers who do see the need for innovative mobile apps still face numerous obstacles. Given the human tendency to seek the path of least resistance, identifying the most effective, "stickiest" mobile apps becomes a real challenge. In *Realizing the Promise of Precision Medicine* [11], we discussed the need to individualize medical care and the importance of improving patient engagement. When choosing mobile health apps to meet patients' needs, it is critical to keep both goals in mind. Each patient is at a different stage in their journey, with some lacking basic knowledge about the disorder and others almost as well informed as their providers. With that in mind, the prescription of health apps should be geared to an individual's level of patient engagement.

Mobile apps can be divided into several broad categories based on the level of engagement that each patient has reached. Patients will likely lose interest in a health app if it is not consistent with their level of engagement [12]. Among the categories that can meet patients' needs are apps that

- Provide educational information
- Alert patients to take some specific action
- Track their health or medical data
- Present patients with data that they have put into their mobile device
- Offer advice based on the data that patients input into their device
- Allow patients to send information to their family or health-care provider
- Provide social network support
- Reward patients for changing their behavior [12].

An activated, fully engaged patient will likely know most of the basics that would be provided in a mobile app that only offers educational information and will lose interest in the digital tool quickly. Conversely, a patient who is only modestly interested in managing a chronic condition may not benefit from a more in-depth app that tracks their medical data or physiological parameters. They must learn to "crawl before they walk."

The second category on the list, namely, alerting patients to take some action, requires a closer look as well. No doubt many patients have benefited from mobile apps that remind them to take their medication on time or to make an appointment for their periodic mammogram or colonoscopy. Forgetfulness is a normal human failing, and these apps can address that. But to be realistic, most nonadherence is *not* driven by poor memory. It's driven by far more complex and entrenched motives, and the reason many patients fail to heed their provider's advice is because it is just not that important to them, or because in their minds the risks outweigh the benefits, or because they can't afford the prescribed intervention, or because they didn't fully understand the advice offered or . . .. The list is long.

Addressing the first issue, Ira Wilson, an authority on patient adherence, points out that "we don't forget to pick up our kids from day care or to make dinner or anything else that's really important." [13]. With that reality in mind, it's not surprising that reminder apps that send patients alerts frequently fall short. This once again emphasizes the point we have made elsewhere in this text: Mobile tools can only supplement medical care, not replace it. And for clinicians to motivate such uncooperative patients will require *time*, a precious commodity in today's health-care environment.

Time is required to ask patients about why they don't want to follow a prescribed course of action. Time is required to query patients about possible obstacles to adherence: "Can you afford this medication?" "Does it cause unbearable GI reactions?" "Do you have a way to get to your next appointment or would it mean losing a day's pay and possibly termination?" "Do you think your hypertension requires medication even though it's not causing you any pain or discomfort?" We obviously can't solve all our patients' problems, but knowing what's behind their noncompliance is the first step toward resolving it.

Ira Wilson takes this type of deeper probing to heart when he works with patients:

*Wilson doesn't push reluctant patients to take their medications. During a visit with a man with poorly controlled hypertension, for example, Wilson began by asking, "What does hypertension mean to you?" The man replied, "I'm kind of a hyper guy. And sometimes I get tense." He explained that he takes his medications only when he feels both hyper and tense. In such situations, I [the author of a* New England Journal of Medicine *editorial] would probably reply, "That's not how it works," but Wilson gently asks, "May I share a different perspective?" And patients usually say, "Of course, that's why I'm here."*

*People like Wilson don't need a digital reminder to have these conversations or to abandon the "doctor knows best" dynamic. For those of us who struggle, the most effective adherence booster may be giving doctors and patients the time to explore the beliefs and attributions informing medication behaviors. These conversations can't happen in a 15-minute visit [13].*

Another issue that clinicians and app developers need to be concerned about is the medical dictum to do no harm. Many physicians and nurses hesitate to recommend health apps because they not only worry that patients will be wasting their time, but that the advice offered will hurt them. Developers must be certain that if their app collects patient's data, it also alerts users when they enter dangerous data, including severely abnormal blood levels or signs and symptoms suggesting an emergency is about to unfold. Singh et al evaluated 121 health apps that collected health information but found only 28 that offered users an appropriate response when they entered information that required immediate attention from a health professional. They point out that "For only three target populations—people with a history of stroke, those with asthma or chronic obstructive pulmonary disorder, and the elderly—did at least 50 percent of the apps react appropriately to relevant health information." [12].

The need to alert app users to seek immediate medical attention or call 911 applies in a wide variety of situations. If an asthma patient tells a mobile app that their shortness of breath is severe, the app should be advising the person to contact their provider or call 911. Similarly, if a patient reports they have chest pain, suicidal thoughts, very elevated or depressed blood pressure or blood glucose levels, or significant short-term changes in body weight, a health app should be designed to catch these problems and advise the patient appropriately. Many mobile apps do not. When Singh et al. reviewed 121 health apps, they found that only about 20% provided an appropriate response to such health dangers. That statistic varied widely, however, depending on specialty. For example, 60% of the apps that targeted stroke patients provided appropriate advice to patients who entered dangerous information. For cancer and diabetes, it was less than 20%. With disturbing numbers like this, it is not surprising that some health authorities have referred to mobile health apps as "digital snake oil."

But such indictments go too far, placing responsible, well-documented mobile apps in the same category as poorly conceived apps. There are criteria available to help separate "snake oil" from valuable mobile resources, including usability testing, observational studies, content analysis, and randomized controlled trials (RCTs) [14]. For clinicians, content analysis and RCTs are near the top of this list. Clinicians want to be assured that the content and advice provided by these digital tools are consistent with published clinical guidelines and rely on strong scientific evidence. And when recommending mobile apps to engaged patients that also encourage behavior change, providers want to know that the behavior change techniques are well grounded in behavioral science—not voodoo science.

Unfortunately, too few commercially available apps have done their due diligence and incorporated the relevant clinical guidelines that would make their product a top choice among medical professionals. For instance, when 227 diabetes self-management apps were compared to evidence-based guidelines published by the American Association of Diabetes Educators (AADE), many came up short. AADE lists seven behaviors that it considers essential to any self-management program, regardless of the platform in which it exists. The program should encourage [15]:

- Healthy eating
- Physical activity
- Self-monitoring
- Taking one's medication
- Reducing risk
- Healthy coping

The aforementioned analysis of 227 diabetes apps found not a single one encouraged all seven basic behaviors, and few included more than two of the behaviors; fewer than half promoted healthy eating (44.9%); biomarker self-monitoring was featured in 48%, while medication adherence was 46.7% [16]. Among all the apps reviewed, self-monitoring—mostly in the form of blood glucose monitoring—was the most frequent feature. On a more positive note, this study was conducted in 2013. Diabetes apps have matured considerably in the intervening years, which we will discuss in more detail in Chapter 5.

A content analysis of self-help mobile apps that are designed to address the needs of patients with clinical depression has also been revealing. Cognitive behavioral therapy (CBT) and behavioral activation (BA) have the most scientific evidence to support their effectiveness in alleviating mental depression. A review of 117 apps that focused on depression found that only 12 apps (10.26%) delivered CBT or BA [17]. A closer look at these 12 apps can help clinicians determine the extent to which each of these evidence-based apps adhere to the core components of a CBT or BA approach to psychiatric care.

Huguet et al. list the following as essential to the CBT approach: Education about depression; an explanation of how the CBT approach works; depression rating; monitoring cognitions; emotions, physical sensations, and behaviors; conceptualization; behavioral, and cognitive techniques. The core ingredients of BA also include education about depression and explanation of the model, as well as "depression rating, activity monitoring, giving each activity a rating for pleasure, giving each activity a rating for mastery, activity scheduling of pleasant behaviors, and activity scheduling of avoided behaviors." On average, the 12 reviewed apps adhered to CBT principles by 15% (median) with a range of 0 to 75%, and BA principles by 18.75% (range 6.25%–25%). As Table 3.1 points out, two mobile apps—eCBT Mood and Depression CBT

**Table 3.1** When researchers reviewed a list of mobile apps, two apps—eCBT Mood and Depression CBT Self-Help Guide—scored best for cognitive behavioral therapy and Activity Diary and Overcome Depression Pro received the best rating for behavioral activity.

| Name | Author | Commercial Market | | Scientific Literature | Cost | Popularity | | | Adherence With the Core Ingredients | |
|---|---|---|---|---|---|---|---|---|---|---|
| | | iTunes | Google Play | | | ASR[a] | # of Reviews | # of Downloads | CBT (%) | BA (%) |
| Depression Cure: The Free 12 Week Course | Archie's Empire | ✓ | ✗ | ✓ | $8.99 | 4.5 | 29 | n/a[b] | 10 | 18.75 |
| iCounselor: Depression | iCounselor | ✓ | ✗ | ✓ | $1.19 | 2.5 | 9 | n/a[b] | 5 | 6.25 |
| MoodMaster antidepression app | MoodMaster | ✓ | ✗ | ✓ | $4.59 | n/a[b] | n/a[b] | n/a[b] | 15 | 18.75 |
| eCBT Mood | MindsApps LLC | ✓ | ✗ | ✓ | $1.19 | 2.5 | 12 | n/a[b] | 55 | 25 |
| Activity Diary | Happtic Pty. Ltd | ✓ | ✗ | ✗ | $3.49 | n/a[b] | n/a[b] | n/a[b] | 0 | 18.75 |
| Antidepression | Dion LLC | ✓ | ✓ | ✗ | $0 | 3.7 | 250 | 10,000 − 50,000 | 25 | 25 |
| MoodTools—Depression Aid | MoodTools | ✓ | ✓ | ✗ | $0 | 4.3 | 1,466 | 50,000 − 100,000 | 10 | 12.5 |
| Mood Sentry | Mood Apps LLC | ✗ | ✓ | ✓ | $1.97 | 5.0 | 3 | 50 − 100 | 25 | 6.25 |
| Depression | AppCounselor | ✗ | ✓ | ✓ | $0.99 | 4.0 | 5 | 500 − 1000 | 15 | 6.25 |
| Depression CBT Self-Help Guide | Excel at Life | ✗ | ✓ | ✓ | $0 | 4.2 | 1154 | 100,000 − 500,000 | 75 | 25 |
| Overcome the Depression Pro | Zanapps | ✗ | ✓ | ✗ | $0 | 4.2 | 5 | 100 − 500 | 20 | 18.75 |
| Positive Activity Jackpot | T2 | ✗ | ✓ | ✓ | $0 | 3.4 | 74 | 10,000 − 50,000 | 0 | 12.5 |

[a]ASR, Average satisfaction rating.
[b]Some apps do not have enough user reviews to have an average rating, stated by n/a.
Huguet A, Rao S, McGrath PJ, et al. A systematic review of cognitive behavioral therapy and behavioral activation apps for depression. PLoS One, <https://doi.org/10.1371/journal.pone.0154248>; 2016 [accessed 09.01.18].

Self-Help Guide—scored best for cognitive behavioral therapy and Activity Diary and Overcome Depression Pro received the best rating for behavioral activity.

Although content analysis favors a few of the mental health apps reviewed by Hugurt et al., there are no RCTs that we are aware of that support the efficacy of these apps. Other investigators, on the other hand, have found the mobile medicine approach to depression effective in an RCT. A chatbot called WoeBot, which we discussed in Chapter 1, is a text-based conversational agent that relies on the principles of CBT. Kathleen Fitzpatrick, PhD and her colleagues at the Stanford School of Medicine tested Woebot on students between 18 and 28 years of age who were recruited from a university community social media site. Seventy recruits were split into two groups, either given access to the bot or directed to an eBook called Depression in College Students, from the National Institute of Mental Health. The researchers found the bot group reported significant improvement when compared to controls after 2–3 weeks, as measured by the 9-item Patient Health Questionnaire, the 7-item Generalized Anxiety Disorder scale, and the Positive and Negative Affect Scale [18].

Several other RCTs have been conducted that support the efficacy of mobile medical apps and related mHealth initiatives in patient care. A. DeVito Dabbs, RN, PhD, from the University of Pittsburgh School of Nursing and her associates have tested a mobile app called Pocket PATH in patients who received a lung transplant [19]. Pocket PATH was distributed to 99 lung transplant patients, while 102 similar patients received routine care. Receiving a lung transplant poses numerous self-care challenges for patients after discharge, including the need to track potentially dangerous signs and symptoms, reporting abnormalities to their transplant coordinator, taking vital signs, and using a spirometer. Pocket PATH was designed to meet these challenges with the help of several user-friendly features. The smartphone platform provided patients with screens that let them record daily measurements, including spirometry, vital signs, and symptoms. It also displayed data graphically, so patients could see their readings over time, allowing them to detect positive and negative trends. The graphs even marked upper and lower limits of normal ranges so that patients could spot problems quickly. When the app recorded parameters that were dangerously abnormal, it automatically sent the user an alert so they knew to reach out to their provider.

Patients in the Pocket PATH group were more than five times as likely to do self-monitoring, when compared to the control group [odds ratio (OR) 5.11, $P < .001$]. Similarly, patients who used the mobile app were more likely to adhere closely to the prescribed postdischarge regimen (OR = 1.64), and more than three times as likely to report critical abnormal health indicators. Unfortunately, the researchers were not able to document any differences in hospital readmissions or differences in mortality.

Francis Plow, PhD, and Meghan Golding from Case Western Reserve University School of Nursing enrolled 46 patients with musculoskeletal and neurologic disorders in an RCT to test whether mobile apps that encourage physical activity have a measurable effect [20]. They compared an mHealth-based self-management program that included Lose it! from FitNow, Inc, iPro Habit Tracker Free from IntelliPro, and Memories: The Diary, against a paper-based self-management program, and a control group. All three groups attended an in-person session and participated in three follow-up phone calls over 6 weeks. A Google Nexus 7 tablet was used to track patients' progress in the mobile app arm of the study.

In the final analysis, the mobile app and paper-based groups saw significant increases in planned exercise, compared to the control group. Plow and Golding also found "There were small and nonsignificant changes between the mHealth-based and paper-based groups with regard to most outcomes. However, the mHealth-based group had moderate effect size increases ($d = 0.47$) in planned exercise and leisure-time physical activity compared with the paper-based group." Since digital and paper-based programs worked, the study suggests that clinicians need to be selective when they choose a self-management regimen for their patients. One size does not fit all.

mHealth initiatives have also proven effective in pediatric care. B.T. Nezami from the University of North Carolina at Chapel Hill and associates performed an RCT among overweight or obese mothers with children between ages 3 and 5 to determine if such a program would reduce the children's intake of sugar-sweetened beverages and juice [21]. At baseline, the children were consuming at least 12 ounces of these drinks a day. A wait list control group was compared to a group that received one group educational session, lessons on a mobile website, and text messages. Six months into the program, children on the mHealth program had significantly reduced their intake of sweet beverages, and mothers in the program had lost 2.4 kg, compared to 0.9 kg in the control group.

A second pediatrics-related mHealth initiative launched by Chinese researchers also showcases the potential of mobile medicine, in this case by addressing the harm done by second-hand smoke. This RCT used face-to-face counseling and mobile phone-based education to reduce the exposure of infants to second-hand smoke and to encourage fathers in such households to quit smoking. At 12 months, mothers also reported less exposure to second-hand smoke [22].

Finally, a systematic review of RCTs that evaluated mHealth interventions against noncommunicable diseases (NCDs) in developing countries looked at eight trials that encompassed more than 4000 patients. The studies tested a variety of programs ranging from health promotion, appointment reminders, medication adjustments, to clinical decision support and addressed diabetes, asthma, and hypertension. It concluded that "Except for one study all showed rather positive effects of mHealth interventions on reported outcome measures. Furthermore, our results suggest that particular types of mHealth interventions that were found to have positive effects on patients with communicable diseases and for improving maternal care are likely to be effective also

Exhibit 11: Number of published digital health efficacy studies over time
Total: 571 efficacy studies between 2007~2017 (YTD)
140
120
100
80
60
40
20
0
2007
2008
2009
2010
2011
2012
2013
2014
2015
2016
2017 YTD
Observational study
Randomized controlled trial
Systematic review or critically appraised topics
Meta analysis

**Figure 3.9** Analysis excludes accuracy studies, only includes studies with hard outcomes. "Observational Study" includes all trials examining interventional value or impact of an app excluded from the other three categories regardless of design. *IQVIA AppScript Clinical Evidence Database, August 14, 2017.(Used with permission)*

for NCDs." [23]. (Additional mHealth studies that have incorporated the RCT methodology will be discussed in the chapters on individual health conditions that follow.)

In total, there have been at least 571 studies conducted to rate the efficacy of mobile health apps since 2007, with one fourth of those investigations occurring in 2017 as of August. More importantly, about 44% of these studies were RCTs and metaanalyses [24] (Fig. 3.9).

The IQVIA Institute for Human Data Science has performed a detailed analysis of the clinical evidence supporting mobile health apps, rating their maturity and relative quality. Its rating scale places a single observational study near the bottom of the scale, progressing upward through multiple observational studies, a single RCT, multiple RCTs, a single metaanalysis, and several metaanalyses. Using this methodology, it organized mobile apps into several categories. In the category called "Potential disappointments—more study required" are apps for exercise, pain management, dermatology, autism, schizophrenia, multiple sclerosis, and autism. In the category called "Candidates for [clinical] Adoption" were mobile apps for weight management,

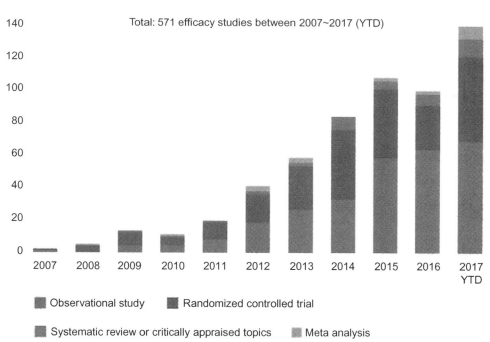

asthma, COPD, congestive heart failure, stroke, arthritis, cancer, PTSD, insomnia, smoking cessation, stress management, cardiac rehabilitation, and hypertension. The most important categories listed in the IQVIA analysis, which it considered candidates for inclusion in clinical guidelines, were diabetes, depression, and anxiety.

IQVIA has also generated of list of "Top-rated apps" for 2017, taking into account their top clinical rating and the fact that they are free and publicly available. Top-rated apps in the free list includes Runkeeper by FitnessKeeper, Inc, Headspace, for stress management, Kwit, for smoking cessation, My Spiritual Toolkit, an AA 12 step program, mySuga, for diabetes management, and SmartBP for hypertension. In the top clinical rating list are Omada, for diabetes prevention, BlusStar Diabetes by WellDoc, Kardia by AliveCor, for atrial fibrillation and dysrhythmias, MoovCare for cancer patients, AiCure for medication management, and Walgreens medication refill app.

It is also important to keep in mind that discarding digital tools just because they are not supported by RCTs is somewhat shortsighted. As we have pointed out before [11], RCTs may be the gold standard by which we judge the value of therapeutic interventions, but they are not the only metrics to consider. RCTs have significant limitations. They are very expensive to perform; the results sometimes do not apply to individual patients in community practice because the inclusion and exclusion criteria that existed when the RCT was conducted do not reflect real-world conditions; and some treatments cannot be adequately tested in RCTs for ethical reasons or because there are too few subjects available, which is usually the case with rare diseases or uncommon adverse drug reactions. Unfortunately, many thought leaders in clinical medicine believe the only justification for recommending a treatment protocol is an RCT. They insist that since the RCT is the most effective way to arrive at scientific truth, any less rigorous evidence cannot be used as the basis for recommending therapy. This black or white approach to reliable medical treatment deprives patients of many options that have persuasive but not definitive evidence to support them. Among these, "silver-standards" and "bronze-standards" are open clinical trials that do not include a placebo arm, case-control studies, animal experiments, test tube studies that confirm the mechanism of action for a therapeutic agent, and observational data derived from Big Data analytics. When taken together, evidence from these diverse sources can be very persuasive.

The fact that a treatment doesn't produce statistically significant results in a clinical study doesn't necessarily mean it will not benefit an individual patient. If a clinical trial enrolls too few subjects, it is possible to falsely conclude that the intervention has no effect because the results of the trial yielded statistically insignificant results, a Type II error. Put another way, if the intervention benefits only a very small number of patients, a very large number of subjects have to be enrolled in the study to reach statistical significance. If for example, a specific mobile app will benefit 1 in 1000 patients but a clinical trial tests it in only 300 patients, the odds of detecting the therapeutic effect are very small.

## THE ROLE OF N OF 1 STUDIES IN MOBILE MEDICINE

One way to address this statistical shortcoming is to employ an N of 1 study, which repeatedly measures an individual's response to treatment or other intervention and then compares it to the person's response to no treatment or another control arm. Some investigators use this type of A/B; others use an A/B/A design in which the patient is put back on the experimental intervention a second time. The N of 1 study design is especially useful as we gradually transition to a personalized medicine model. Nonetheless critics point to one weakness: the inability to generalize the results of N of 1 studies to the general public. But if we are aiming for personalized care, this objection is almost irrelevant. If the goal of personalized medicine is to locate a specific treatment regimen that suits an individual's genetic and environmental peculiarities, including their psychosocial needs, nutritional profile, microbiome, cognitive skills, preferences and so on, one would expect such regimens would *not* be generalizable—by definition. Criticizing the results of an N of 1 trial because it cannot be applied to the general public is like criticizing a master tailor who creates a well-crafted one-of-a-kind suit because it can't be sold to the masses at Walmart.

That said, there are other weaknesses in the N of 1 design that are more substantive, including the so-called digital placebo effect. Many mobile phone users are overly enthusiastic about what their apps can accomplish, and such expectations can result in falsely positive study results. However, as is the case with the placebo effect in more traditional studies, these positive effects tend to fade over time, which is one reason to conduct long-term experiments to test the value of mobile medicine.

Including a control arm in an N of 1 study would also help eliminate any overly optimistic expectations on the part of patients, especially if the patient is blinded to experimental and control interventions. But that's often impractical or impossible to do when testing the value of a mobile health app. It may be more realistic to conduct comparative effective studies with individual patients in which they first use a scientifically well-documented program and then switch off to an untested app. For instance, in diabetes care, that's feasible because there are a few well-documented medical apps.

The value of an N of 1 study can also be bolstered by using some of the methodological tools used in conventional clinical trials. Lillie et al. [25] discuss the advantage of using sequence randomization in choosing how the A/B comparisons are conducted. Creating an A/A/B/A/A/B/B sequence, for example, in which the patient is randomly switched back and forth between two mHealth programs may be useful. So would a washout period between the experimental and control apps so that patients can "recover" from their expectations—much like a subject in a drug trial who loses the physiological effects of the medication he is on as it's washed out of his body before he is moved to the second phase of the trial. Using a metaanalysis to collect data from multiple N of 1 trials may also be worth considering and would address the criticism about these trials not yielding generalizable results.

Finally, the power of an RCT that includes many individuals can be strengthened by increasing the number of participants in the trial, an option that is obviously not available in an N of 1 trial. Instead, its ability to persuade us of the value of the tested intervention can be bolstered by increasing the number of observations in the one test subject over time. In other words, a study that exposes a patient to a mobile health intervention 10 or 20 times and taking measurements each time will be more convincing than a simple A/B/A/B trial that includes only 4 observations. Since any one individual is likely to experience natural variability in their response to treatment, the more observations the better.

## USABILITY, USER RATINGS, AND OBSERVATIONS STUDIES

Although efficacy and evidence-based content are top priorities for clinicians as they evaluate mobile health apps, usability ratings and observational studies also have their place. Jake-Schoffman et al. explain that "Usability or user testing refers to how well an app functions and whether or not it serves its intended purpose. Typically, usability is measured across dimensions such as user ratings of app flexibility, operability, understandability, learnability, efficiency, satisfaction, attractiveness, consistency, and error rates." [14]. Standards provided by the International Organization for Standardization are available to help developers as they design and test mobile apps, including ISO 9241 and ISO 25062. App usability can be measured by means of laboratory testing, field evaluations, and user ratings.

Unfortunately, when it comes to functionality and ease of use, mobile health apps vary widely, with some being far more complicated to use than others. If you ask health professionals their preference on what they seek in clinician-facing apps, most want as few mouse clicks as possible. It's unlikely the general public is any more tolerant of health apps that require needless clicks. One lab study that looked at the usability of 11 diabetes, depression, and caregiving apps found about 42% of participants were able to complete tasks without assistance using technology: "Participants were interested in technology, but lacked confidence navigating the apps and were frustrated by design features." [14,26]. A lab test that compared two pain-management mobile apps in patients with chronic pain found it was a lot easier to enter data into an app called Pain Scale than it was for Manage My Pain [27].

Observational studies also offer some clues on the relative worth of mobile health apps. Carpenter et al. looked at data from more than 152,000 users of a mental health app called Happify to determine whether it predicted more positive emotions, which it did [14,28], The app seemed to bolster well-being by about 27% over an 8-week period. Their analysis also supported the value of big data analysis in reviewing mobile apps. As Carpenter and associates state "Using observational analyses on naturalistic big data, we can explore the relationship between usage and well-being among people using an Internet well-being intervention and provide new insights into the underlying mechanisms that accompany it. By leveraging big data to power these new types of analyses, we can explore the workings of an intervention from new angles, and harness the insights that surface to feed back into the intervention and improve it further in the future."

A similar data mining project that looked at weight loss apps suggests they do have value—in distinct subgroups. Katrina Serrano, PhD, with the National Cancer Institute, and her colleagues performed a cross-sectional deidentified analysis of users of Lose it!, a weight loss app. The dataset of more than 12,000,000 divided users into 24 subgroups; Serrano et al.'s analysis looked at 3 subgroups, incorporating nearly 1 million data points. They found that only 4.87% of occasional users of the weight loss app lost weight, while 37.6% of basic users reported successful weight loss. By contrast, 72.2% of power users lost weight. Certain behavioral characteristics also distinguished the three groups [29].

## EXPERT RECOMMENDATIONS

Another metric that many clinicians would like to see is recommendations from experts with medical training. Several organizations are entering this space, including the American Heart Association, the American Medical Association, the DHX Group, and the Healthcare Information and Management Systems Society (HIMSS). All four groups have come together to form an alliance called Xcertia. Its goal is to develop guidelines to evaluate mHealth apps with the hope that such guidelines will improve their quality, safety, and effectiveness. As we go to press, Xcertia is in the early stage of development. Its mission is to use a collaborative approach that will "incorporate feedback from its members in a consensus-driven process to advance the body of knowledge around clinical content, usability, privacy and security, interoperability and evidence of efficacy. Xcertia will not engage in certifying mobile health apps but will encourage others to apply its principles and guidelines in the development and curation of safe and effective mobile health apps." [30]. Xcertia is currently soliciting comments on a list of preliminary guidelines at www.xcertia.com.

The proposed guidelines cover app operability, privacy, security, and content. The guidelines outline several commonsense basics. To meet operability standards, the "mobile health app installs, loads, and runs in a manner that provides a reasonable user experience." For the app to be secure, the application has to protect users from external threats. The guideline for content says "The app is based on one or more credible information sources including, but not limited to, protocols, published guidelines, evidence-based practice and peer-reviewed journals. New sources can be submitted for acceptance with supporting documentation."

The American Psychiatric Association also has a system in place to evaluate mobile health apps. Like Xcertia, APA is not rating mobile health apps but has provided a detailed stepwise process that allows individual clinicians to perform their own evaluation. The five-step evaluation process, which is spelled out in detail on the APA website, includes [31]

- Gather background information,
- Risk/privacy and security,
- Evidence,
- Ease of use,
- Interoperability.

APA illustrates this process by evaluating PTSD Coach, a mobile app available from the US Department of Veterans Affairs [32]. It provides educational resources, a self-assessment tool, and ways to find support and help managing stress for patients with posttraumatic stress syndrome. APA addresses many important questions that developers and clinicians should consider as they design and recommend health apps.

- Does the app collect personal data or is the data deidentified?
- Is collected data encrypted?
- Does the app meet HIPAA requirements if it has been designated as a medical device?
- What are its core functions?
- Is the tool based on peer-reviewed published scientific evidence?
- Is the app easy to use, and customizable?
- Can the app share data with an EHR, or with data tools like Apple HealthKit?

In April 2017, Great Britain's National Health Service took the evaluation of health apps a step further. It launched a mobile service that allows clinicians to prescribe health apps from the NHS Apps Library. The AppScript platform provided by the data science research company IQVIA is available to clinicians so that they can offer apps to patient free of charge. NHS is vetting some of the apps in its Digital Apps Library and marking them as such with the label "NHS Approved," which indicates that there is enough evidence to demonstrate they meet "the high standard of quality, safety, and effectiveness you expect from the NHS." [33].

The Digital Apps Library, located here, is still in beta testing but does include at least one vetted health app called myCOPD [34]. To gain free access to the app, patients have to contact their general practitioner, a COPD health-care team or a clinical commissioning group. If they don't qualify, they can still purchase it on their own. myCOPD includes videos on how to use an inhaler, as well as breathing exercises, a medication diary, and a symptom tracker. Other health apps that are listed on the NHS site include an evidence-based tool to help young persons manage their feelings and avoid self-harm and one that offers a support group for patients with dementia. There are also apps on breast cancer, which allows patients to keep track of their treatment, MyHealth Guide, described as "easy-to-use communication tool for adults with learning disabilities," a telemed app, secure messaging apps, and several apps that address nutritional issues. Developers interested in getting their app into the NHS Apps Library should review the NHS web page, which is designed to help them submit their proposal.

As mentioned above, England's National Health Service has embraced the digital tools available from IQVIA Institute. IQVIA's report on digital health in the United Kingdom provides this rationale for using mobile health apps:

*The overall body of clinical evidence on app efficacy has grown substantially and now includes 571 published studies, enabling the identification of a list of Top Apps with increasingly robust clinical evidence. The use of such Digital Health apps in just five patient populations where they have proven reductions in acute care utilisation (diabetes prevention, diabetes, asthma, cardiac rehabilitation and pulmonary rehabilitation) could save the U.K. healthcare system an estimated £170 million per year. This represents about 1.1% of total costs in these patient populations. If this level of savings could be extrapolated across total national health expenditure, annual cost savings of £2 billion could be achieved.*

*Efforts by patient care organisations to fit Digital Health tools into clinical practice has progressed, with 860 current clinical trials globally incorporating these tools. Despite progress to date, a number of barriers still exist to widespread adoption by patient care institutions, and only an intermediate level of adoption has yet occurred. A variety of industry and policy initiatives have now emerged to address these barriers and accelerate the ongoing adoption of Digital Health tools by care provider organisations [24].*

The National Institute for Health and Care Excellence (NICE), United Kingdom, has also made real progress in evaluating mobile health apps. One of its missions is to provide guidelines for the use of health technologies within the NHS. NICE reviews data on drugs, medical devices, diagnostic techniques, surgical procedures, and health promotion activities, basing its recommendations on clinical evidence that demonstrates these treatments and activities are effectives, and on economic evidence that shows they are cost effective [35].

The Institute has evaluated numerous mHealth services, with very detailed reviews of each service or mobile app. Among the apps that have been studied: GDm-Health, which is intended for women with gestational diabetes, AliveCor Health Monitor and AliveECG app for monitoring cardiac function, Sleepio, for adults with sleeping problems, VitalPAC, for assessing vital signs in hospital patients, LATITUDE NXT Patient Management System, which allows clinicians to monitor cardiac devices at home, and numerous others [36].

To illustrate the depth and thoroughness of the NICE reviews, consider its analysis of GDm-Health. The review explains the app's purpose, which is to download data from a patient's blood glucose meter and send it to a secure website where it can be monitored by clinicians. The website also lets clinicians send text messages to patients to help them manage their condition. But NICE does not stop there. It also evaluates the app's clinical effectiveness, user benefits, and the impact that its use would have on costs and resources. It then puts the mobile app into the context of NICE's guideline for gestational diabetes, explains several of the app's features in detail, and goes into an extensive discussion of the evidence supporting the app, including summaries of each of the clinical trials that support its use, the key outcomes, and its strengths and limitations. Its overall assessment of the evidence concludes in the following way:

- The evidence suggests that GDm-Health is a reliable and user-friendly method of remote blood glucose monitoring, and that it improves communication between health-care professionals and people with gestational diabetes.
- There is a high degree of patient compliance and satisfaction with using the system
- An ongoing randomized trial comparing GDm-Health with standard care has completed data collection, and publication of results will add to the current body of evidence particularly in relation to improving clinical outcomes [37].

An equally impressive review of Sleepio is available from NICE. It explains that the app is intended for adults with poor sleep and may help them through the use of cognitive behavioral therapy. The self-help program costs £200 per user per year for individual purchases. The app is supported by good quality evidence, but the review points out that the effect size varies among studies, none of which compared Sleepio to CBT that was provided through in-person therapy. Like many other mHealth resources evaluated by NICE, Sleepio underwent a technical evaluation using the NHS "Digital Assessment Questions." That tool enabled reviewers to look at clinical safety, security and privacy, information governance, usability, accessibility, technical stability, updates and version control, and regulatory approval. Sleepio passed the assessment. The app is available through the NHS system through 10 clinical commission groups and "It has the potential to increase the availability of CBT-I and there is some evidence of good user engagement and experience."

The well-respected Cleveland Clinic has also given its blessing to several health apps, all of which were apparently developed by the Clinic itself. Some are relevant to patients who are attending the clinic and others can be used by the general public. Among the apps offered by the Clinic: MyEpilepsy, an iPad app that provides details on facts, misconceptions, diagnosis and treatment options for the disorder; ORAnywhere, which targets clinicians, includes a scheduling tool that lets them know what operating rooms and endoscopy suites are available for us. Available apps from the Cleveland Clinic can be located in the Apple Apps store and on iTunes.

Iltifat Hussain, MD, an assistant professor of emergency medicine and Director of the Mobile App Curriculum at the Wake Forest School of Medicine, is also a good source to turn to when seeking expert recommendations on both clinician-facing and patient-facing health apps. He. and his colleagues have created a web service called imedicalapps.com, which includes pages and pages of reviews. A recent sample from imedicalapps.com included EBM Stats Calc, designed to help clinicians and students calculate number needed to treat, pretest probability, and positive and negative predictive values, all of which are essential calculations for anyone interested in evidence-based medicine and scientific research [38]. The purpose of Gas Guide: Quick Anesthesia, on the other hand, is to help medical students and residents learn the basics of anesthesiology, while M.B.C.T. Syllable Drilling was designed to help speech pathologists teach children to speak. The credo of imedicalapps.com is summed up this way: "Unlike other medical review and mHealth sites, the imedicalapps Editors do not make medical apps and institute strict conflict of interest policies enabling us to provide an unbiased view of mobile medical technology. . .."

There is little doubt that health professionals need services like imedicalapps.com, the Cleveland Clinic's app store, and the advice from groups like the AHA, AMA, and HIMSS. A recent survey from the Medical Group Management Association found that fewer than 20% of physicians were recommending health-related mobile apps to patients while more than half said they were not [39]. A separate poll from QuantiaMD found about 4 out of 10 physicians refused to prescribe an app to their patients because there was no regulatory oversight of these digital tools. About one in five physicians chose not to recommend an app because there was no long-term data to support the effectiveness [39]. That last statistic remains a concern despite all the expert advice mentioned above because these expert reviews and advice cannot take the place of controlled studies that evaluate the effects of each app on clinical outcomes, health-care costs, clinician workflow, patient loyalty, administrative burden, and so on.

But as we said earlier, many mobile apps are not supported by RCTs. One alternative research methodology that is slowly emerging relies on mechanistic reasoning rather than population-based data [40]. Mechanistic reasoning may be especially valuable in evaluating precision medicine therapies that benefit very small numbers of patients. Currently, this approach has merit in the study of physiological and genomic-related interventions—for example, precision cancer therapy. Its role in studying digital interventions like mobile medical apps remains to be seen. But there are several other research methodologies available that can be used to evaluate mHealth programs. Despite these innovations, the vast majority of efficacy studies of mHealth still rely on traditional RCT design [41].

Among the alternatives to the RCT worth considering when evaluating mobile health apps are time-series, stepped-wedge, regression discontinuity, and the previously discussed N of 1 study design. In fact, RCTs may be incompatible and impractical for evaluating many mHealth apps because they are constantly being updated, ungraded, and revised at a fast pace. And with the help of machine learning and artificial intelligence, some apps have the ability to learn from past experience, making traditional research methods even more problematic.

The rigid protocols associated with RCTs do not have the ability to handle such "moving targets." The National Institutes of Medicine's mHealth Evidence Workshop emphasized that existing research designs—including the RCT design—are not keeping pace with innovations in mobile medicine [42]. The Chicago-based Center for Behavioral Intervention Technologies has been concentrating its efforts on ways to create research methodologies that are more appropriate for testing mHealth. Researchers have also developed a framework, the Continuous Evaluation of Evolving Behavioral Intervention Technologies (CEEBIT) as an alternative to RCTs [43]. But for stakeholders who still believe that RCTs should continue to be used for evaluation, there are also ways to improve the efficiency of traditional RCTs that may facilitate their use in mHealth research, including the use of within-group designs, fully automating the recruitment of subjects, and shortening follow-up by modeling long-term outcomes.

Several innovative thinkers are now trying to design unique digital tools to help researchers and clinicians use some of these alternative approaches to determine which treatment options are best for individuals. Their goal is to not just find the best research methodology to evaluate health apps but to create applications, wearable monitoring devices, and protocols that will enable providers to manage N of 1 studies in everyday medical practice. A case in point: Katrina Davidson, PhD, with Columbia University's College of Physicians and Surgeons, has received a 2017 Transformative Research Award from the National Institutes of Health. The project's aim is to develop an electronic platform for clinicians and patients to order a single N of 1 trial. The platform will then be used to help validate and individualize treatment for hypertension, clinical depression, and chronic insomnia [44]. Creative minds like Dr. Davidson are helping to transform mobile medicine into an invaluable supplement to routine patient care.

# REFERENCES

[1] Task Force on Sudden Infant Death Syndrome. SIDS and other sleep-related infant deaths: updated 2016 recommendations for a safe infant sleeping environment. Pediatrics 2016;138(5):e20162938.

[2] HIMSS. HIMSS mobile technology survey infographic, <http://www.himss.org/2015-mobile-survey/infographic>; 2015.

[3] Ernsting C, Dombrowski SU, Oedekoven M, et al. Using smartphones and health apps to change and manage health behaviors: a population-based survey. J Med Internet Res. 2017;19(4):e101.

[4] Krebs P, Duncan DT. Health app use among US mobile phone owners: a national survey. JMIR mHealth uHealth 2015;3(4):e101.

[5] Murnane EL, Huffaker D, Kossinets G. Mobile health apps: adoption, adherence, and abandonment. UbiComp/ISWC Adjunct 2015;. Available from: https://www.semanticscholar.org/paper/Mobile-health-apps-adoption-adherence-and-abandonm-Murnane-Huffaker/39ae91f6c5ae e4d222bae4b8a1de9e81614293be.

[6] Levine DM, Lipsitz SR, Linder JA. Trends in seniors' use of digital health technology in the United States, 2011–2014. JAMA. 2016;316:538–40.

[7] Kleinsinger E. Working with the noncompliant patient. Perm J. 2010;14:54–60.

[8] Popovich N, Schwartz J, Schlossberg T. How Americans think about climate change, in six maps. New York Times December 31, 2017;F13. Available from: https://www.nytimes.com/interactive/2017/03/21/climate/how-americans-think-about-climate-change-in-six-maps.html?_r = 0.

[9] Accenture Consulting. Insight driven health losing patience: why healthcare providers need to up their mobile game, <https://www.accenture.com/t20160118T135036__w__/us-en/_acnmedia/Accenture/Conversion-Assets/DotCom/Documents/Global/PDF/Dualpub_24/Accenture-Losing-Patience.pdf> 2015 [accessed 04.02.18]

[10] Deloitte. The four dimensions of effective mHealth: people, places, payment, and purpose, <https://www2.deloitte.com/us/en/pages/life-sciences-and-health-care/articles/center-for-health-solutions-four-dimensions-effective-mhealth.html>; 2014.

[11] Cerrato P, Halamka J. Realizing the promise of precision medicine. New York: Elsevier/Academic Press; 2017.

[12] Singh K, Drounin K, Newmark LP, et al. Many mobile health apps target high-need, high-cost populations, but gaps remain. Health Affairs. 2016;35:2310–18.

[13] Rosenbaum L. Swallowing a spy—the potential uses of digital adherence monitoring. N Engl J Med. 2018;378:101–3.

[14] Jake-Schoffman DE, Silfee VJ, Waring ME, et al. Methods for evaluating the content, usability, and efficacy of commercial mobile health apps. JMIR Mhealth Uhealth. 2017;5:e190.

[15] American Association of Diabetes Educators. AADE7 self-care behaviors, <https://www.diabeteseducator.org/living-with-diabetes/aade7-self-care-behaviors>; 2017 [accessed 08.01.18].

[16] Breland JY, Yeh VM, Yu J. Adherence to evidence-based guidelines among diabetes self-management apps. Trans Behav Med. 2013;3:277–86.

[17] Huguet A, Rao S, McGrath PJ, et al. A systematic review of cognitive behavioral therapy and behavioral activation apps for depression. PLoS One. 2016; https://doi.org/10.1371/journal.pone.0154248 [accessed 09.01.18].

[18] Fitzpatrick KK, Darcy A, Vierhile M. Delivering cognitive behavior therapy to young adults with symptoms of depression and anxiety using a fully automated conversational agent (Woebot): a randomized controlled trial. JMIR Mental Health. 2017;4:e19.

[19] Dabbs AD, Song MK, Myers BA, et al. A randomized controlled trial of a mobile health intervention to promote self-management after lung transplantation. Am J Transplant. 2016;16:2172–80.

[20] Plow M, Golding M. Using mHealth technology in a self-management intervention to promote physical activity among adults with chronic disabling conditions: randomized controlled trial. JMIR mHealth uHealth. 2017;5:e185.

[21] Nezami BT, Ward DS, Lytle LA, et al. A mHealth randomized controlled trial to reduce sugar-sweetened beverage intake in preschool-aged children. Pediatr Obes. 2018;13(11):668–76. Available from: https://doi.org/10.1111/ijpo.12258.

[22] Yu S, Duan Z, Redmon PB, et al. mHealth intervention is effective in creating smoke-free homes for newborns: a randomized controlled trial study in China. Sci Rep 2017;7:9276. Available from: https://doi.org/10.1038/s41598-017-08922-x.

[23] Stephani V, Opoku D, Quentin W. A systematic review of randomized controlled trials of mHealth interventions against non-communicable diseases in developing countries. BMC Public Health. 2016;16:572.

[24] IQVIA Institute. The growing value of digital health in the United Kingdom evidence and impact on human health and the healthcare system. Report summary, <https://www.iqvia.com/institute/reports/the-growing-value-of-digital-health-in-the-united-kingdom>; 2017.

[25] Lillie E, Patay B, Diamant J, et al. The n-of-1 clinical trial: the ultimate strategy for individualizing medicine?. Per Med. 2011;8:161−73.

[26] Sarkar U, Gourley GI, Lyles CR, Tieu L, Clarity C, Newmark L, et al. Usability of commercially available mobile applications for diverse patients. J Gen Intern Med 2016;31(12):1417−26.

[27] Reynoldson C, Stones C, Allsop M, Gardner P, Bennett MI, Closs SJ, et al. Assessing the quality and usability of smartphone apps for pain self-management. Pain Med 2014;15(6):898−909.

[28] Carpenter J, Crutchley P, Zilca RD, Schwartz HA, Smith LK, Cobb AM, et al. Seeing the "big" picture: big data methods for exploring relationships between usage, language, and outcome in internet intervention data. J Med Internet Res 2016;18(8):e241.

[29] Serrano KJ, Yu M, Coa KI, Collins LM, Atienza AA. Mining health app data to find more and less successful weight loss subgroups. J Med Internet Res 2016;18(6):e154.

[30] American Medical Association. Alliance forms to develop guidelines for evaluation of mHealth apps. <https://www.ama-assn.org/alliance-forms-develop-guidelines-evaluation-mhealth-apps>; 2016

[31] American Psychiatric Association. App evaluation model, <https://www.psychiatry.org/psychiatrists/practice/mental-health-apps/app-evaluation-model>; 2018 [accessed 26.01.18].

[32] U.S. Department of Veterans Affairs. National center for PTSD. Mobile app: PTSD coach, <https://www.ptsd.va.gov/public/materials/apps/PTSDCoach.asp>; 2018 [accessed 26.01.18].

[33] National Health Service. About us, <https://apps.beta.nhs.uk/>; [accessed 27.01.18].

[34] National Health Service. Find digital tools to help you manage and improve your health, <https://apps.beta.nhs.uk/#!>; n.d.[accessed 27.01.18].

[35] NICE. Technology appraisal guidance, <https://www.nice.org.uk/about/what-we-do/our-programmes/nice-guidance/nice-technology-appraisal-guidance>; 2018[accessed 06.02.18].

[36] NICE. Mobile health technology search results, <https://www.nice.org.uk/search?q = mobile + health>; 2018 [accessed 06.02.18].

[37] [NICE3] NICE. Health app: GDm-Health for people with gestational diabetes, <https://www.nice.org.uk/advice/mib131/chapter/Evidence-on-effectiveness>; 2017 [accessed 06.02.18].

[38] Bagby K. Best medical apps of the week, <https://www.imedicalapps.com/2018/01/best-medical-apps-week-1-26-2018/>; 2018.

[39] Tennant RM. MGMA poll finds about one out of five providers "prescribing" health-related apps to their patients. MGMA Connection Plus 2017;. Available from: https://www.mgma.com/practice-resources/mgma-connection-plus/online-only/2017/august/mgma-poll-finds-about-one-out-of-five-providers-prescribing-health-related-apps-to-their-patients.

[40] Tonelli MR, Shirts BH. Knowledge for precision medicine mechanistic reasoning and methodological pluralism. JAMA 2017;318:1649−50.

[41] Pham Q, Potts H, Azevedo N, Larsen M. Beyond the randomized controlled trial: a review of alternatives in mHealth clinical trial methods. JMIR mHealth uHealth. 2016;4:e107.

[42] Kumar S, Nilsen WJ, Abernethy A, Atienza A, Patrick K, Pavel M, et al. Mobile health technology evaluation: the mHealth evidence workshop. Am J Prev Med 2013;45(2):228−36.

[43] Mohr DC, Cheung K, Schueller SM, Hendricks BC, Duan N. Continuous evaluation of evolving behavioral intervention technologies. Am J Prev Med 2013;45(4):517−23.

[44] Columbia University Medical Center. CUMC researcher receives NIH "High-Risk, High-Reward" grant, <http://newsroom.cumc.columbia.edu/blog/2017/10/05/cumc-researcher-receives-nih-high-risk-high-reward-grant/>; 2017.

# CHAPTER FOUR

# Mobile Apps: Heart Disease, Hypertension, and Atrial Fibrillation

It is the rare healthcare professional who is not aware of the enormous toll that heart disease takes on the American population. The Centers for Disease Control and Prevention estimates that 610,000 people die of the disease in the United States every year, which is the equivalent of one in every four deaths [1]. But that statistic pales in comparison to the damage done by cardiovascular diseases (CVDs) worldwide. This family of disorders, which includes coronary artery disease and stroke, is the number 1 cause of death globally, felling about 17.7 million people in 2015 alone. That translates to nearly a third (31%) of all deaths globally [2].

What bothers clinicians most about these disturbing numbers is that so many of the deaths could be avoided by addressing risk factors and contributing causes such as tobacco use, poor diet, obesity, lack of exercise, and overuse of alcohol. And among those individuals who develop CVD despite taking reasonable precautions, many of the most devastating consequences can be averted with the help of early detection, management of hypertension, stress management, nutritional therapy, medication, and a variety of other therapies. There is no doubt that a close face-to-face relationship between clinicians and patients is the key to reducing the impact of CVD worldwide, but there is also persuasive evidence to show that several mobile health tools can supplement the efforts. It is important to point out, however, that supplemental is not synonymous with trivial. As the evidence discussed below indicates, many of these tools can have a significant impact on patient care, especially for certain subgroups. What remains to be determined is *which* tools are most effective and which ones are a waste of time.

There is evidence to suggest that text messaging, health apps, and other digital tools can personalize care for patients with coronary heart disease (CHD) and hypertension and affect clinical outcomes. For example, the tobacco, exercise, and diet messages or TEXT ME trial, a large single-blind randomized study, found that texting semipersonalized health messages to patients with preexisting heart disease reduced low density lipoprotein (LDL) cholesterol levels by 5 mg/dL and systolic blood pressure (BP) by 7.6 mmHg after 6 months. It also increased physical activity by 345 METs (metabolic equivalents) minutes/week and significantly reduced smoking ($P < .001$) [3].

In this trial, Clara Chow, MBBS, with the George Institute for Global Health, Sydney Medical School in Australia, and her colleagues conducted a single-blind,

*The Transformative Power of Mobile Medicine.*
DOI: https://doi.org/10.1016/B978-0-12-814923-2.00004-0

randomized clinical trial (RCT) that recruited 710 patients with a mean age of 58 years [3]. About half of patients, all of whom had already been diagnosed with coronary artery disease, received their usual care while half received four text messages a week for 6 months, along with their usual care. The messages offered heart-friendly advice, motivational reminders, and support to change their behavior. The messages were somewhat personalized based on each patient's known risk factors. At the end of 6 months, LDL cholesterol levels were significantly lower in the intervention group—by 5 mg/dL—and there were also significant drops in systolic BP and body mass index compared to control patients. Although these improvements were modest, they would likely have an impact on clinical outcomes over time—if patients continued to follow the advice once the program ended. And although the researchers who conducted this trial refer to their results as a "modest improvement in LDL cholesterol," previous studies have demonstrated that every 1% drop in LDL level results in a 1% reduction in CHD deaths and nonfatal myocardial infarction [4].

This text messaging experiment involved an automated electronic delivery system that sent out four messages a week for 24 weeks and used an algorithm that was able to personally address some messages and personalize the content of the message based on each patient's baseline characteristics. Some messages, for instance, focused on smoking if the subject used tobacco. One of the limitations of the studies, however, was its short-term nature. It was not possible to determine if the effects the text messages had on behavior and the clinical benefits would last over time. This is an important issue because mobile health apps seem to engage many patients because they are a relatively new way to interact with their healthcare provider. When the novelty wears off, patients may lose interest and see diminishing returns. The relatively short duration of Chow's study gives pause to third party insurers who are looking for digital tools that they can rely on to provide cost-effective care. They are disinclined to support any program that doesn't generate long-term benefits.

mHealth critics often bemoan the fact that many studies have not proven the effects of such programs over the long-term, and with that in mind, Canadian researchers have managed to demonstrate that text messaging's benefits can be extended to at least 12 months. Pandey et al. [5] conducted two randomized controlled pilot trials over a year period, using text messaging to encourage cardiac medication compliance and exercise among patients undergoing rehabilitation after being discharged from the hospital following myocardial infarction. Thirty-four patients who received text reminders during the day and were supposed to take their medication had a 14.2 percentage point improvement in medication adherence compared to controls. Among 50 patients who received messages to exercise as directed, they spent an additional 4.2 days per month following the prescription.

The American Heart Association (AHA) has done an exhaustive review of the research on the role of mobile technology, concentrating on the prevention of CVD.

AHA focused on how mobile technology might influence the risk factors most likely to contribute to heart disease, including obesity, lack of physical exercise, hypertension, and elevated cholesterol levels [6]. The results were mixed, which suggests that these tools work in some populations and not others, and that different types of mobile interventions produce different results.

Five of eight randomized controlled trials conducted in the United States found significantly more weight loss occurring in patients using mobile technology than in controls. Many of the positive studies used text messaging or text messaging plus Facebook to encourage weight loss.

For clinicians and technologists searching for a common denominator for success among mobile weight loss tools, an analysis by Khaylis et al. is useful. They identified five features that have been linked to effective technology-based weight loss programs [7]:

- A structured approach
- Self-monitoring
- Feedback and communication
- Social support
- The ability to individualize the intervention

Elsewhere in its review, AHA concludes that:

*Mobile interventions can produce weight loss in motivated populations, albeit at a lower magnitude relative to traditional treatment approaches. The characteristics of successful mobile interventions are quite comparable to those of their offline counterparts: The largest weight losses are produced by comprehensive, multicomponent interventions that are personally tailored, promote regular self-monitoring, and involve a qualified interventionist. The accumulated evidence, although limited, supports intervention delivery through a range of technology channels (including the Web, SMS, e-mail, telephone, and IVR), with limited variability in the magnitude of weight loss outcomes.*

But on a cautionary note, it also states that although the evidence strongly supports the value of texting when supported by phone calls, web sites, and social media, "there is no evidence to suggest that SMSs as a stand-alone intervention are effective."

Finally, as providers consider using mobile technology, it is important to remember that weight loss programs do not have to result in a huge weight reduction to have benefits. AHA points out that a sustained weight loss of only 3%−5% can have an impact, significantly reducing the risk of CVD. In practical terms, that means a 250 lb person only needs to lose between 7.5 and 12.5 lb to see results.

Similarly, when evaluating mobile-enhanced programs that encourage exercise, there's no need to reach for the moon. The Centers for Disease Control and Prevention recommends at least 30 minutes of moderate intensity physical activity on most days of the week. And AHA reminds readers that sustained exercise reduces the risk of Type 2 diabetes, stroke, osteoporosis, and depression. It also reduces the risk of

CVD by lowering BP. AHA reported the results of 14 RCTs it considered of high quality, which used texting on a mobile phone, email, a pedometer, and the Internet. Nine of the 14 reported the programs were effective in increasing physical activity.

## HYPERTENSION

The use of mHealth interventions to help patients gain control over their hypertension also may have merit. There is ample evidence to demonstrate that self-measured BP (SMBP) monitoring is valuable in managing hypertension, which is why the seventh report of the Joint National Committee on prevention, detection, evaluation, and treatment of high BP recommended its use. But while SMBP monitoring, strictly speaking, is considered a mobile technology, it's not exactly the cutting edge. To date, however, research on more sophisticated digital tools has suffered from one major weakness. Most high-quality studies have only lasted 6 months or less. Since hypertension is a chronic disease requiring long-term solutions, we need to establish the effect of mobile technology over many years.

Despite this shortcoming, it is worth mentioning that five high-quality studies using SMBP plus support found a reduction in systolic BP of 2.1 and 8.3 mmHg. (Only one of the studies included mHealth support.) To put these numbers into perspective: a 1 mmHg drop in systolic BP has been associated with about 20 fewer cases of heart failure (HF) per 100,000 person-years in African Americans and about 13 fewer HF deaths in whites [8].

Since those findings were reported, others have done independent research on the subject. For instance, Yoon-Nyun Kim, with Keimyung University College of Medicine in Daegu, Korea, and his colleagues conducted a well-designed RCT to test the effectiveness of remote patient monitoring for lowering patients' BP [9]. They divided a group of 374 adult patients with hypertension into three groups.

- The first group measured their BP at home in the usual way, without the help of remote monitoring and served as controls. They received office follow-up at 8-week intervals for 24 weeks. These patients were expected to record their BP readings in a diary and bring that log with them to each office visit.
- The second group was remotely monitored with the help of the LG Smart Care system but didn't get any remote physician care. However, like group 1, they did receive in person follow-up care every 8 weeks for 24 weeks.
- The third group received remote BP monitoring and remote physician care but without follow-up in person care from a physician.

Kim et al. found that remote BP monitoring with or without remote physician monitoring was as efficacious as routine office care for lowering BP. A subgroup analysis found that patients over age 55 years actually did better when they had remote BP monitoring, either with or without remote physician monitoring, when compared to controls. They reached their BP target levels faster and the absolute values were lower. The investigators postulated that "The significant efficacy in the subgroup of patients over the age of 55 might be explained by the significantly better adherence to the home healthcare device, as demonstrated by the significantly higher number of home BP measurements in the group of patients over 55 years age."

Alexander Logan from Mount Sinai Hospital Toronto in Ontario, Canada, and his associates have tested the effects of a mHealth-based program for patients with both hypertension and diabetes [10]. Their RCT included 110 patients in a 1 year trial in which half the group had their BP telemonitored and received self-care messages on their smartphones *immediately* after they took the BP readings at home while the second group were instructed to measure their BP but did not receive the self-care messages. Both groups collected their readings with the use of a Bluetooth-enabled home BP device that was linked to their cell phone and which automatically transmitted their readings to a server that stored the results.

All patients initially started out with systolic BP readings at or above 130 mmHg, but those in the experimental group experienced a decrease that was 9.1 mmHg greater than that seen in control patients. In addition, more than half of the patients in the experimental program (51%) reached the BP levels recommended in guidelines, namely, <130/80, compared to only 31% in the control group.

It is likely that the patients who received the self-care messages experienced greater improvement due to the nature of the messages. The researchers designed an application that ran on the Blackberry phone and paired it with a BP measuring device that sent measurements to a centralized server. But the application server also had the ability to process and analyze incoming data to look for BP trends. With the help of built-in clinical decision rules, the system could send a customized message to the patients' smartphone screen, telling them how to respond to these trends. The messages relied on a set of care plan pathways to predefine low and high values. When patients in the experimental group reported BP readings outside the normal range, they were told to take additional measurements and then to follow-up with the clinician if there was an urgent need to do so. In addition, "Nonadherence to the preset home BP measurement schedule triggered an automated voice message that was sent to the patients' home telephone, requesting them to check the smartphone for a message. Critical alerts were automatically sent to their physician's office by fax whenever BP readings exceeded predetermined threshold values. Simultaneously an automated voice message was left on the patients' home telephone advising them to check their smartphone for a message, which instructed them to contact their doctor immediately for advice."

While customized apps like this one demonstrate the efficacy of a mobile BP monitoring, they have little practical merit for small or medium size medical practices with no technological savvy or an IT team to help design such tools. A more practical solution would be to download a commercially available mobile app from iTunes or Google Play that's supported by good evidence. As we discussed in Chapter 3, the IQVIA Institute for Human Data Science has performed a detailed analysis of the clinical evidence supporting mobile health apps, rating their maturity and relative quality. IQVIA has generated of list of "Top rated apps" for 2017, taking into account their top clinical rating and the fact that they are free and publicly available. The list includes SmartBP for monitoring BP [11].

SmartBP is being used in over 100 countries according to its developers and can be synched with a variety of wirelessly enabled BP devices. Version 2.1 for iOS can also read and write data through the Apple Health app. It lets patients track their progress with graphic displays of the BP readings over time and share this data with clinicians [12].

Of course, if your organization does have the resources to create a customized mobile platform to help hypertensive patients self-manage, there are guidelines available to ease the way. Hannah Kang, RN, MSN, and her colleagues at Systems Biomedical Informatics Research Center, College of Nursing, Seoul National University, Seoul, Republic of Korea provide a useful blueprint by outlining how their organization created its own application [13].

Kang et al. began the development process by insisting that the app be firmly grounded in good science. With that in mind, they reviewed the medical literature to locate the relevant clinical practice guidelines, which served as the underpinning for the app. They also started out with a fairly obvious assumption, namely that managing high BP requires a two-pronged approach: lifestyle improvement and, when medication is required, adherence to the drug regimen. Unfortunately, most mobile apps that attempt to improve hypertension care do little more than record BP readings and manage records. Folding clinical practice guidelines into the equation has the potential to do more. And if the app is designed properly, it can also provide tailored recommendations for subgroups of patients with various degrees of risk. Details on the development process used by Kang et al. go beyond the scope of this book but include planning, analysis, design, implementation, and evaluation phases. Fig. 4.1 contains the schema that they used to develop the application.

Once the app was created, it was tested with 38 patients, 29 of whom took part in the medication adherence component. Kang et al. concluded that "Medication adherence, as measured by the Modified Morisky Scale, was significantly improved in these patients after they had used the hypertension management app (HMA) ($P = .001$). The perceived usefulness score was 3.7 out of 5."

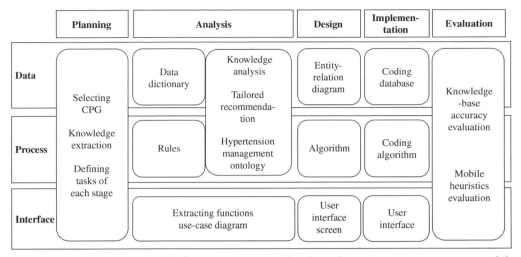

**Figure 4.1** Kang and Park used a five-step process to develop a hypertension management mobile app that incorporated clinical practice guidelines. *Originally published in Kang H, Park H-A. A mobile app for hypertension management based on clinical practice guidelines: development and deployment. JMIR mHealth uHealth 2016;4(1):e12. Copyright ©Hannah Kang, Hyeoun-Ae Park <https://www.ncbi.nlm.nih.gov/pmc/articles/PMC4756253/>.*

The aforementioned research projects strongly suggest that mobile tools can play an important role in managing hypertension. The next challenge is to find the best practices that will make these tools an integral part of routine patient care. One way to address this issue is to fold hypertension management apps into one's electronic health record (EHR) system. As we have stated earlier in the book, clinicians do not want to move outside their EHR, open up a separate application, and transfer data from that app into the EHR. And if the patient has several comorbidities requiring additional mobile apps that are also available outside the EHR, e-management becomes too burdensome and most clinicians will balk. To get physicians and nurses on board, we need a single button in the EHR to give them direct access to each disease specific app.

Several innovative thinkers and organizations have been working on best practices, including Palo Alto Medical Foundation (PAMF) Research Institute, Sutter Health in Mountain View, CA, and Stanford University School of Medicine. Nan Lv, PhD, with PAMF and colleagues, has studied an EHR-integrated hypertension management protocol, for instance, that generated measurable benefits. After 6 months on a program that included home-monitored BP, office-measured weight, and personalized advice on diet, exercise, smoking, and patient education, 55.9% of 149 patients were able to lower their BP to less than 140/90 mmHg and 86% experienced a reduction of 5 mmHg or more systolic pressure and 3 mmHg or more diastolic readings [14].

Realistically speaking, this program, although had an impact on patient care, is too expansive to be easily adopted by small to medium size practices. But it may serve the needs of healthcare systems looking to build a cost-effective population health software system. Lv et al. used the EMPOWER-H protocol, which involved a care team that included two nurse care managers, a registered dietitian, and a pharmacist consult. It also relied on theoretical constructs, including perceived severity of a health threat, self-efficacy, perceived barriers to action, and social cognitive theory. And lastly, it used the seventh report of the Joint National Committee on prevention, detection, evaluation, and treatment of high BP as the clinical practice guideline.

During the experiment, patients were monitored with the help of a provider dashboard, which enabled clinicians to obtain a 14-day average of their home BP data, which in turn let them prioritize patients as low, medium, or high risk. Using those risk categories, the software could send alerts to patients when BP readings were at a critical level.

## ATRIAL FIBRILLATION

Because this abnormal heart rhythm can lead to thromboembolism, stroke, HF, and other cardiovascular complications, it requires prompt medical attention. Atrial fibrillation (aFib) doubles a person's risk of heart-related death and increases the risk of stroke fivefold [15]. The fact that aFib is the most common type of arrhythmia and that it affects an estimated 2.7−6.1 million Americans has put it near the top of the list of priorities for clinicians [16]. With the introduction of novel anticoagulants such as dabigatran, rivaroxaban, edoxaban, and apixaban, in addition to the standard agent, warfarin, clinicians are eager to detect aFib as early as possible so it can be managed before serious complications develop.

An international team of researchers has developed a mobile app to help manage the condition and has randomized about 200 patients to either use the program or receive routine care [17]. Among patients using the mobile app, adherence to the drug regimen and satisfaction with their anticoagulant was significantly better, as were quality of life scores. Patients using the app, average age 67.4 years, reported less anxiety and depression.

Guo et al.'s RCT featured a smartphone loaded with the Android operating system and contained a clinical decision support component and patient-facing component. Clinicians were able to obtain well-documented risk scores from the app, including $CHA_2DS_2VASc$, HAS-BLED, and $SAMe-TT_2R_2$. The app also included patient education materials, a way to conduct structured follow-up, and self-care components. It is also important to point out that the program was sophisticated enough to automatically calculate the clinical risk scores above using data from the patient's personal health record. As healthcare slowly transitions to a precision medicine model, that's an important feature to have in place. One of the objections voiced by many healthcare professionals is that the emergence of a data–intensive precision medicine approach is going to overwhelm them with mountains of data that they have no time to interpret. Incorporating digital tools into the workflow that do some of the "heavy lifting" will make the transition easier. As the report explains,

> Clinical decision support provided by the mAFApp streamlined guideline-based decision-making for stroke prevention in patients with atrial fibrillation and was easily handled by doctors and understood by patients. The clinical decision support tools in the mAF App automatically assessed stroke and bleeding risk, and stratified the patients with high-risk stroke/thromboembolism to anticoagulant treatment, while balancing the bleeding risk. Bleeding risk factors were labeled and could be reviewed by doctors and patients. Personalized choice of oral anticoagulants would be advised on the basis of the SAMe-TT2R2 score, resulting in rational decision making on anticoagulant management options.

Julian Halcox, MD, and his United Kingdom colleagues have also tested the value of mobile screening for patients at risk for aFib. Their RCT recruited about 1000 patients, median age 73 years, with elevated risk scores (mean CHAD-VASc was 3.0) [18]. They used the AliveCor Kardia monitor connected to a Wi–Fi-enabled iPod to collect electrocardiograph readings from outpatients, comparing the group to control patients receiving routine care over 12 months. The iECGs were transmitted to a secure server and analyzed with the help of an automated aFib detection algorithm and by a physiologist or cardiologist. aFib was detected in 19 patients in the iECG group, compared to only 5 in the control group.

As was the case with the Guo et al. study, Halcox et al. used a mobile medicine tool that did much of the electrocardiogram (ECG) analysis, which can ease some of the workflow for busy clinicians. It is also important to note that most patients were satisfied with the device and found it "easy to use without restricting activities or causing anxiety." Given the average age of the patients in this study, that's very encouraging since older adults tend to be resistant to new technology.

The AliveCor system used in these two studies has received Food and Drug Administration (FDA) approval as a one lead ECG monitor. The small device is attached to a patient's Apple or Android phone or placed near it. The patient places at least one finger from each hand on each of two pads on the device, which then sends a signal to the AliveCor app on the phone and displays the ECG tracing after a 30 seconds recording. The vendor has also developed the technology to record ECGs on Apple's smart watch, called KardiaBand. The device combines the ECG device with analysis algorithms to monitor a patient's heart rate and activity level.

The system uses a deep neural network to compare data from the watch's heart rate sensor and accelerometer, looking for anomalies that might suggest an abnormal heart rhythm. If the neural network detects an atypical pattern, it alerts the user to record a 30 seconds ECG. The watch's analysis algorithm will detect normal sinus rhythm or alert the user that he or she may be experiencing a possible aFib, displaying the waveform directly on the watch's screen.

KardiaBand can detect abnormal rhythms with the help of a photoplethysmogram (PPG) built into the back of the watch. The PPG uses green and infrared light emitting diodes to shine light into the user's skin, which in turn can sense changes in light that bounce off the user's arteries as they pulsate. The watch's PPG interprets these changes in reflected light as changes in heart rate and heart rate variability. When heart rate anomalies are detected, in the context of a patient's activity level as measured by the accelerometer, it recommends the patient record an ECG. The ECG is then processed through the watch's analysis algorithms to determine if aFib may have occurred. The watch can also forward those readings to a personal physician.

There is evidence to suggest that the Apple Watch, combined with machine learning, can even detect aFib even in the absence of a built-in ECG. As part of a cardiovascular study organized by the University of California, San Francisco, more than 9700 patients were recruited into the Health eHeart Study. Investigators remotely measured heart rate, feeding 139 million measurements into a deep neural network for training. The deep neural network provided a machine learning algorithm that is capable of recognizing distinct patterns in medical data and was used to detect aFib from data coming from patients' smart watches [19].

To access heart rate data from the smart watches, patients' heart rates were detected by the phone's photoplethysmography sensor and their activity level was measured by the watch's accelerometer. Tison et al. used a mobile app called cardiogram to collect both sets of data points and fed them into the deep neural network. As Tison et al. explain, "We used a purpose-built neural network consisting of 8 layers, each of which had 128 hidden units, for a total of 564,227 parameters ... that transformed raw sensor measurements—heart rate and step counts—into a sequence of scores corresponding to probabilities that a participant was in AF at each time interval. Our primary classification task was to passively detect atrial fibrillation (AF) from Apple Watch data while in Workout mode. The network was trained using an unsupervised approach, which we call heuristic pretraining, using Google's TensorFlow framework. This training used 57,675 person-weeks of unlabeled data from the remote cohort ($n = 6682$) to compute several representations approximating $R-R$ intervals (i.e., time between heartbeats). Modeled after a heuristic previously used for AF detection, we calculated the average absolute difference between successive heart rate measurements across window sizes of 5 seconds, 30 seconds, 5 minutes, and 30 minutes."

A second cohort was also included in the clinical trial to evaluate the value of the neural network. Fifty-one patients with preexisting aFib underwent electrical cardioversion to convert the abnormal heart rhythm to normal sinus rhythm. Each of these patients also had a 12-led ECG performed in addition to using the Apple Watch for at least 20 minutes while the watch was in workout mode. The watch data was fed into the neural network. With the help of this machine learning, the researchers were able to detect the vast majority of patients with aFib, with a sensitivity of 98% and a specificity of 90%.

## DYSLIPIDEMIA, STRESS, AND REMOTE MONITORING

There have been some attempts to enlist the help of mobile technology to manage dyslipidemia and related cardiac problems, with promising but tentative results. There are home lipid testing kits for use with a smartphone for instance, but the 2015 AHA guidelines concluded that "the amount of evidence-based literature in this area remains surprisingly low."

In addition to mobile technology designed to address weight gain, hypertension, and other individual risk factors for heart disease, there are also applications that measure one's overall risk of heart disease. The Marshfield Clinic's HeartHealth Mobile app is a well-respected tool in this category. It is available for Apple devices and a web version also exists. Users can insert statistics on their height, weight, cholesterol level, smoking status, the presence of diabetes, hemoglobin A1c level, and BP and obtain a risk score. The app joins a growing number of digital tools that have been designed with gamification principles in mind with the hope that it will keep users entertained while it improves their health.

One area of concern for persons at risk of heart disease that was not addressed by the AHA mobile technology review in any depth is emotional health. The evidence linking psychosocial stress to heart disease is undeniable. And new data from the long-running INTERHEART study only supports the relationship. Analysis of over 12,000 cases of acute myocardial infarction (AMI), conducted in 52 countries, has found that the odds of having an AMI are three times greater among individuals who were angry and involved in heavy physical exertion within an hour of having the attack, when compared to AMI patients who did not share these risk factors [20]. The study paints a dramatic picture: Imagine a spouse arguing with his or her mate, boiling over with contempt and frustration, and then storming out of the house to relieve their pent-up emotions by vigorously shoveling snow or retreating to the gym to furiously run on a treadmill, only to fall victim to their own sympathetic nervous system and its effects on the myocardium. As Smyth et al. explain in their INTERHEART study report, "Physical exertion and emotions (including anger and emotional upset) are reported to cause sympathetic activation, catecholamine secretion, systemic vasoconstriction, and increase heart rate and BP, thereby modifying myocardial oxygen demand, which may precipitate the rupture of an already vulnerable atherosclerotic plaque."

In light of such evidence, an assessment of mobile cardiac medicine would be incomplete without the use of a measuring stick to assess an individual's ability to manage stress and other psychosocial problems. The data from Smyth et al. further highlights the importance of such an assessment tool. While they found an odds ratio of 3.05, they also found that only 14.4% of the study population who were angry or emotionally upset experienced an AMI, which implies that nearly 85% did not. Identifying those who are most sensitive to extreme physical exertion and anger will require a sensitive screening system.

Brent Winslow from Design Interactive Inc., in conjunction with colleagues from the Philadelphia VA Medical Center and the University of Pennsylvania, have developed a wearable sensor that may have value in measuring a person's stress response and serve as a monitoring device. They used the Biopac MP-150 system to collect physiological data—including cardiovascular and electrodermal activity—both of which signal changes in a person's response to stress. To compare these readings against a standard parameter that indicates a stress reaction, the researchers also measured salivary cortisol levels.

The system was tested in a group of armed forces veterans who were undergoing cognitive behavioral therapy (CBT) for stress and anger management, and on healthy controls. The system was able to detect physiological stress in more than 90% of the controls, and veterans who used the system while undergoing therapy were significantly improved on measures of stress, anxiety, and anger, when compared to veterans who underwent CBT alone [21].

Wearable sensors are also finding a place in pediatric medicine. Children's of Alabama, located in Birmingham, is providing the parents of children with congenital heart disease with a remote monitoring kit from Vivify Health that includes a tablet and sensors to measure patients' weight, pulse, and oxygen saturation. The "Hearts at Home" program helps parents cope with the most vulnerable stages of postsurgery and recovery, and gives clinicians immediate access to vital signs that may require prompt action [22].

As we enter the era of personalized patient care, mobile apps are helping clinicians and patients understand which patients are responding to medications and which ones are not. Pharmacogenomics can play an important role in determining individual response to medication. But at a much more basic level, knowing which patients are actually taking their medication is just as important. There are numerous digital tools available that can help in this regard. They include smartphone apps such as MyMedSchedule, MyMeds, and RemindMe, which can remind patients to take their medication. Other tools include "smart pill bottles" that keep track of when patients open and close their pill vials. There is even a "smart necklace" called WearSens that contains a piezoelectric sensor that allows clinicians to monitor patients' medication adherence by detecting a person's neck movements when they swallow a pill [23].

Not all the research on such "smart" remote monitoring devices has been positive, however. Kevin Volpp, MD, PhD, with the Perelman School of Medicine, University of Pennsylvania, and his associates conducted a large RCT to test the effectiveness of an Internet connected pill bottle, used in conjunction with financial incentives and social support in patients who had had a myocardial infarction [24]. The 12 month investigation—the HeartStrong Trial—recruited over 1500 patients between the ages of 18 and 80 years who had survived an acute MI, were taking a least two cardiac drugs and had been discharged from the hospital within 180 days of have the MI. Unfortunately, they were unable to confirm that this combined approach had on impact on clinical outcomes. There were no differences in rehospitalization for vascular problems or death between the experimental group and those on routine care. Similarly, the researchers found no differences in first all-cause hospitalization or total number of repeat hospitalizations. Equally disappointing was the finding that medication adherence did not differ despite the use of the "smart" pill bottles, which were provided by Vitality GlowCaps. The caps fit onto regular pill bottles and use light, sound, and phone reminders to alert patients to take their medication at specific times. The technology also shares the patient's adherence rate with his physician. The platform includes a DeviceConX mobile app, and a medication adherence portal. Although the HeartStrong Trial was not able to confirm the efficacy of the e-pill cap, an unpublished randomized 6-month study performed at Partners Healthcare in Boston found that 86% of patients who used GlowCaps without an additional financial incentive to remain compliant achieved an overall 80% medication adherence rate, compared to 45% in a control group. (A summary of the study did not provide the number of patients involved in the trial or any additional statistics.)

With so many remote sensors available to measure a wide variety of physiological parameters and limited regulation on the industry generating these sensors, critics have rightly asked whether these products produce accurate readings. Robert Wang, MD, a cardiologist with the Cleveland Clinic, and his associates addressed this issue by testing the accuracy of heart rate monitoring available in wearables from Apple Watch, Fitbit Charge, Mio Alpha, and Basis Peak, comparing their readings to the heart rate recorded by a standard ECG machine as the gold standard. Volunteers were tested while at rest and while on a treadmill at 2, 3, 4, 5, and 6 mph. When they tested 50 healthy adults, they found the Apple Watch and Mio Fuse readings correlated closely to the ECG readings (concordance correlation coefficient 0.91 for each). The Fitbit and Basic Peak were less accurate (0.84 and 0.83). While such variance is of little concern when the devices are used for recreational purposes, some clinicians are now using them to monitor cardiac patients in rehabilitation, situations in which accuracy is much more important. In the case of the Basis Peak device, the researchers found a median difference of $-8.9$ and $-7.3$ bpm at 2 and 3 mph [25]. And since this experiment included only healthy adults, it is entirely possible the results would have been worse in cardiac patients with damaged blood vessels.

Fitness apps that measure heart rate do not require FDA approval, and as such do not have to reach the high standard of the medical devices that have met FDA standard. Pulse oximeters, ECG monitors, and several other remote sensing devices do have to meet this higher standard, which means clinicians can have more confidence in their reliability.

A pulse oximeter, for instance, must meet a series of criteria to gain FDA clearance, including accuracy testing, as explained in the Agency's guidelines. Meeting this higher standard gives health insurers the confidence to recommend their use in home care, as illustrated in Aetna's stated policy [26]. It also offers a measure of assurance that using such devices can individualize patient care, at the same time increasing the likelihood that patients can be reimbursed for the cost of the equipment, under specified conditions. Home monitoring devices that have also meet FDA criteria include the smartphone-based AliveCor ECG and the HeartCheck handheld ECG device.

## ROOT CAUSE ANALYSIS

In addition to the studies we have discussed above, there are several others that suggest mobile technology can have a positive impact on the prevention and treatment of heart disease. A mobile app called SaltSwitch, for instance, allows users to obtain a more accurate estimate of how much sodium they are consuming by enabling shoppers to scan the barcodes of packaged goods to determine their sodium content. The app generates a traffic light style alert about the item and offers suggestions for healthier lower-salt alternatives. For salt-sensitive hypertensive patients, this type of digital tool will likely offer tangible benefits [27]. Similarly, a mobile app called HeartMapp has been developed to help patients with HF to improve their self-management [28].

Several mobile apps to assist patients with HF are also available from the Heart Failure Society of America. They include a medication tracker, a symptom tracker, a program that lets patients keep a record of relevant vital signs, a physical activity tracker, low sodium guidelines, and an app to monitor one's moods [29]. The apps, which were developed by Self Care Catalysts, Inc., are available in Apple's App Store and Google Play.

There are physician-facing apps to assist with the management of HF as well. For instance, investigators from Intermountain Healthcare in Salt Lake City have developed a clinical decision support app that alerts clinicians when their HF patients deteriorate and require more specialized care. It identifies HF patients with new echocardiogram results that include a left ventricular ejection fraction below 35%. The app collects and analyzes patient demographics, lab test results, diuretic use, emergency department (ED) visits, previous hospitalizations, and a variety of other variables that may affect their cardiac status. The app's algorithms analyze all these elements, taking into account published guidelines on advanced HF, and then send a secure email to the patient's physician about the need to refer to a specialized HF unit that is better qualified to manage advanced disease. Evans et al. [30] found that patients in the intervention arm of their study were more likely to be referred to a specialized HF facility within 30, 60, 90, and 180 days, when compared to control patients. They were also more likely to live longer.

Since poor nutrition and a sedentary lifestyle are among the root causes of heart disease, it is only fitting to discuss mobile apps that can help patients address these issues. The AHA offers a free app for patients who have already experienced a myocardial infarction. My Cardiac Coach provides evidence-based advice on secondary prevention, helps patients keep track of their medication and log their physical activity, and tracks their doctor appointments. It also lets survivors connect with others who have had an MI through the AHA's Support Network [31]. The AHA's sodium tracker is useful for patients who are salt sensitive as well.

Among the nutrition-related apps often recommended by cardiac experts are those that help users count calories. While these digital tools may have a place in promoting a heart healthy lifestyle, a recent study has challenged the calorie-counting approach to weight management and will likely change the way heart healthy nutrition is viewed [32].

Chris Gardner, PhD, and his colleagues from the Stanford Prevention Research Center, Department of Medicine, Stanford University Medical School, randomized about 600 overweight and obese participants in a trial that compared a healthy low-fat regimen to a healthy low-carbohydrate regimen. After a year, both groups lost about the same amount of weight. But the most revealing aspect of the experiment was the fact that "No explicit instructions for energy (kilocalories) restriction were given. Both diet groups were instructed to (1) maximize vegetable intake; (2) minimize intake of added sugars, refined flours, and trans fats; and (3) focus on whole foods that were minimally processed, nutrient dense, and prepared at home whenever possible." Despite the fact that these 600 adults paid little attention to the number of calories they consumed each day, after 12 months, they had lost 5.3 kg (the low-fat group) and 6 kg (low-carbohydrate group).

What's the mechanism of action for such a "calorie-blind" approach to weight loss? A closer look at the permitted food choices tells the story. Whole grain breads and cereals contain enough dietary fiber to cause satiety early on, making it less likely that study participants would overeat. Similarly, a diet high in fiber-rich vegetables blunts a person's appetite for high-calorie alternatives. Avoiding packaged foods with added sugar no doubt helped reduce their calorie intake as well. And the patient education sessions that study participants received helped them make wise food choices. In total, they received 22 instructional sessions over the 1 year period, with only 17 participants attending each class. And therein lies the problem. Applying the results of this study to the general public will require they be taught how to distinguish high quality, nutrient dense foods and beverages from all the more tempting choices offered in the supermarket. Even health-conscious patients are easily tricked into buying poor quality items that are deceptively labeled as natural, multigrain, low fat, or low carbohydrate. None of these terms indicate a food item is high quality, fiber-rich, or nutrient dense.

While mobile health apps should have a role in cardiac care, it should not distract clinicians and technologists from the bigger picture. Mortality from heart disease has steadily declined in recent decades—with the exception of the last few years [33] (see Box 4.1 for more details on heart disease facts and figures). That trend has been the result of addressing a variety of health risks from clinical, social, legislative, and cultural perspectives. Among the contributing factors responsible for this decline: fewer Americans smoke and fewer are exposed to secondhand smoke. Heart disease is being better managed in the ED and before patients reach the ED. Laws have been put in place over the years to address air pollution and tobacco use in public places; food labeling has improved, giving consumers better understanding of the fat, sugar, and sodium content of their food; and public education has made Americans more aware of the importance of stress, diet, obesity, and exercise in preventing and treating heart disease. Public health campaigns are helping people control their risk factors. For example, the Heart Truth, an NIH-sponsored national awareness campaign about women and heart disease, has provided tools to help women reduce their risks of heart disease [34]. Most of these influences occurred without the aid of mobile apps, remote patient monitoring, or other digital tools. These efforts must continue to capture the public's attention if we hope to see continued progress.

No doubt, the right digital tools can supplement all these efforts, but they cannot replace clinicians willing to "annoy" their patients with advice on losing weight and reducing the intake of empty calories. Nor will it take the place of law makers who have the moral fiber to challenge soda makers, polluters, junk food purveyors, and tobacco companies with legislature that further restricts their marketing and exploitation of the public. Nor can they take the place of advocacy groups like the Center for Science in the Public Interest (CSPI), which regularly exposes dishonest food companies that continue to misrepresent their nutritionally depleted products.

CSPI's *Nutrition Action* newsletter regularly highlights vendors, multinational food companies, distorted news stories, and politicians who would like us to believe that our food supply is heart healthy. A case in point: The newsletter has called attention to a provision in the Affordable Care Act that was supposed to be implemented in May of 2017 [36]. It would have required major restaurants, supermarkets,

## BOX 4.1  Heart Disease Facts and Figures

For decades, deaths from heart disease continued to decline, from 520.4 deaths/100,000 in 1969 to 169.1 in 2013 [33]. Unfortunately, that decades-long trend may be coming to an end. In 2014, the rate was 167.0 but that went up to 168.5 in 2015, as depicted in Fig. 4.2 [35].

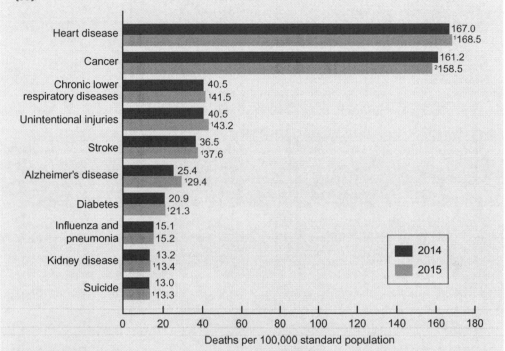

**Figure 4.2** Age-adjusted death rates for the 10 leading causes of death in 2015: United States, 2014 and 2015.
[1]Statistically significant increase in age-adjusted death rate from 2014 to 2015 ($P < .05$).
[2]Statistically significant decrease in age-adjusted death rate from 2014 to 2015 ($P < .05$).
*Notes:* A total of 2,712,630 resident deaths were registered in the United States in 2015. The 10 leading causes accounted for 74.2% of all deaths in the United States in 2015. Causes of death are ranked according to the number of deaths. *Source: http://www.cdc.gov/nchs/data/databriefs/db267_table.pdf#3. NCHS, National Vital Statistics System, Mortality. (From CDC. Mortality in the United States, <https://www.cdc.gov/nchs/products/databriefs/db267.htm>; 2015).*

convenience stores, and movie theater chains to list the number of calories in their products. Unfortunately, on May 4, the US FDA delayed the deadline by a year and then the House of Representatives of the US Congress passed a bill entitled "Common Sense Nutrition Disclosure Act," which would allow restaurants to give diners misleading serving sizes. It would also let supermarkets and convenience stores tuck calorie counts in hard to find places. In practical terms, that means a company can say its muffin only contains 100 calories per serving, but then define a serving as one-fifth of a muffin—not what most consumers would call a common-sense approach to food labeling. The newsletter also publishes a regular column called *Food Porn*, which features products that are anything but heart healthy. A recent installment in the column included a description of a popular pizza that comes in a single serving size. The only problem with the single serving is it contains 2000 calories, which is the calorie allowance for an entire day, 4240 g of sodium, and 2 days' worth of saturated fat!

The Centers for Disease Control and Prevention reports that about 610,000 people die of heart disease in the United States every year, that is, 1 in every 4 deaths.

Heart disease is the leading cause of death for both men and women. More than half of the deaths due to heart disease in 2009 were in men.

CHD is the most common type of heart disease, killing over 370,000 people annually.

Every year about 735,000 Americans have a heart attack. Of these, 525,000 are a first heart attack and 210,000 happen in people who have already had a heart attack.

Heart disease is the leading cause of death for people of most ethnicities in the United States, including African Americans, Hispanics, and whites. For American Indians or Alaska Natives and Asians or Pacific Islanders, heart disease is second only to cancer.

High BP, high cholesterol, and smoking are key risk factors for heart disease. About half of Americans (47%) have at least one of these three risk factors.

Several other medical conditions and lifestyle choices can also put people at a higher risk for heart disease, including diabetes, overweight and obesity, poor diet, physical inactivity, and excessive alcohol use.

# REFERENCES

[1] Centers for Disease Control and Prevention. Heart disease facts, <https://www.cdc.gov/heartdisease/facts.htm>; 2017 [accessed 16.02.18].
[2] World Health Organization. Cardiovascular diseases (CVDs). Fact sheet updated May 2017, <http://www.who.int/mediacentre/factsheets/fs317/en/>; 2017 [accessed 16.02.18].
[3] Chow CK, Redfern J, Hillis GS, et al. Effect of lifestyle-focused text messaging on risk factor modification in patients with coronary heart disease: a randomized clinical trial. JAMA 2015;314:1255—63.
[4] Gotto AM. Jeremiah Metzger lecture: cholesterol, inflammation and atherosclerotic cardiovascular disease: is it all LDL? Trans Am Clin Climatol Assoc 2011;122:256—89. Available from: https://www.ncbi.nlm.nih.gov/pmc/articles/PMC3116370/.
[5] Pandey A, Krumme A, Patel T, Choudhry N. The impact of text messaging on medication adherence and exercise among postmyocardial infarction patients: randomized controlled pilot trial. JMIR mHealth uHealth. 2017;5:e110.
[6] American Heart Association. Current science on consumer use of mobile health for cardiovascular disease prevention: a scientific statement from the American Heart Association. Circulation 2015;132:1157—213. Available from: https://www.ncbi.nlm.nih.gov/pubmed/26271892.

[7] Khaylis A, Yiaslas T, Bergstrom J, Gore-Felton C. A review of efficacious technology-based weight-loss interventions: five key components. Telemed J E Health 2010;16:931—8.

[8] Hardy ST, Loehr LR, Butler KR, et al. Reducing the blood pressure—related burden of cardiovascular disease: impact of achievable improvements in blood pressure prevention and control. J Am Heart Assoc 2015;4:e002276. Available from: http://jaha.ahajournals.org/content/4/10/e002276.full.pdf + html.

[9] Kim Y-K, Shim DG, et al. Randomized clinical trial to assess the effectiveness of remote patient monitoring and physician care in reducing office blood pressure. Hypertens Res 2015;38:491—7.

[10] Logan AG, Irvine MJ, McIsaac WJ, et al. Effect of home blood pressure telemonitoring with self-care support on uncontrolled systolic hypertension in diabetics. Hypertension 2012;60:51—7.

[11] IQVIA Institute. The growing value of digital health in the United Kingdom evidence and impact on human health and the healthcare system. Report Summary, <https://www.iqvia.com/institute/reports/the-growing-value-of-digital-health-in-the-united-kingdom>; November 7, 2017.

[12] Smart BP. The all new SmartBP — smart blood pressure, <http://www.evolvemedsys.com/blog/2018/1/30/the-all-new-smartbp-smart-blood-pressure.html>; 2012 [accessed 20.03.18].

[13] Kang H, Park A-E. A mobile app for hypertension management based on clinical practice guidelines: development and deployment. JMIR mHealth uHealth 2016;4(1):e12.

[14] Lv N, Xiao L, Simmons ML, et al. Personalized hypertension management using patient-generated health data integrated with Electronic Health Records (EMPOWER-H): six-month pre-post study. J Med Internet Res 2017;19:e311.

[15] American Heart Association. Atrial fibrillation, <http://www.heart.org/HEARTORG/Conditions/Arrhythmia/AboutArrhythmia/Atrial-Fibrillation-AF-or-AFib_UCM_302027_Article.jsp?gclid = Cj0KCQjw-uzVBRDkARIsALkZAdld91ep3sLDSQMzCvqW1nGJLzvk1-GzbcvD3elB5blcFoDU0XMqC4MaAgnuEALw_wcB#.WruWEIjwa1t>; 2018 [accessed 28.03.18].

[16] Centers for Disease Control and Prevention. Atrial fibrillation fact sheet, <https://www.cdc.gov/dhdsp/data_statistics/fact_sheets/fs_atrial_fibrillation.htm> 2017 [accessed 28.03.18].

[17] Guo Y, Chen Y, Lane DA, et al. Mobile health technology for atrial fibrillation management integrating decision support, education, and patient involvement: mAF App Trial. Am J Med. 2017;130:1388—96.

[18] Halcox JP, Wwareham K, Cardew A, et al. Assessment of remote heart rhythm sampling using the AliveCor heart monitor to screen for atrial fibrillation: the REHEARSE-AF study. Circulation 2017;136:1784—94.

[19] Tison GH, Sanchez JM, Ballinger B, et al. Passive detection of atrial fibrillation using a commercially available smartwatch. JAMA Cardiol. 2018;3(5):409—16. Available from: https://doi.org/10.1001/jamacardio.2018.0136.

[20] Smyth A, O'Donnell M, Lamelas P, et al. Physical activity and anger or emotional upset as triggers of acute myocardial infarction: the INTERHEART study. Circulation 2016;134:1059—67.

[21] Winslow BD, Chadderdon GL, Dechmerowski SJ, et al. Development and clinical evaluation of an mHealth application for stress management. Front Psychiatry 2016;7:130. Available from: https://doi.org/10.3389/fpsyt.2016.00130.

[22] Vivify Health. High risk patients, <http://www.vivifyhealth.com/childrens-alabama-deploys-vivify-health-solution-closely-monitor-infants-congenital-heart-disease-home/> 2018.

[23] Kalantarian H, Motamed B, Alshurafa N, et al. A wearable sensor system for medication adherence prediction. Artif Intell Med 2016;69:43—52.

[24] Volpp KG, Troxel AB, Mehta SJ, et al. Effect of electronic reminders, financial incentives, and social support on outcomes after myocardial infarction: the HeartStrong Randomized Clinical Trial. JAMA Intern Med 2017;177:1093—101.

[25] Wang R, Blackburn G, Desai M, et al. Research letter: accuracy of wrist-worn heart rate monitors. JAMA Cardiol 2017; Jan 1;2(1):104—106. doi: 10.1001/jamacardio.2016.3340.

[26] Aetna. Pulse oximetry for home use, <http://www.aetna.com/cpb/medical/data/300_399/0339.html> 2018.

[27] Eyles H, McLean R, Neal B, et al. Using mobile technology to support lower-salt food choices for people with cardiovascular disease: protocol for the SaltSwitch randomized controlled trial. BMC Public Health 2014;14:950.

[28] Athilingam P, Jenkins B, Johansson M, et al. A mobile health intervention to improve self-care in patients with heart failure: pilot randomized control trial. JMIR Cardiol 2017;1:e3.

[29] Heart Failure Society of America. Patient app, <http://www.hfsa.org/patient/patient-tools/patient-app/>; [accessed 05.04.18]. n.d.

[30] Evans RS, Kfoury AG, Horne BD, et al. Clinical decision support to efficiently identify patients eligible for advanced heart failure therapies. J Card Fail 2017;23:719—26.

[31] American Heart Association. AHA introduces smartphone app to help heart attack survivors manage their heart health, <https://news.heart.org/aha-introduces-smart-phone-app-to-help-heart-attack-survivors-manage-their-heart-health/>; 2017 [accessed 05.04.18].

[32] Gardner CD, Trepanowski JF, Del Gobbo LC, et al. Effect of low-fat vs low-carbohydrate diet on 12-month weight loss in overweight adults and the association with genotype pattern or insulin secretion the DIETFITS randomized clinical trial. JAMA 2018;319:667—79.

[33] American Heart Association. Heart disease death rate continues to drop, <https://www.heart.org/en/news/2018/05/01/heart-disease-death-rate-continues-to-drop>; 2015 [accessed 02.04.18].

[34] NIH National Heart, Lung, and Blood Institute. Make a commitment to your heart, <https://www.nhlbi.nih.gov/health/educational/hearttruth/>; 2016 [accessed 06.04.18].

[35] CDC. Mortality in the United States, <https://www.cdc.gov/nchs/products/databriefs/db267.htm>; 2015 [accessed 06.04.18].

[36] Lurie PG. Hold the information and pass the salt. Nutrition Action Healthletter, Center for Science in the Public Interest; April 2018.

# CHAPTER FIVE

# A Mobile Approach to Diabetes and Asthma

The adage about an ounce of prevention being worth a pound of cure certainly applies to Type 2 diabetes mellitus. The Western diet is one of the leading causes of the disorder, as is a lack of adequate exercise [1]. Any strategy that addresses the disorder needs to include both its prevention and treatment and should include both mobile technology and nontechnological measures.

Unfortunately, most of the attention in the mHealth community has been on managing preexisting diabetes rather than preventing it. The association between a Western diet and Type 2 diabetes is primarily related to the fact that it encourages the overconsumption of calorie-rich but nutrient-poor food, which in turn results in the epidemic of overweight and obesity now prevalent in many developed countries. If there is any doubt that improving lifestyle factors such as diet and physical exercise can prevent Type 2 diabetes, it should have been eliminated by the Diabetes Prevention Program (DPP), a randomized controlled trial that was published in 2002 and then updated in 2009. Both studies have been supported by several e-based programs that confirmed its effectiveness.

## PREVENTING TYPE 2 DIABETES

In 2002, the DPP Research Group published its landmark study "Reduction in the incidence of Type 2 diabetes with lifestyle intervention or metformin" in *The New England Journal of Medicine* [2]. The project involved more than 3000 nondiabetic adults who were at risk for the disease because they had three risk factors: they were overweight, had elevated fasting glucose levels, and an abnormal glucose tolerance test. More specifically, their body mass index was 24 or higher, fasting plasma blood glucose was 95–125 mg/dL, and glucose levels were 140–199 mg/dL 2 hours after a glucose load.

One-third of the patients were given metformin, a popular antidiabetic agent, plus standard lifestyle recommendations; one-third served as a control group and received standard lifestyle advice plus placebo; and the final third was enrolled in an intensive lifestyle modification program. The latter attempted to reduce patients' weight by at

*The Transformative Power of Mobile Medicine.*
DOI: https://doi.org/10.1016/B978-0-12-814923-2.00005-2

least 7% with the help of a healthy low-fat, low-calorie diet, and moderate intensity exercise, which might include brisk walking for at least 150 minutes a week. This group also received a 16-week course that discussed diet, exercise, and behavior modification; participants received instruction on a one-to-one basis for 24 weeks. The researchers emphasized the fact that the instruction was "flexible, culturally sensitive, and individualized."

After nearly 3 years of follow-up, the intensive lifestyle modification program reduced the incidence of diabetes by 58% and metformin by 31%, when compared to controls. In absolute numbers that meant 400 of the 1082 patients in the placebo group eventually developed diabetes, while only 215 of the 1079 patients in the intensive program did, and among those on metformin, 300 of the 1073.

In 2009, the DPP team published the results of its 10-year follow-up study, which demonstrated that nutritional therapy and exercise were still having an impact. While patients in the intensive program had gained some of their lost weight, the incidence of diabetes was 4.8 cases per 100 person-years in the intensive lifestyle modification group, compared to 7.8 in the metformin group and 11 in the placebo group [3].

In 2015, Jeremy Sussman, a research scientist at the University of Michigan and his associates performed a reanalysis of the raw data from the DPP and were able to focus more precisely on patients at greatest risk of developing diabetes. Their analysis also weeded out those less likely to benefit from intervention. To accomplish that, Sussman et al. [4] evaluated 17 risk factors for Type 2 diabetes rather than just the 3 that were originally taken into account and found that 7 of these 17 more accurately identified patients who would benefit from the intensive lifestyle modification program and from metformin. The seven risk factors that increased an individual's chances of developing diabetes were fasting blood glucose, hemoglobin A1c (HbA1c), a family history of elevated blood glucose, blood triglyceride level, waist measurement in centimeters, waist to height ratio, and height. When the investigators divided the subjects into quarters, from lowest to highest risk of disease, they found ". . . the lifestyle intervention provided a sixfold greater absolute risk reduction in the highest risk quarter than in the lowest risk quarter." However, they also discovered that "patients in the lowest risk quarter still received substantial benefit (3-year absolute risk reduction 4.9% vs 28.3% in highest risk quarter; numbers needed to treat of 20.4 and 3.5, respectively)." The benefits of metformin were more unevenly distributed, with its value almost entirely confined to patients in the top quarter of risk for diabetes.

Kevin Joiner from the Yale University School of Nursing and his colleagues have performed a systematic review and metaanalysis of DPP lifestyle programs that were delivered through a variety of electronic, mobile, and telehealth platforms to determine how effective they were in promoting weight reduction [5]. Their analysis looked at 22 studies, including over 2000 patients, and found that on average the programs reduced body weight by 3.98% after 15 months of follow-up. The interventions included web-based applications, video conferencing, the use of mobile phones, voice response—automated telephone calls, and text messaging. In some cases, participants had face-to-face access to educators who would provide baseline orientation on how to use the eHealth application and what the dietary and exercise goals were. In other cases, they received behavioral support remotely, either through video conferencing or personalized emails. Some patients received face-to-face behavioral support.

When Joiner et al. did a subgroup analysis, they found relatively minor differences in the way patients responded to various interventions. Although the overall change in weight was 3.98%, those who used programs that offered face-to-face behavioral support experienced a 4.65% drop. It is also important to note that the demographics of most study populations were quite different than the demographics of the populations most at risk for Type 2 diabetes. The majority of patients in the electronic DPP initiatives were white and college educated. Diabetes disproportionally afflicts Asian Americans, Hispanics, and non-Hispanic black adults.

## ADDRESSING PREDIABETES

2002 not only marked the year the first DPP trial was published, it was also the year the American Diabetes Association (ADA) put a new term into circulation: prediabetes, which it defined as impaired fasting glucose (IFG) and/or impaired glucose tolerance (IGT). The association defined IFG as 100—125 mg/dL and IGT as 140—199 mg/dL 2 hours after drinking a glucose drink—thresholds very close to those used in the DPP trial. ADA later added an HbA1c level of 5.7%—6.4% as prediabetic [6].

Although not all experts agree that prediabetes should be viewed as a distinct entity, there is little doubt that having the values set out by ADA put individuals at greater than average risk of developing full blown disease. About 5%—10% of persons who have prediabetes present with diabetes each year [7]. In addition to the e-DPP studies described above, there are studies to suggest mobile apps that monitor physical activity in prediabetics have merit. The Diabetes and Technology for Increased Activity or DaTA study found that at risk patients who track their activity levels with smartphones and pedometers saw a positive impact on daily physical activity. Such monitoring also made them more cognizant of the effects of a healthy lifestyle on health outcomes [8]. The same approach has been used in an randomized controlled trial (RCT) of 149 patients at risk for heart disease and Type 2 diabetes. That investigation found small but significant improvements in HbA1c levels at 24 and 52 weeks [8].

## MANAGING TYPE 2 DIABETES

Of all the disorders that may respond to the individualized care afforded by mobile apps, diabetes mellitus likely tops the list. One of the reasons the disease is such a good fit for mobile technology is its very nature of demanding a great deal of self-management, in contrast to acute conditions such as appendicitis or abdominal hernia, for which the clinician plays the dominant role.

There is ample evidence to show that diabetes self-management combined with diabetes education is a cost-effective way to lower HbA1c readings, the best metric we have to monitor a patient's glucose control [9]. What remains unresolved is how much of an impact mobile apps and other computer-assisted protocols have on improving diabetes self-management and clinical outcomes. One review of 16 randomized controlled trials that recruited over 3500 patients with Type 2 diabetes found that computer-assisted self-management levels lowered HbA1c by 0.2%. The same analysis found that smartphone-based programs in particular lowered HbA1c levels by 0.5% [10]. To put those findings into context, consider an analysis of over 4500 patients from 23 hospital-based clinics, which found that "Any reduction in HbA1c is likely to reduce the risk of complications, with the lowest risk being in those with HbA1c values in the normal range (<6.0%)." More specifically, a 15% drop in HbA1c was associated with a 37% decrease in the risk of microvascular complications and a 21% drop in diabetes-related death [11]. A decrease from about 9.5% to 9%, the equivalent of a 0.5% drop, was associated with a decrease in the adjusted incidence of microvascular complications from $\sim$100 per 1000 person-years to $\sim$75 per 1000 person-years ([11,12]).

A reduction of 0.5% in HbA1c is generally considered the benchmark of clinical effectiveness. With that in mind, a 2017 systematic review of 11 diabetes mobile apps found that they all helped lower HbA1c levels, but with a wide range of results, from 0.15 to 1.95 [13]. Only four of the studies produced statistically significant results, and all four apps had the greatest interactive features. HbA1c reductions in these four trials ranged from 0.4% to 1.9%.

Some studies have suggested that having Type 2 diabetics patients check their own blood glucose with a home monitor is not especially cost-effective, especially if they are not on insulin therapy [14,15]. On the other hand, researchers who asked Type 1 diabetic patients to attach a device (iBGStar) that can send blood glucose readings to an iPhone reported better glycemic control according to Shah et al. [16]. Similarly, positive data has been published to demonstrate that a system such as the BlueStar mobile app, which provides personalized behavioral intervention to Type 2 diabetics, can improve the interaction between patient and provider and reduce HbA1c levels over 1 year. The coaching app reduced these levels by 1.9% in the group in the maximum treatment arm, compared to only 0.7% in the group receiving usual care [17]. Maximal treatment included the use of the mobile app, web-based self-management, and provider assistance. Unlike many mobile diabetes apps, BlueStar has received the Food and Drug Administration (FDA) clearance as a medical device and must be prescribed by a health professional. The reports generated by the software are sophisticated enough to serve as clinical decision support (CDS) to tailor each patient's treatment plan.

The Boston Consulting Group's evaluation of the mHealth movement summed up the challenge of surviving and succeeding in this market. Innovative thinking isn't enough to create a financially viable mobile app and platform. The product has to be easy for patients to use and appeal to a variety of stakeholders, including clinicians and third-party payers, who have to be willing to invest time and money. Equally important, the product has to fit into the infrastructure of the healthcare system or medical practice that uses it. Boston Consulting Group states, "Most important, while examples are rare, some companies have managed to achieve early success despite an imperfect regulatory environment. For example, WellDoc's BlueStar 'mobile pre-scription therapy' provides diabetes patients with evidence-based, real-time feedback when they use their phone, PC, or tablet to input information about their medica-tions, glucose level, diet, and activity level. BlueStar also provides clinical-decision support to patients' physicians so that treatment changes can be optimized. Some payers have agreed to reimburse the product in a manner comparable to a monthly drug prescription. However, the jury is still out as to whether these solutions will be able to generate revenues over the long term." [18].

The BlueStar platform includes three components: the self-care system; BlueStar Rx, which includes an insulin bolus dose calculator; and the Diabetes Wellness Program. Its SMART Visit reports let patients share diabetes data and trends with any member of the care team. It is also possible to access several interactive tools, articles, and videos from diabetes experts. Relatively personalized messages are also sent to patients depending on their blood glucose readings, including more than 12,000 mes-sages sent in real time as they are needed. A patient whose readings drop too low, for instance, may be told to consume 15 g of fast-acting glucose to avoid the symptoms of hypoglycemia and then recheck their readings 15 minutes later.

Several other investigators have explored the value of mobile medicine in manag-ing Type 2 disease. Sarah Wild, with the Usher Institute of Population Health Sciences and Informatics, University of Edinburgh, and colleagues recently tested the value of telemonitoring in patients with poorly controlled Type 2 diabetes [19]. Patients were asked to measure their blood glucose levels at least twice weekly, includ-ing a fasting and one nonfasting reading. They were instructed to transmit those readings via Bluetooth technology through a supplied modem to a remote server that was monitored by nurses. Over a 9-month intervention period, the nurses checked the data weekly to make changes in patients' treatment regimen when warranted, based on national guidelines. When HbA1c data was tabulated for 146 patients on the experimental program and 139 controls, the researchers discovered that the readings declined by a clinically significant 0.51% in the telemonitored patients (63 vs 67.8 mmol/mol or 8.9% vs 9.4%). It is important to note, however, that the success of this particular program did require clinician support, which would not be feasible if a medical practice did not have the resources to employ qualified nurses to redirect treatment choices. But it is worth mentioning that the 95% confidence interval for the percentage change in HbA1c was 0.22%−0.81%, which implies that some patients saw much better results than others. The mixed results from all aforementioned studies suggest that clinicians need to choose a mobile solution that fits each individual's needs and preferences.

One mobile solution worth considering for patients on insulin therapy is continuous glucose monitoring (CGM). At least three companies—Dexcom, Medtronic, and Abbott—make systems that include a beneath-the-skin sensor, transmitter, and wireless monitor that continuously records blood glucose levels and generates detailed trending data. In 2015, the FDA approved the first mobile medical app platform for CGM, created by Dexcom Inc. The Dexcom Share Direct lets patients share real-time data through an Apple device such as an iPhone. The system is especially helpful for parents who want to remotely monitor their child's glucose levels. According to FDA, "The Dexcom Share system displays data from the G4 Platinum CGM System using two apps: one installed on the patient's mobile device and one installed on the mobile device of another person. Using Dexcom Share's mobile medical app, the user can designate people ('followers') with whom to share their CGM data. The app receives real-time CGM data directly from the G4 Platinum System CGM receiver and transmits it to a Web-based storage location. The app of the 'follower' can then download the CGM data and display it in real-time." [20].

Systems such as this can help personalize diabetes care in two respects. The fact that they provide clinicians, families, and patients more detailed information on blood glucose readings over time allows them to fine-tune insulin therapy, food intake, and activity levels. But the settings on the devices themselves can also be personalized by dialing in specific alarm thresholds for hypo- and hyperglycemia. The American Association of Clinical Endocrinologists and the American College of Endocrinology recommend CGM for all adult patients with Type 1 diabetes and in patients with Type 2 diabetes who are required to take several insulin injections daily, and those on basal insulin or sulfonylureas (a type of oral medication that lowers blood glucose) who are likely to be unaware of impending hypo- or hyperglycemia. Similarly, the ADA recommends that Type 1 patients who experience hypoglycemia unawareness or experience frequent episodes of hypoglycemia also use CGM [21].

A recent randomized controlled study conducted by the well-respected Joslin Diabetes Center in Boston is worth consideration [22]. As most clinicians who care for Type 2 diabetic patients know, one of the most difficult periods for patients is when they are required to add insulin to a treatment regimen that includes an oral agent such as metformin. Titrating the dose is challenging for patients and physicians alike, and incorrect insulin use remains one of the main reasons patients end up in the emergency room. The experts at Joslin have devised a creative way to utilize mobile technology to assist with this transition, easing the burden on clinicians and empowering individual patients to take on more of the responsibility for adjusting their basal insulin dose.

William Hsu, MD, and his colleagues designed the system using a software platform from Massachusetts Institute of Technology's Media Lab called CollaboRhythm. The cloud-based diabetes management system makes use of an individualized treatment plan agreed on between clinician and patient, a plan that patients access on their tablet. A wireless glucose meter is patched into the system to transmit blood glucose readings.

Their program is unique in that it incorporates situated learning theory to help patients learn to be relatively self-sufficient in managing their condition. The clinician explains their decision-making process for choosing an insulin dose and then encourages the patient to develop the same skill by active participation rather than through lectures or handouts, gradually developing the expertise needed to adjust their dose. The study, which took place over an average of 12 weeks and included 40 patients, was able to lower HbA1c levels by 3.1%, compared to 2% in the control group. Equally important was the fact that practitioners were able to spend less time with the experimental group, about 66 versus 82 min/patient. Although their approach is probably too complex to incorporate into a primary care practice, it is certainly worth considering in a busy specialty practice. It may ease the time commitments for clinicians while giving committed patients a sense of self-empowerment.

Of course, clinicians are not the only ones who can encounter problems using mobile apps to monitor diabetes management. Patients who attempt to use apps sometimes complain that they are not very user friendly, which is why evaluating app usability is just as important as studying their clinical effectiveness. Among seven usability studies, usability was rated poor (38%) to average (80%) [13].

Having to manually enter data into an app, for instance, is less convenient than working with one that automatically transfers blood glucose or other parameters directly from a device to the app. The former increases the likelihood of making errors. Some patients also complain about poor system navigation and the need for several steps to accomplish what they perceive as a simple task.

The labor-intensive process of manually entering blood glucose readings into a log or mobile device did not go unnoticed when Atrius Health was choosing a mobile platform for their patients with diabetes [23]. Atrius is a healthcare system located in the greater Boston area, comprising 29 clinical sites, 50 specialties, and over 675,000 patients. Because so many patients with diabetes have to cope with a wide variety of management challenges, including logbooks and diaries, Atrius was looking for a system that wirelessly synchs with a patient's mobile phone or tablet to automatically recorded blood glucose readings, and one that is device agnostic. They chose the Glooko system, which accepts data from more than 50 m, insulin pumps, and CGM systems. It also lets patients share data with clinicians and gives providers a risk stratified view of the patient panel they are working with.

Atrius Health tested the FDA-cleared Glooko system in its endocrine clinic during the pilot phase of their evaluation and then among its obstetric patients for the larger Phase-2 evaluation. To make it easier for clinicians, Atrius integrated Glooko into its EHR system so that they would not have to log into a separate digital platform. That meant they could click directly into each patient's glycemic data from within their chart. "To help clinicians more easily keep track of their patients, a report was developed to show all patients of that clinician being monitored by Glooko. Clinicians used this report to see patient status and sort patients by site."

Using this glucose management system in its obstetrical patients, the health system found that patients doubled the frequency of their daily blood glucose testing, and this increase was sustained for up to 20 weeks after starting to use the program.

Another mobile platform that looks promising is the FreeStyle Libre from Abbott, the first system approved in the United States that does not require patients to regularly prick their finger to obtain a drop of blood for its glucose meter, eliminating the pain and inconvenience that turn many patients away from self-management. The FreeStyle Libre system includes a thin filament sensor inserted under the skin of the upper arm to continuously measure glucose and send data to a handheld reader and smartphone app. The filament sensor measures interstitial glucose rather than plasma glucose.

Although this new system has the potential to transform diabetes self-management, there are some important caveats to keep in mind. The sensor readings may not always be accurate and should be compared to finger prick readings from a traditional glucose meter. If a patient's blood glucose levels change rapidly, these changes may not be reflected in readings from the FreeStyle Libre system because interstitial glucose takes time to catch up with blood glucose levels [24].

## CREATING THE NEXT GENERATION DIABETIC MOBILE APP

If we were to look back at how diabetes was managed before the discovery and isolation of insulin, we would find several bizarre recommendations, including the oat cure, potato therapy, and the starvation diet. But if we were to fast forward 5−10 years from today, chances are clinicians would look back at our current approach to diabetes and see it as primitive and uninformed. One can imagine tomorrow's physician or nurse practitioner spending an hour or more with each at-risk patient to explain what they can expect if they ignore their condition and how to prevent that eventuality. In that more informed future, clinicians would be afforded the needed time for patient education because third-party insurers had finally come to realize that reimbursing clinicians for the time and resources needed to educate at-risk patients is a form of enlightened self-interest, reducing the financial burden of paying for years of treatment to manage cardiovascular complications, neuropathy, and related problems.

In this future, our patient would also have access to a *clinician-prescribed*, evidence-based mobile app that does far more than keep track of blood glucose readings from a traditional glucose meter. This second-generation app would be synched with a mobile device that no longer requires several finger pricks daily, perhaps one similar to the Abbott's FreeStyle Libre mentioned earlier.

This futuristic diabetic app, when used in combination with face-to-face clinical consultation, would also be equipped with algorithms that measure several risk factors ignored by today's primitive apps. It would recognize that diabetes is more than just a disturbance in the way the body metabolizes glucose but a systemic disorder that requires a holistic, systems biology approach to prevention, and treatment. With that realization in mind, the app would take advantage of machine learning and neural networks and would assess and monitor a variety of contributing causes, including genetic mutations, the impact of physical and psychosocial stress, nutritional deficiencies, the effects of weather extremes, activity level, food quality and availability, and body weight.

To factor these contributing causes into the equation, app developers would have incorporated environmental risk scores, genomic risk scores, and diabetes prediction tools into their software to help guide clinician and patient decisions. Some of the foundational research for this next-generation program have already been done. The data analysis performed by Sussman et al. discussed earlier in this chapter, generated a diabetes risk prediction tool, which we elaborated on during a 2018 oral presentation at the Healthcare Information Management Systems Society (HIMSS) annual conference [4,25]. The tool includes a point system to give relative weights to the seven risk factors that their analysis found most relevant, namely, fasting blood glucose; HbA1c, which represents long-term glycemic control; a family history of elevated blood glucose; blood triglycerides level; waist measurement; height; and waist-to-hip ratio. If a prospective study confirms the tool's predictive ability, it would be a perfect fit for our futuristic app.

Similarly, a genetic risk score for Type 2 diabetes would likely include mutations in *TCF7LA, ABCC8, CAPN10, GLUT2, and GCGR* [26]. By one estimate, there are at least 150 DNA variants that have been linked to the disease and most have only been shown to subtly increase the risk of developing it. But when these variations are factored into a larger risk assessment, they may be clinically meaningful [27]. (For details on the strengths and limitations of genetic risk scores, see Box 5.1.)

## BOX 5.1  What Role Should Genomic Risk Scores Play?

While there is little doubt that the future of mobile medicine will include genomic risk scores to help prevent diabetes and other degenerative diseases, the current state of the science is more tenuous. Because most degenerative diseases are polygenic in origin, the specific genes and single nucleotide polymorphisms (SNPs) that contribute to these disorders have been much more difficult to identify. Monogenic disorders such as sickle cell anemia and cystic fibrosis have been linked to single mutations, but all the evidence points to the role of numerous genetic variants as contributors to coronary artery disease, Type 2 diabetes, and other hard to manage diseases.

Nonetheless, we are making progress. Amit V. Khera, MD, a cardiologist at the Center for Genomic Medicine and Cardiology Division, Massachusetts General Hospital in Boston, and his colleagues have developed a polygenic risk score by combining data from 6.6 million common SNPs and testing its validity in over 400,000 persons whose genetic data is stored in the UK Biobank [31]. Their score can identify individuals who are four times more likely to develop coronary artery disease than the general public. The distribution of risk forms a normal distribution, with the subgroup most at risk representing the top 2.5% of the population analyzed, compared to the remaining 97.5% on the distribution curve. The increased risk associated with this combination of SNPs is similar in magnitude to the risk incurred by the monogenic mutation for familial hypercholesterolemia, which is about 1 in 250. Unfortunately, there is no practical way to apply this revelation in clinical practice at this point in time. While it is possible to test a patient for a single mutation that causes familial hypercholesterolemia, short of analyzing a patient for 6.6 million SNPs, it is difficult to see how this new information can be put to use at the bedside—yet.

The field of genomic medicine is also making headway in Type 2 diabetes. A genetic risk score that takes into account 1000 SNPs has been developed by analyzing a population of about 10,000 individuals whose genetic data has been sorted in the Estonian Biobank, including 1181 patients with Type 2 diabetes and 9092 controls [32].

The doubly weighted genetic risk score derived from this analysis can separate high and low risk individuals. As Lall et al. explain, "The hazard for incident T2D [type 2 diabetes] was 3.45 times (95% CI: 2.31—5.17) higher in the highest GRS [genetic risk score] quintile compared with the lowest quintile, after adjusting for body mass index and other known predictors." In other words, patients with a genetic risk score in the top quintile were more than three times as likely to develop diabetes, when compared to those with the lowest scores. And when this genetic risk score was added to the standard 5-year diabetes risk algorithm—which include a patient's age and body mass index—there was an improvement of 0.324 (effect size).[1] The analysis also revealed that the impact of measuring these genetic markers was similar in strength and perhaps even stronger than other more traditional diabetes risk factors. In other words, using a genetic risk score improved the ability to predict who would and would not develop the disease. One rather obvious weakness in this analysis is that it was performed among the Estonian population, so whether it can be applied more widely in the United States, other parts of Europe, or elsewhere is unknown.

---

[1] An effect size of 0.2 is considered small while 0.5 represents a medium size effect.

This same app would factor in nutritional imbalances, including magnesium (Mg) deficiency. Individuals who consume high quantities of foods rich in Mg are less likely to develop Type 2 diabetes [28]. Similarly, low blood Mg levels may exacerbate insulin resistance, one of the precursors of diabetes. It is also possible that insulin resistance itself precipitates an Mg deficit. A metaanalysis that included more than 286,000 patients and almost 11,000 cases of diabetes found that adding 100 mg a day of the mineral significantly decreased the risk of diabetes [29].

A separate metaanalysis that included over 271,000 men and women found a significant inverse association between dietary magnesium intake and the risk of Type 2 diabetes, with a relative risk reduction of 23% when highest and lower intakes were compared [30].

As this scenario illustrates, the future of mHealth will involve leveraging innovation, seizing opportunities, and overcoming obstacles, as the subtitle of our book states.

## MANAGING ASTHMA WITH MOBILE TECHNOLOGY

Like diabetes, asthma affects millions of people worldwide. About 25 million Americans have asthma, including 6 million children; the disease has also been increasing since the early 1980s [33]. As many as 334 million people worldwide have asthma according to a report from the Global Asthma Network [34].

The challenge of managing asthma is especially acute in geographic areas with the worst air quality. In the United States, the distinction of being the worst city to live in if you have the disorder is Memphis, Tennessee. Richmond, Virginia; Philadelphia, Pennsylvania; Detroit, Michigan; Atlanta, Georgia; and Louisville, Kentucky are also on the 2015 list [35]. The Air Louisville Project was launched to address the challenge in this city, which was ranked 21 on the Asthma and Allergy Foundation of America List of Asthma Capitals; the project has made good use of mobile technology to address the issue [36].

Louisville, KY, is an especially problematic area for asthmatics to live in because it is an airshed, an atmospheric bubble created as a result of the presence of coal-fired power plants, temperature inversions—which trap air pollution near the ground—and an overabundance of pollution-spewing cars. Air Louisville was the result of an innovative collaboration among city leaders, nonprofit organizations, and a digital health company called Propeller Health. After a pilot project that generated positive results, the Robert Wood Johnson Foundation took notice and helped launch a full-scale 2.5-year investigation of nearly 500 participants that also recruited local business leaders and municipal stake holders. Its goal was to not only evaluate clinical effectiveness but also to find geographic hotspots that might be causing asthmatic symptoms, and to use the data collected to make policy recommendations.

Study participants were given electronic sensors to attach to their medication inhalers. That enabled the devices to track the use of their medication, including the date and time they took a puff. (For details on additional sensor attachments used in the management of asthma, see Box 5.2.) The data was collected via Bluetooth, paired with a smartphone, and sent to servers. With the help of this digital platform, subjects were encouraged to self-manage because they were now receiving additional information about the severity of their condition and how well it was being controlled. Meredith Barrett, vice president of research at Propeller Health, and associates state, "Participants could authorize health care providers to view their data and summary reports through a secure web dashboard to inform clinical treatment, such as medication adjustments or early intervention at the sign of acutely increasing SABA [short-acting beta agonist] use." [short-acting beta agonists (SABAs) include albuterol and levalbuterol].

By the end of the study, rescue inhaler use had declined by 78%, including an 84% drop in nighttime use of SABA drugs, there was a 48% improvement in the number of symptom-free days. Similarly, 80% of patients who reported feedback about their experience in the program said they were satisfied with the sensor and found it easy to use. The data analysis also revealed several asthmatic hotspots, including areas in central and western Jefferson County, which are exposed to larger than average levels of pollutants from nearby major roadways and from industrial activity.

Unlike many clinical studies, this project took things a step further by making policy recommendations based on their findings. Evidence suggests that the planting of trees in urban locations reduces mortality and lowers the prevalence of asthma, especially in children. The researchers identified neighborhoods most in need of assistance and recommended tree planting in those areas. More specifically, the research team and their community stakeholders recommended land development codes be revised to include stricter tree coverage policies. At the time of the AIR Louisville Project, only 15% of trees that were removed during land development had to be replaced in Jefferson County. The team suggested it be increased to 45%. They also recommended creating buffers zones between sources that spewed pollutants and housing, schools, and day care centers.

The AIR Louisville Project is impressive on many levels, but its results beg the question: Is it generalizable to other patient populations? Would they apply to other communities in which the socioeconomic mix is different? Would the same benefits be seen in groups that use a different mobile platform? Would the study results apply to a different age group—the mean age in the AIR Louisville Project was 38 years and most were adults. Chi Yan Hui, with the Asthma UK Centre for Applied

## BOX 5.2 A Smarter Approach to Asthma Management

While smartphones are slowly finding their way into asthma self-management, a few innovative companies have created attachments to make these mobile devices even smarter. Two examples worth consideration are the peak.me by breathe.me and Smart Peak Flow.

Peak.me, which is depicted in Fig. 5.1, is a spirometer that connects directly to a smartphone. When a patient exhales into the attachment, the device converts the exhalation air flow rate into an acoustic signal. A mobile app then uses an algorithm to analyze the signal and give patients feedback. Accumulated spirometric values provide a detailed snapshot of the patient's respiratory status, which can be uploaded to a cloud service and electronic medical record (EMR) system and shared with clinicians for further analysis. He or she in turn can send the patient their interpretation of the data and any relevant advice to their mobile phone to complete the loop. The software lets clinicians perform a trend analysis, enabling actionable early recognition of disease flare-ups and improvements. There is also a diary to let patients record lung function improvements, symptoms, triggers, and medications. An alert system reminds patients to take their medication and perform tests.

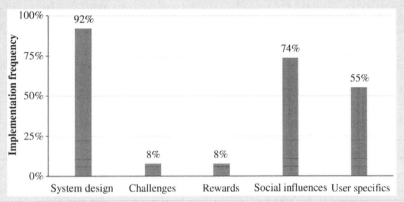

**Figure 5.1** Percentage of apps which applied at least one component fully from the corresponding gamification component category. *From Tinschert P, Jakob R, Barata F, et al. The potential of mobile apps for improving asthma self-management: a review of publicly available and well-adopted asthma apps. JMIR Mhealth Uhealth 2017;5:e113. <https://www.ncbi.nlm.nih. gov/pmc/articles/PMC5559650/#app3>. Copyright ©Peter Tinschert, Robert Jakob, Filipe Barata, Jan-Niklas Kramer, Tobias Kowatsch.*

Smart Peakflow provides a similar function. It too is a spirometer that is attached directly to a smartphone, and it also generates charts to help patients and clinicians monitor changes in peak flow rate and take appropriate action.

Research, University of Edinburgh, UK, and associates provide a partial answer to this issue. Their analysis of 12 randomized controlled trials and 3 metaanalyses found inconsistent results. For instance, overall clinical effectiveness of digital technology that focused on asthma varied.

The 12 RCTs included 3 mobile phone apps, 4 web applications, 3 texting interventions, 1 electronic inhaler reminder system that was linked to a web app and a customized monitoring system that included data entry and transmission over phone lines [37].

The studies reviewed by Hui et al. included a variety of features that fell into seven broad categories: education, monitoring/electronic diary, action plans, medication reminders, professional support, raising patient awareness, and decision support for clinicians. The investigators found that the most successful programs incorporated several of these features but in the final analysis "effects on health-related outcomes were inconsistent . . . . Our findings suggest that mobile apps have the potential to be effective in supporting self-management and are an option that may be preferred by some people and their clinicians. However, these studies of multifaceted interventions did not provide clear evidence on which of the range of ICT [information and communication technology] features were essential for effectiveness."

On the other hand, the American Lung Association (ALA) takes a more positive position on mobile apps for children with asthma [38]. Because so many children love smartphones, tablets, and other digital devices, ALA is encouraging the use of educational games on these devices to help them learn about asthma and how to manage it. The benefits seen among children with cancer, including a 16% improvement in medication adherence and a better understanding of that disease, have prompted the association to recommend their use in respiratory disorders as well. ALA reports that "An asthma game shows better child to parent communication, improved self-care and self-efficacy. Over 170 studies have already been done on gaming applications and asthma alone with many more studies in the works as well as asthma games being developed."

One leading mobile app listed in the ALA recommendations, called SPARX, gamifies the management of diabetes, asthma, and other chronic disorders with the help of a video game that includes a three-dimensional interface that will remind young patients of the popular World of Warcraft game. One of its goals is to relieve the depression and anxiety often experienced by children with diseases they may find bewildering. A more practical approach is taken by an app called Assist Me with Inhalers. It provides images and text to help patients use their inhalers correctly. It discusses 11 types of devices, including closed and open-mouthed metered dose inhalers (MDIs), MDI spacers, aerolizers, autohalers, diskus, flexhaler, and others. Considering how many patients misuse their inhalers, this app certainly has merit. By one estimate, 93% of asthma patients use the wrong technique [39].

Another barrier to good asthma control for many patients is the tedious process of keeping a paper and pencil log of symptoms, triggers, and medications. While these diaries can provide invaluable insights for clinicians trying to adjust a medication regimen, they do have their shortcomings. For computer-savvy patients, a mobile tool such as Asthma Journal Pro, which is also on the ALA list of useful apps, can make a difference. It provides patient education, tracks symptoms, medication use, and triggers. It sends journal entries from an iPhone to a Google Health account.

As we discussed earlier in the chapter, studies that evaluated the clinical effectiveness of asthma mobile apps have produced inconsistent results. But effectiveness is not the only metric health care providers will want to look at when considering these digital tools. It is also important to evaluate functionality, their potential to change behavior, how likely the app is to encourage its use—with the help of gaming, for instance—and overall quality. One standard way to assess app quality is the mobile application rating scale (MARS) metric, which consists of 19 parameters measured on a 5-point Likert scale. MARS measures patient engagement, functionality, esthetics, and information quality. A review conducted by German and Swiss technologists has shed light on all of these metrics [40]. (A chart rating the reviewed apps' gamification components is depicted in Fig. 5.2.)

Tinschert et al. reviewed 38 asthma-related apps and found they made use of about 7 of 26 behavior change techniques and about 5 of 31 available gamification components. They judged overall app quality as acceptable. An app called Asthma Health by

**Figure 5.2** Peak.me is a spirometer that connects directly to a smartphone. When a patient exhales into the attachment, the device converts the exhalation air flow rate into an acoustic signal. (Used with permission of Breathe.me http://breatheme.net/)

Mount Sinai received some of the best scores on the MARS quality scale and for behavior change techniques, gamification components, and available functions. One of the lowest rated apps was "Asthma Treatment." The authors provided detailed rankings of all 38 apps, including their names, in an appendix.

## THE ROLE OF MOBILE TECHNOLOGY IN ASTHMA RESEARCH

We have concentrated our discussion on the role of mobile technology in direct patient care, but it can also play an important role in medical research. The recently published Asthma Mobile Health Study illustrates its valuable place in the research community.

Yu-Feng Yvonne Chan, with the Department of Genetics and Genomics at the Icahn School of Medicine at Mount Sinai, New York, and her colleagues have completed the first phase of a large study using Apple's ResearchKit. The mobile platform was used to complete the entire recruitment, consent, and enrollment process, allowing participants to walk through these steps on their smartphones. Anyone who has ever tried to recruit study subjects using more traditional methods knows what a challenge it can be. Chan et al. seem to have bypassed many of the obstacles with the help of a mobile app called Asthma Health Application (AHA). Using AHA and ResearchKit, they were able to obtain patient consent electronically, administer questionnaires and collect the results, send subjects reminders and notifications, and send secure data back and forth from a central repository that stored all the research [41]. The research project enrolled nearly 7600 participants, 88% of whom agreed to share that deidentified data with the research team. Among the 7593 subjects, 6470 responded to at least one study survey. There was also a smaller group of more than 2300 who were more fully involved in the project and who completed at least five daily or weekly surveys. One of the shortcomings of using an online approach to research, however, appears to be its attrition rate. By the end of the 6-month study, only 175 participants were still committed enough to fill out the final milestone survey. Another limitation of the mobile app method of research is the demographics of the study population, which differed significantly for the average patient with asthma. AHA users were younger, wealthier, better educated, and more often male, when compared to the typical asthma population documented by the Centers for Disease Control and Prevention.

The results of the research project suggest that a mobile-only approach can generate useful data. For instance, the Asthma Health app allows patients to track their symptoms, provides feedback on a person's progress, and offers personalized medication reminders. With the help of the app and input from researchers, study participants found that the activity limitations brought on by asthma were reduced from 25% to 20%. During summer months, it went from 25% to 13%. Among the smaller subgroup that endured to the 6-month mark, "asthma control substantially improved over the study period" with the percentage of subjects who had uncontrolled asthma dropping from 42% to 24% ($n = 173$).

The online analysis also confirmed the role of asthma triggers in this population. Animals, pollen, and upper respiratory tract infections were listed as the three most troublesome triggers by participants when the study started. Among 545 participants who gave the researchers permission to gather geolocation data for asthma triggers, this data collection was revealing. In the Southern United States, where pollen counts are the highest, investigators found that more participants suffered from the effects of pollen before April 1 of the year, when compared to those in Northern regions. Similarly, there was a correlation between maximum daily temperature trends and complaints about extreme heat as a trigger for the asthmatic symptoms.

## REFERENCES

[1] Fernberg AP. The key role of epigenetics in human disease prevention and mitigation. N Engl J Med 2018;378:1323—34.

[2] Diabetes Prevention Program Research Group. Reduction in the incidence of type 2 diabetes with lifestyle intervention or metformin. N Engl J Med 2002;346:393—403.

[3] Diabetes Prevention Program Research Group. 10-year follow-up of diabetes incidence and weight loss in the Diabetes Prevention Program Outcomes Study. Lancet 2009;374:1677—786.

[4] Sussman JB, Kent DM, Nelson JP, Hayward RA. Improving diabetes prevention with benefit based tailored treatment: risk based reanalysis of Diabetes Prevention Program. BMJ 2015;350:h454. Available from: https://doi.org/10.1136/bmj.h454.

[5] Joiner KL, Nam S, Whittemore R. Lifestyle interventions based on the diabetes prevention program delivered via eHealth: a systematic review and meta-analysis. Prev Med 2017;100:194—207.

[6] American Diabetes Association. History of diabetes, <http://www.diabetes.org/research-and-practice/student-resources/history-of-diabetes.html>; 2018 [accessed 17.04.18].

[7] Bansal N. Prediabetes diagnosis and treatment: a review. World J Diabetes. 2015; 6:296—303.

[8] Coughlin SS, Stewart JL. Toward research-tested mobile health interventions to prevent diabetes and cardiovascular disease among persons with pre-diabetes. J Hosp Manag Health Policy 2017;1:7.

[9] Shah VN, Garg SK. Managing diabetes in the digital age. Clin Diabetes Endocrinol 2015;1:16.

[10] Pal K, Eastwood SV, Michie S, Farmer A, et al. Computer-based interventions to improve self-management in adults with type 2 diabetes: a systematic review and metaanalysis. Diabetes Care 2014;37:1759—66.

[11] Stratton IR, Adler AI, Neil HW, et al. Association of glycaemia with macrovascular and microvascular complications of type 2 diabetes (UKPDS 35): prospective observational study. BMJ 2000;405:321. Available from: http://www.bmj.com/content/321/7258/405.

[12] Stratton IR, Adler AI, Neil HW, et al. Updated mean hemaglobin A1c concentration, Figure 1. BMJ 2000;321:407.

[13] Fu H, McMahon SK, Gross CR, et al. Usability and clinical efficacy of diabetes mobile applications for adults with type 2 diabetes: a systematic review. Diabetes Res Clin Pract 2017;131:70—81.

[14] Cypress M, Tomky D. Using self-monitoring of blood glucose in noninsulin-treated type 2 diabetes. Diabetes Spectr 2013;26(2):102—6.

[15] Klonoff DC. New evidence demonstrates that self-monitoring of blood glucose does not improve outcomes in type 2 diabetes—when this practice is not applied properly. J Diabetes Sci Technol 2008;2(3):342—8.

[16] ShahV HW, Gottlieb P, Beatson C, Snell-Bergeon J, Garg S. Role of mobile technology to improve diabetes care in adults with type 1 diabetes: the Remote-T1d study. Diabetes Technol Ther 2015;17:A25—6.

[17] Quinn CC, Shardell MD, Terrin ML, et al. Cluster-randomized trial of a mobile phone personalized behavioral intervention for blood glucose control. Diabetes Care 2011;34(9):1934—42.

[18] Lindgardt Z, et al. Fulfilling the promise of mHealth through business model innovation. Boston Consulting Group, <https://www.bcg.com/publications/2014/innovation-medical-devices-technology-fulfilling-the-promise-of-mhealth-through-business-model-innovation.aspx>; April 3, 2014 [accessed 24.04.18].

[19] Wild S, Hanley J, Lewis SC, et al. Supported telemonitoring and glycemic control in people with type 2 diabetes: the Telescot diabetes pragmatic multicenter randomized controlled trial. PLoS Med 2016. Available from: http://journals.plos.org/plosmedicine/article?id = 10.1371/journal.pmed.1002098.

[20] FDA permits marketing of first system of mobile medical apps for continuous glucose monitoring, <http://www.fda.gov/NewsEvents/Newsroom/PressAnnouncements/ucm431385.htm>; January 23, 2015.

[21] Dexcom. Professional society positioning statements on continuous glucose monitoring system benefits and use recommendations, <https://s3-us-west-2.amazonaws.com/dexcompdf/HCP_Website/Professional + Societies + Positioning + Statement.pdf>; (n.d.).

[22] Hsu WC, Lau KH, Huang R, et al. Utilization of a cloud-based diabetes management program for insulin initiation and titration enables collaborative decision making between healthcare providers and patients. Diabetes Technol Ther 2016;18:59—67.

[23] Glooko. Case study: diabetes remote patient monitoring at Atrius Health, <https://www.glooko.com/resource/case-study-diabetes-remote-patient-monitoring-atrius-health/>; (n.d.).

[24] Kishimoto M, Tamada S, Oshiba Y. Successful glycemic control using a flash glucose monitoring system for a pregnant woman with diabetes: a case report. J Diabetes Metab Disord 2017;16:44.

[25] Halamka J, Cerrato P. Precision medicine: separating hype from reality. HIMSS18, <http://365.himss.org/sites/himss365/files/365/handouts/550237064/handout-98.pdf?_ga = 2.239840067.1327743195.1524226792-2070743236.1523809997>; March 7, 2018 [accessed 20.04.18].

[26] Winter S. Is type 2 diabetes caused by genetics? Healthline, <https://www.healthline.com/health/type-2-diabetes/genetics>; Nov 21, 2016 [accessed 20.04.18].

[27] NIH National Library of Medicine Genetics Home Reference. Type 2 diabetes, <https://ghr.nlm.nih.gov/condition/type-2-diabetes#genes>; 2018 [accessed 20.04.18].

[28] National Institutes of Health Office of Dietary Supplements. Magnesium fact sheet for health professionals, <https://ods.od.nih.gov/factsheets/Magnesium-HealthProfessional/>; [accessed 4.05.18].

[29] Song Y, Liu S. Magnesium for cardiovascular health: time for intervention. Am J Clin Nutr 2012;95:269—70.

[30] Schulze MB, Schulz M, Heidemann C, Schienkiewitz A, Hoffmann K, Boeing H. Fiber and magnesium intake and incidence of type 2 diabetes: a prospective study and meta-analysis. Arch Intern Med 2007;167:956—65.

[31] Khera AV, Chaffin M, Aragam KG, et al. Genome-wide polygenic score to identify a monogenic risk-equivalent for coronary disease. BioRxiv 2017. Available from: https://doi.org/10.1101/218388.

[32] Lall K, Magi R, Morris A, et al. Personalized risk prediction for type 2 diabetes: the potential of genetic risk scores. Genet Med 2017;19:322—9.

[33] Asthma and Allergy Foundation. Asthma facts and figures, <http://www.aafa.org/page/asthma-facts.aspx>; 2018 [accessed 30.04.18].

[34] Global Asthma Network. The global asthma report 2014, <http://www.globalasthmareport.org/2014/about/executive.php>; 2014 [accessed 30.04.18].

[35] Asthma and Allergy Foundation of America. Asthma Capitals 2015, <http://www.aafa.org/media/Asthma-Capitals-Report-2015-Rankings.pdf>; 2015 [accessed 30.04.18].

[36] Barrett M, Combs V, Su JG, et al. AIR Louisville: addressing asthma with technology, crowdsourcing, cross-sector collaboration, and policy. Health Aff 2018;37:525—34.

[37] Hui CY, Walton R, McKinstry B, et al. The use of mobile applications to support self-management for people with asthma: a systematic review of controlled studies to identify features associated with clinical effectiveness and adherence. J Am Med Inform Assoc 2017;24:619—32.

[38] American Lung Association. Mobile apps and asthma management: why educational games matter in asthma care, <http://www.lung.org/local-content/illinois/documents/mobile-apps-and-asthma.pdf>; (n.d.) [accessed 02.05.18].

[39] Thompson J. Asthma: most people don't correctly use their inhalers. HealthCentral, <https://www.healthcentral.com/article/asthma-most-people-dont-correctly-use-their-inhalers>; 2015[accessed 03.05.18].

[40] Tinschert P, Jakob R, Barata F, et al. The potential of mobile apps for improving asthma self-management: a review of publicly available and well-adopted asthma apps. JMIR Mhealth Uhealth 2017;5:e113.

[41] Chan YY, Wang P, Rogers L, et al. The asthma mobile health study, a large-scale clinical observational study using ResearchKit. Nat Biotechnol 2017;35:354—65.

CHAPTER SIX

# Mental Health

It is estimated that the financial burden of mental illness worldwide will reach $16 trillion by 2030 [1]! The World Health Organization reports that over 300 million people suffer from depression alone, making it the leading cause of disability worldwide [2]. That projection is not only disturbing but emphasizes the need to seek disruptive, innovative approaches to psychiatric disease. Mobilehealth can help fill this need for at least two reasons: given the number of available mental health professionals, it is virtually impossible for all those in need of these services to be cared for face-to-face, a dilemma that is especially acute in low and middle-income countries. And there is also some evidence to suggest that many patients are more willing to open up about their psychological concerns online during an anonymous consultation.

In Chapter 1 and Chapter 3, we discussed WoeBot, a text-based conversational agent that is based on the principles of cognitive behavioral therapy (CBT). In one study led by Kathleen Fitzpatrick, the program delivered measurable improvements on the 9-item Patient Health Questionnaire, the 7-item Generalized Anxiety Disorder scale, and the Positive and Negative Affect Scale among college students who had not been officially diagnosed with depression or anxiety [3]. Created by Alison Darcy, PhD, a clinical psychologist at Stanford University, Woebot uses natural language processing and a knowledge base derived from the psychological literature on CBT. It lets users have what almost feels like a human, two-way conversation with an automated "therapist," although the program is quick to point out that is not designed to replace a human therapist. It's available on Facebook Messenger, and iPhones, iPads, and Android devices.

## MOBILE APP CRITERIA

As we have discussed elsewhere in the book, there are several criteria to be considered when assessing the value of mobile health apps for patients, including randomized controlled trials (RCTs), observational studies, content analysis—which includes an evaluation to determine if the mobile app relies on nationally accepted clinical guidelines—usability analysis, expert recommendations, and user reviews. The aforementioned study by Fitzpatrick et al. was an RCT.

*The Transformative Power of Mobile Medicine.*
DOI: https://doi.org/10.1016/B978-0-12-814923-2.00006-4

A content analysis of depression-related mobile apps found that CBT and behavioral activation (BA) have the most scientific evidence to support their effectiveness. A review of 117 apps that focused on depression found that only 12 apps (10.26%) delivered CBT or BA [4]. On average, the 12 reviewed apps adhered to CBT principles by 15% (median) with a range of 0%—75%, and BA principles by 18.75% (range 6.25%—25%).

Other sources worth considering as one judges the merits of a mental health mobile apps include The United Kingdom's National Health Service (NHS), which has put a great deal of thought and analysis into its selection of mobile health apps, many of which are intended to improve mental health. Its apps library (version 2) includes Chill Panda, which is being tested by NHS to help users learn to relax, manage their worries, and improve well-being; Feeling Good: Positive Mindset, a relaxation program designed to help manage stress; and https://apps.beta.nhs.uk/iprevail/, which NHS says "provides mental health support whenever you need it. Connect with a community of people who have experienced issues such as stress, anxiety and depression, and learn how to manage your feelings."

The United Kingdom's National Institute for Health and Care Excellence (NICE) recently recommended that the NHS conduct an in-depth evaluation of Deprexis, a mobile app and online program designed to help adults manage depression. NICE believes Deprexis may serve as an "effective alternative therapy for adults with mild to moderate depression."

Deprexis, which is based on CBT and other therapeutic approaches, provides users with simulated conversations that can last as long as 60 minutes. Its developers claim it can adjust its response based on a user's learning style and cognitive capabilities. A meta-analysis of eight RCTs concluded that the automated "therapist" was moderately effective in relieving the symptoms of depression [5]. A second analysis looked at the effectiveness of mental health apps, including Deprexis and Mental Health Online, using the number needed to treat metric to judge their worth [6]. Mary Rogers, MS, PhD, and her colleagues in the Department of Internal Medicine, University of Michigan, concluded that for every four persons with depression that used Deprexis, one recovered from depression when compared to those who didn't use the program. However, some experts believe this claim is too bold.

There are RCTs that challenge positive evaluations of CBT-based mobile apps. For example, Robyn Whittaker, with New Zealand's National Institute for Health Innovation, and her associates, tested a CBT-based mobile program called MEMO CBT against a control intervention among 855 students at 15 high schools [7]. The purpose of the trial was to determine if a multimedia mobile phone program designed to prevent depressive symptoms would have a measurable impact at 12-month follow-up. It did not. But it is important to point out that MEMO CBT took a very different approach than the interactive approach featured in

Woebot and Deprexis. MEMO CBT delivered text messages, video diary messages from celebrities, cartoons, and the like. On the other hand, it is also important to state that Woebot does not deliver therapy for patients with diagnosed mental health disorders.

In the realm of expert recommendations, clinicians may look to groups like the American Psychiatric Association and evaluation websites like https://psyberguide.org/, which is directed by Stephen Schueller, PhD, an assistant professor of preventive medicine at Northwestern University's Feinberg School of Medicine. The nonprofit organization's app guide relies on three criteria: a credibility score, a mobile app rating scale (MARS), and a transparency score. The credibility score is calculated by (1) reviewing the scientific research on each product and its research funding; (2) its proposed intervention, for example, is it intended to improve a specific condition or symptom, or provide a nonspecific benefit like improve one's mood; (3) consumer ratings; (4) clinical input in development; and (5) software support.

MARS, a well-known scale created to validate eHealth and mHealth tools, measures user engagement, functionality, esthetics, information content, subjective quality, and the app's perceived impact. Psyberguide.org's transparency rating measures an app's data storage and collection policies and how willing the app's developers are to share this information with their users. An app is rated as either acceptable, questionable, or unacceptable on this metric depending on its privacy policies and policies on collection, storage, and exchange of health information.

When one dives into the app guide, he or she can choose from a list of relevant apps based on its platform, that is, iOS, Android, etc.; cost, target audience, target conditions, and types of treatment.

Psyberguide.org has rated WoeBot, giving it a 3.47 out of 5 rating on its credibility scale and an acceptable rating for transparency. It has yet to offer a MARS rating because it has too little data to form a judgment. Koko, another mental health app reviewed on the PsyberGuide website, received a high credibility rating (3.95) but an unacceptable transparency score. Its MARS score was 3.63/5. The review explains "Koko is a crowdsourced mental health app ideal for individuals struggling with depressive or mood disorders. The app allows anonymous users to connect with social networks to share concerns ranging from stress management skills to suicidal ideation. The application utilizes artificial intelligence learning to detect high-risk clients and scales up the type of source provided based on the level of distress. Koko starts out with a text-like conversation to better understand the user's specific needs and goals, establishing that the forum serves as a safe space for individuals." [8]

Some of the app evaluations on the PsyberGuide site also include expert reviews and/or a synopsis of the scientific research supporting the app. For example, the review of Tactical Breather, which is intended for users who want to learn how to develop mindfulness and other stress management skills, provides a summary of the research papers that has been published on the app.

One note of caution with regards to Psyberguide.org and other organizations that apply a point-based rating system to mental health apps: these systems have their limitations. John Torous, MD, professor of psychiatry at Harvard Medical School, and his colleagues explain "One weakness of these assessments is that they all appear to experience lower interrater reliability when assessed in the real world. For example, a study applying point-based metrics from existing mental health app rating frameworks including the ADAA and PsyberGuide to popular depression and smoking cessation found overall poor interrater reliability when used by mental health clinicians" [9].

The American Psychiatric Association has also developed a mental health mobile app evaluation process. Although APA does not recommend specific apps, it has created a detailed evaluation protocol that it recommends to clinicians before they consider suggesting specific apps to their patients. It advises clinicians to look at the app's privacy and security safeguards, as well as evidence that the app is supported by clinical trials. By way of example, it points out that the company Lumosity was making unsubstantiated claims that its brain training apps could delay the symptoms of dementia. The Federal Trade Commission went after the vendor, requiring it to pay $2 million in fines because it could not provide the evidence to support that claim [10]. APA provides an App Evaluation Form that lets users plug in the name of a specific app for evaluation. The online form asks users to fill in a series of boxes about privacy and safety features, ability to delete data, use of cookies, data encryption, HIPAA requirements, types of evidence supporting the app, data sharing, and so on.

The IQVIA Institute for Human Data Science offers guidance on mobile health apps, including those relevant to mental health. Its report, *The Growing Value of Digital Health in the United Kingdom*, was produced without industry or government funding and includes input from Dr. Michael Hodgkins, Vice President and Chief Medical Information Officer, American Medical Association [11]. The report points out that since 2007, peer-reviewed studies that evaluated the efficacy of mobile health apps have increased significantly, with at least 571 efficacy studies published during this period. Included in its list of evidence-based mental health apps is Start, by Iodine Labs, which allowed patients on antidepressants to track the effectiveness and adverse effects of new antidepressants, explaining that "Users can see how their results change over time as an objective measure of whether their medication may be working. This information may help patients communicate their symptoms to clinicians at their next office visit, potentially accelerating the process of finding an appropriate antidepressant." (The app is no longer available.) On a less positive note, the report criticized at least one app that was designed to provide self-monitoring and clinical feedback from a physician for patients with depression or mania because an RCT failed to demonstrate any benefits relative to a control group.

The same report provided a list of top-rated apps that included a stress management program called Headspace, one that helps users moderate their intake of alcohol, called Drinkaware, and an app to assist with smoking cessation called Clickotine.

## HOW STRONG IS THE EVIDENCE?

While RCTs are considered the gold standard by which physicians judge medical interventions, a meta-analysis, which combines the results of several RCTs, might be called the "platinum" standard. Its advantage is that it combines analyses of the individual populations studied in each RCT, thus increasing the sample size that can be evaluated, which in turn can increase statistical and clinical significance. Joseph Firth, with NICM, School of Science and Health, Western Sydney University, Campbelltown, Australia, and his colleagues recently conducted a meta-analysis of smartphone apps designed to treat depression [12]. They were able to combine the results of 18 RCTs on 22 mobile mental health apps that generated outcome data for over 3400 users. They found that overall, the apps significantly reduced depressive symptoms with a moderate positive effect size when compared to inactive control participants ($g = .56$). Participants who had been classified as inactive had received no intervention during their respective studies, as opposed to active participants, who either used a smartphone app not designed to treat depression, received face-to-face intervention, or had other types of activity. Firth et al. found less impressive differences between subjects who used mental health apps and active controls ($g = .22$).

A closer look at this meta-analysis, including several subgroup analyses, reveals important insights. The RCTs that looked at smartphone apps lasted from 4 to 24 weeks, and depressive symptoms were measured using a variety of well-documented tools, include the Depression Anxiety Stress Scale, the Patient Health Questionnaire (PHQ-9), and the Beck Depression Inventory II scale. The analysis also found that the mobile apps were only effective in users who had self-reported mild-to-moderate depression. They had no significant impact on patients with major depression, bipolar disorder, or anxiety disorders. Some of the subgroup analyses were unexpected. Apps that did not involve any in-person feedback generated statistically significant moderately positive effects, while those that did include human feedback did not. Apps that delivered their content entirely through a mobile device appear to have been more effective than those that were not self-contained, though the difference was just short of reaching statistical significance ($P = .07$). Finally, those apps that offered cognitive training had less of an impact on users than those that focused more generally on mental health.

Although Firth et al.'s exhaustive review of mental health apps did not uncover any that had a significant therapeutic effect in patients with major depression, the Patient Health Questionnaire (PHQ-9), designed as a professional assessment tool for major depressive disorder, has been validated as a smartphone app. It is available in Depression Monitor and MoodTools [13]. However, Michael Van Ameringen, MD, with the Department of Psychiatry and Behavioural Neurosciences at McMaster University, and his colleagues did not find any studies validating assessment apps for anxiety disorders, bipolar disorder, or obsessive compulsive disorder in their review of the literature. A mobile version of an assessment tool for posttraumatic stress disorder does exist, called PTSD Checklist-Civilian. It is used in PTSD Coach and PE Coach, both of which were developed by the US Department of Veterans Affairs.

RCTs and meta-analyses give clinicians the most assurance of efficacy, but less rigorous studies should not be ignored when evaluating a mental health app. Consider Mobilyze, for example, an app developed by the Center for Behavioral Intervention Technologies (CBITS), Northwestern Medicine. In a small, controlled trial that evaluated this depression-management tool, seven patients with major depression experienced significant improvements in depressive and anxiety symptoms by the end of the 8-week experiment and no longer met the criteria for depression (PHQ-9 scores had dropped from 17.1 in week one to 3.6 by week 8 $P < .0001$) [14]. Like many other mental health apps, Mobilyze required patients to log their thoughts, mood, and activities; it also provided reminders to help them cope with their feelings. Equally important, the app provided "context sensing." With the help of a mobile phone's GPS, Bluetooth, and accelerator, the app was able to make predictions about a person's emotional state based on their location, movements, and daily rhythms. While the small number of patients involved in the trial limits its generalizability, the rationale and mechanics of the app are scientifically sound.

Although Mobilyze is no longer available from the App Store or Google Play, Northwestern University and Northwestern Medicine have developed several next generation "intellicare" apps to take its place, including Worry Knot, Boost Me, Thought Challenger, and iCope [15].

There is little doubt that evidence-based mental health apps can help many patients, but most make the same mistake that health apps focusing on physical disease make. They fail to see the whole person and ignore the fact that psychiatric disease is a systemic problem that requires systemic solutions. These solutions require addressing a long list of contributing causes, including psychosocial stress—which many existing apps do address—and physical stress, dietary deficiencies, sleep deprivation, adverse reactions to medication, genetic predisposition, and lack of physical activity—which they do not. A case in point is vitamin B12 deficiency. A mobile app that teaches patients CBT techniques will have a very limited impact on someone experiencing the psychiatric effects of a cobalamin deficit. By one estimate, the deficiency affects about 12% of older, noninstitutionalized adults [16]. Among vegetarians, the prevalence ranges between 21% and 85% [17]. It can cause a variety of neuropsychiatric signs and symptoms, including cognitive impairment, irritability, peripheral neuropathy—a sensation of pins and needles in the hands and feet—and weakness. Patients taking metformin, one of the most commonly prescribed drugs for type 2 diabetes, are at risk for B12 deficiency, but too few clinicians take the time to order a serum B12 level for patients on the drug to monitor for the problem. How many mental health mobile apps ask providers or patients to consider this problem as they search for solutions?

Similarly, any disorder that causes chronic pain has to be viewed as a potential cause of depression and anxiety. Patients experiencing chronic pain are three times as likely to develop depression or anxiety and a mobile app that does not factor in pain or other physical stressors as triggers does not provide a holistic approach to mental health. The same can be said for insomnia.

As developers embrace the concept of systems biology and take a more holistic approach, it is likely we will gradually see mobile apps to address all these issues and more.

## REFERENCES

[1] Jones SP, Patel V, Saxema S, et al. How Google's 'ten things we know to be true' could guide the development of mental health mobile apps. Health Affairs 2014;33:1603—11.

[2] World Health Organization. Depression: key facts, <http://www.who.int/news-room/fact-sheets/detail/depression> [accessed 19.07.18].

[3] Fitzpatrick KK, Darcy A, Vierhile M. Delivering cognitive behavior therapy to young adults with symptoms of depression and anxiety using a fully automated conversational agent (Woebot): a randomized controlled trial. JMIR Mental Health 2017;4:e19.

[4] Huguet A, Rao S, McGrath PJ, et al. A systematic review of cognitive behavioral therapy and behavioral activation apps for depression. PLoS One 2016;. Available from: https://doi.org/10.1371/journal.pone.0154248 Accessed January 9, 2018.

[5] Twomey C, O'Reilly G, Meyer B. Effectiveness of an individually-tailored computerised CBT programme (Deprexis) for depression: a meta-analysis. Psychiatr Res 2017;256:371—7.

[6] Rogers MA, Lemmen K, Kramer R, et al. Internet-delivered health interventions that work: systematic review of meta-analyses and evaluation of website availability. J Med Internet Res 2017;19: e90.

[7] Whittaker R, Stasiak K, McDowell H, et al. MEMO: an mHealth intervention to prevent the onset of depression in adolescents: a double-blind, randomised, placebo-controlled trial. J Child Psychol Psychiatr 2017;58:1014—22.

[8] Psyberguide. Koko, <https://psyberguide.org/apps/koko/> [accessed 05.07.18].

[9] Torous J, Firth J, Huckvale K, et al. The emerging imperative for a consensus approach toward the rating and clinical recommendation of mental health apps. J Nerv Mental Dis 2018;2016:662—6.

[10] Wang DC. To app or not to app. American Psychiatric Association issues framework for evaluating apps. *Psychology Today*, February 13, 2017. <https://www.psychologytoday.com/us/blog/the-kitchen-shrink/201702/app-or-not-app>.

[11] IQVIA Institute for Human Data Science. The growing value of digital health in the United Kingdom: evidence and impact on human health and the healthcare system. <https://www.iqvia.com/en/institute/reports/the-growing-value-of-digital-health-in-the-united-kingdom>; 2017.

[12] Firth J, Torous J, Nicholas J, et al. The efficacy of smartphone-based mental health interventions for depressive symptoms: a meta-analysis of randomized controlled trials. World Psychiatry 2017;16:287—98.

[13] Van Ameringen M, Turna J, Khalesi Z, et al. There is an app for that! The current state of mobile applications (apps) for DSM-5 obsessive-compulsive disorder, posttraumatic stress disorder, anxiety and mood disorders. Depress Anxiety 2017;34:526—39.

[14] Burns MN, Begale M, Duffecy J, et al. Harnessing context sensing to develop a mobile intervention for depression. J Med Internet Res 2011;13(3):e55. Available from: https://doi.org/10.2196/jmir.1838.

[15] Northwestern Medicine. IntelliCare apps, <https://intellicare.cbits.northwestern.edu/> [accessed 12.07.18].

[16] Langan RC, Zawistoski KJ. Update on vitamin B12 deficiency. Am Fam Physic 2011;83:1425—30.

[17] Guney T, Yikilmaz AS, Dilek I. Epidemiology of vitamin B12 deficiency. In: Epidemiology of communicable and non-communicable diseases. IntechOpen. doi:10.5772/63760. <https://www.intechopen.com/books/epidemiology-of-communicable-and-non-communicable-diseases-attributes-of-lifestyle-and-nature-on-humankind/epidemiology-of-vitamin-b12-deficiency>.

# CHAPTER SEVEN

# Reinventing Clinical Decision Support: What Role for Mobile Technology?

"The complexity of medicine now exceeds the capacity of the human mind." That observation, made by Ziad Obermeyer, MD, and Thomas H. Lee, MD, in the *New England Journal of Medicine*, highlights a dilemma for many clinicians who still believe that even the most challenging diagnostic puzzles can be solved with astute cognitive skills, years of experience in diagnostic reasoning, and access to the medical literature [1]. As Obermeyer and Lee point out, the quantity of data now being generated on many patients is so massive that it is virtually impossible to decipher all the patterns and correlations needed to make an accurate diagnosis or plan the most effective therapeutic regimen. Oftentimes, the sheer volume of information in patient records alone makes it impossible for clinicians to even *read* through all the relevant facts no less do a deep analysis. The consequences of these data avalanche were summed up in a National Academies of Sciences, Engineering and Medicine's report entitled *Improving Diagnosis in Health Care* that states "It is estimated that 5 percent of U.S. adults who seek outpatient care each year experience a diagnostic error. Postmortem examination research spanning decades has shown that diagnostic errors contribute to approximately 10 percent of patient deaths, and medical record reviews suggest that they account for 6 to 17 percent of adverse events in hospitals."[2].

Of course, it's overly simplistic to imply that all the misdiagnoses discussed in this report were the result of physicians not taking full advantage of big data analytics, machine learning, neural networks, and all the other new developments in clinical decision support. There are numerous other reasons why clinicians come to the wrong conclusion when trying to determine the underlying cause of a patient's condition: Some patients lie about their signs and symptoms for various reasons. Clinical laboratories sometimes make mistakes when analyzing tissue samples. Critical imaging test results sometimes fail to reach a clinician in time to make a time-sensitive decision, to name only a few of the obstacles.

Another roadblock to accurate diagnosis is the lack of financial incentives to encourage clinicians to take the time to do a deep study of the patient data in front of them. As the IOM report explains it, there is a need to: "Design a payment and care delivery environment that supports the diagnostic process. Payment likely influences the diagnostic process and the occurrence of diagnostic errors. For example, fee-for-service payment lacks incentives to coordinate care, and distortions between

*The Transformative Power of Mobile Medicine.*
DOI: https://doi.org/10.1016/B978-0-12-814923-2.00007-6

procedure-oriented and cognitive-oriented care may be diverting attention from important tasks in the diagnostic process. A fundamental research need is an improved understanding of the impact of payment and care delivery models on diagnosis."

Nonetheless the inherent limitations of the human brain cannot be discounted among the reasons for the misdiagnosis dilemma. And emerging technology is now addressing these limitations, providing server, desktop, cloud-based, and mobile tools to improve diagnosis and treatment.

## CLINICAL DECISION SUPPORT BASICS

Before exploring the most advanced clinical decision support (CDS) tools, one should first become familiar with the most fundamental components of these systems. Typically, the purpose of CDS is to help clinicians make more informed decisions at the point of care, enabling them to better analyze all the basic input they are gathering from a patient's family and medical history, their physical examination, blood test results, imaging studies, and so on. CDS systems (CDSSs) are usually divided into two broad categories: knowledge-based and nonknowledge based.

Knowledge-based systems consist of three components: the database with all the scientific research on diagnostic criteria to pinpoint specific diseases, best practices about treatment, and so on. Depending on the nature of the CDSS, it will also contain a collection of If/Then statements. For example, *if* a patient consumes large doses of vitamin K while taking the anticoagulant warfarin, *then* the drug will be less effective and will increase the likelihood that the patient will develop a blood clot. The second component of the CDSS, the inference engine, links the scientific research and these algorithms with the individual patient's data to help reach a diagnosis. Component 3 is a communications tool to share the recommendations with the user. (There are also CDS tools that are primarily research repositories and collections of expert interpretations and reviews of said research, for example, UpToDate and ClinicalKey.)

Nonknowledge based CDSSs have also been developed recently that rely on machine learning, neural networks, and artificial intelligence (AI) to detect patterns in patient data. While these tools are less useful at the point of care to assist in diagnosis and treatment, that will gradually change as they become more sophisticated. In some settings, these tools are poised to actually replace the need for a physician's cognitive skills. A case in point: Varun Gulshan, PhD, from Google, in conjunction with investigators from the University of Texas, Austin, have demonstrated that deep learning algorithms can be used to detect diabetic retinopathy with better accuracy than 54 licensed ophthalmologists and ophthalmology senior residents. The machine-learning system accomplished this impressive feat by reviewing over 11,000 retinal fundus images [3]. Similarly, with the use of deep neural networks, it is now possible for computers loaded with the appropriate software to diagnose skin cancer as well as experienced dermatologists can [4].

Using a computational tool called a deep convolutional neural network, Andre Esteva from the Department of Electrical Engineering, Stanford University, and his medical colleagues in the departments of dermatology and pathology tested their algorithms on more than 129,000 clinical images. The neural networks were designed to evaluate the ability of the neural networks to distinguish between keratinocyte carcinomas and benign seborrheic keratosis, and between malignant melanomas and benign nevi. The machine learning—enabled algorithms were as effective as trained dermatologists for accurately identifying both cancers.

## THE TECHNOLOGICAL UNDERPINNING OF NEXT GENERATION CDS

The push into AI, machine learning, and neural networks requires clinicians to have at least a basic understanding of the terminology and principles used in these fields. As the term suggests, AI implies any thinking that is not generated by "unartificial" beings, namely humans. The concept of a thinking machine has been around for centuries but is often traced back to Alan Turing, who published *Computing Machinery and Intelligence* in 1950. The challenge of mechanizing thought has been with us ever since. If one defines AI as a machine that can analyze, experience emotions, is self-aware, and has free will, we are nowhere near developing such an artificial being—Star Trek's Data remains a sci-fi fantasy. But on a more modest scale, technologists have developed some of the components of this artificial life form. Among the most promising are the computer-generated algorithms that comprise machine learning.

The term is somewhat misleading. Machine learning is better referred to as machine self-learning since its purpose is to allow computer software to grow in understanding and analytic skills without the assistance of programmers adding more code; instead it uses the data it analyzes as a self-teaching tool. The data input—for instance, 11,000 medical images of skin lesions—trains the software to recognize characteristics and patterns with the eventual goal of identifying a pathology—melanoma, for example.

One way in which machine learning can be accomplished is with the help of neural networks and backpropagation. Neural networks take their name from the neural networks in the human brain, which are composed of neurons connected to one another by synapses. In a digital neural network, the flesh-and-blood neurons are replaced by software "nodes" that are connected to one another and are arranged in several layers that communicate with one another. (Artificial neural networks are not physical entities, they are software constructs.) Like the brain's neuron, each node gets excited, which is represented by a numerical value, and then it is passed on to the next node [5]. The amount of excitement that is transferred to the next neuron varies and is represented by a specific number as well. The higher the value of that second number, the stronger the connection between neuron one and two.

As the neural network scans a medical image, it analyzes millions of pixels, with the brightness of each pixel corresponding to a specific excitement value. As Fig. 7.1A and B illustrate, neural networks are composed of several layers, each containing several nodes that are connected by the digital equivalent of synapses. In neural networks, there's much discussion of input units, hidden units, and output units. Data representing image pixels may be sent through 100,000 seconds of nodes in the first input layer, which is then transferred to the next layer, with the strength of each signal indicated by specific numerical values. The goal is to eventually reach an output node that offers two choices. In our illustration, they were melanoma or not melanoma.

The operative word in that last sentence is eventually. The algorithms don't get it right the first time through the maze so the neural network goes through a learning process to fix its errors using backpropagation. Early in the image-recognition process, the connections between nodes have random weights. In other words, the numerical values assigned to each connection that indicates how much excitement will be passed on to the next node are random.

Backpropagation is a way to fine tune these values by analyzing all the excitement numbers to estimate which ones suggest the right conclusion and which ones suggest the wrong conclusion—in our illustration, which weighted values concluded that a malignant image was a melanoma or an image of a normal mole was in fact a normal mole, and which mistook a melanoma for a benign nevus or concluded that a normal mole was a cancer. With the help of thousands or millions of training images to look at, the network looks *back* and gradually changes the incorrect values, eventually teaching the algorithm to accurately distinguish cancer from noncancer. For any pathway supporting the wrong diagnosis, the connection gets weaker, while connections that support the correct answer get stronger. In effect, the network is saying "you chose the wrong answer, go back and rethink this." Once the algorithm has been trained on images that are known to be benign and malignant, it is then capable to serving as a diagnostic tool to be used on skin lesions that have not been correctly categorized yet.

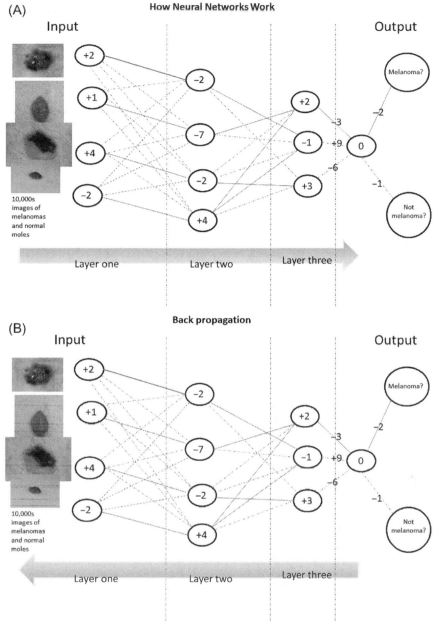

**Figure 7.1** (A) A neural network designed to distinguish melanoma from a normal mole will scan tens of thousands of images to teach itself how to recognize small differences between normal and abnormal skin growths. (B) During the process of differentiating normal from abnormal tissue, a neural network will make many mistakes. Backpropagation looks back at these mistakes to help the program readjust its algorithms and improve its accuracy.

## WHAT IS CDS CAPABLE OF?

The accomplishments of neural networks in healthcare are impressive, and many technologists wonder just how far machine learning and other innovative approaches can take us. At the HealthPartners Institute in Minneapolis, Minnesota, Elyse Kharbanda, MD, and associates from the University of Minnesota, linked a pediatric CDS tool called TeenBP to an electronic health records system to help recognize and manage hypertension, a condition that is often overlooked in children. Twenty primary care practices were assigned to either the CDSS or to routine care. In the former group, the electronic health record (EHR) system automatically displayed patients' blood pressure (BP) and percentiles based on their height. Using this data in over 31,000 pediatric patients between 10 and 17 years of age, they detected 522 cases of hypertension over a 2-year period. In the CDSS arm, clinicians recognized the condition in more than half of patients (54.9%) within 6 months, compared to 21.3% in the children receiving usual care [6]. While the project did not involve a machine-learning algorithm, it was nonetheless an innovative approach to CDS in which it integrated the tool into clinician's workflow, provided alerts and smart order sets, displayed current and previous BP readings for each patient, as well as medications and disorders that can affect BP.

Margaret Meador, MPH, with the National Association of Community Health Centers in Bethesda, Maryland, and her colleagues have demonstrated that using a different set of algorithms programmed into a CDSS and linked to EHRs could identify hypertensive patients at 10 health centers in Arkansas, California, Kentucky, and Missouri [7]. The algorithms increased the prevalence of diagnosed hypertension from 34.5% to 36.7% ($P < .05$). Follow-up evaluation of patients in 8 of 10 health centers led to a firm diagnosis of hypertension in 31.9% of patients. What is significant about this study is that patients with high BP were hiding in plain sight (HIPS), that is, there already were BP readings at or about 140/90 in their records, but they are being ignored. Unfortunately, provider inertia, coupled with a wait and see attitude, often delays treatment of hypertension even after a patient's elevated readings are repeatedly documented. In the Meador et al. study, a quality improvement program and clinical champions helped resolve the issues.

TeenBP and the HIPS program only scratch the surface in terms of what CDS is capable of. It is now possible to use machine learning—assisted CDS to predict which patients with early stage lung cancer would most likely benefit from additional chemotherapy after surgery [8]. A computerized histomorphometric image classifier can analyze biopsy specimens taken from patients during surgery, looking closely at nuclear orientation, texture, shape, and tumor architecture. Using this data, it can predict which patients with early stage nonsmall cell lung cancer are most likely to experience a recurrence, which in turn allows oncologists to plan postsurgical chemotherapy. Like most machine-learning protocols, the software used by Xiangxue Wang from Case Western Reserve University in Cleveland, OH, and associates was initially trained with a collection of biopsy samples and then validated in two separate data collections. The system predicted the recurrence of cancer with an accuracy of 81% in the training cohort and 82% and 75% in the validation cohorts. It is also important to note that this approach to prognosis accurately predicted who was most at risk of cancer recurrence *independent* of the usual predictive parameters used by oncologists, including gender, cancer staging, and histologic subtype.

Innovative researchers and clinicians are also starting to use machine-learning algorithms to help predict the onset of severe sepsis. The condition affects over 700,000 Americans a year and costs more than $20 billion annually. There are several risk-scoring systems in place in US hospitals to help detect severe sepsis, including the Sequential Organ Failure Assessment, the Systemic Inflammatory Response Syndrome criteria, and the Modified Early Warning Score. A machine-learning enabled system called InSight has been shown to outperform these scoring systems in a randomized controlled clinical trial in medical/surgical ICUs at the University of California, San Francisco Medical Center. The average length of stay for patients evaluated with the InSight software was about 20% lower than that observed in the control arm of the trial (10.3 vs 13.0 days). Equally impressive was the fact that in-hospital mortality was 8.96% in the machine-learning group versus 21.13% in those evaluated with the more traditional assessment tools [9].

It is important to note that the machine-learning program was folded into the hospital's EHR system, eliminating the need for clinicians to move outside the patient record to access a separate system, an obstacle that physicians and nurses often complain about. Over the years, we have heard countless complaints from clinicians about too many mouse clicks slowing down their productivity and interfering with fact-to-face time with patients. By one estimate, physicians spend only 27% of their time with patients while nearly 50% of their time is consumed with EHRs and other desk work. Giving them easy access to CDS tools within the EHR they are already working with helps mitigate that problem.

The vital signs and related lab results needed to conduct the assessment in this study were readily obtained from the EHR system; in this trial, it was APeX from Epic. Shimabukuro et al. also note that "Patients in the experimental group additionally received antibiotics an average of 2.76 hours earlier than patients in the control group and had blood cultures drawn an average of 2.79 hours earlier than patients in the control group." A more in-depth explanation of how the algorithms were developed and implemented is provided by Thomas Desautels of Dascena Inc, which created the program [10].

Neural networks are also gaining ground in the field of pancreatic cancer, improving the ability of radiologists to detect the malignancy at an earlier stage. Currently, the disease carries a very poor prognosis and is rarely detected early enough to make a significant difference in patient survival. Part of the problem is the location of the pancreas, which is tucked away in a part of the abdomen where it is difficult to properly visualize on computerized tomography (CT) scans. Elliot Fishman, MD, a radiologist at Johns Hopkins Hospital, has been developing a way to segment the pancreas on scans using deep learning in the hope that it will let his colleagues see small abnormalities more clearly. With the assistance of the DGX-1 AI supercomputer, Fishman and his associates have been feeding data on pancreatic cancer to train the neural network algorithms to detect small textual changes in pancreatic tissue images and differentiate these changes from nearby tissues. "In the first year of the project, the team trained an algorithm to recognize the pancreas and the organs that surround it, achieving a 70 percent accuracy rate. In tests this year, the deep learning model has accurately detected pancreatic cancer about nine times out of 10." [11,12].

## WHAT IS THE HUMAN BRAIN CAPABLE OF?

"What a piece of work is a man! How noble in reason, how infinite in faculty! In form and moving how express and admirable! In action how like an angel, in apprehension how like a god! The beauty of the world. The paragon of animals." When William Shakespeare put those words into Hamlet's mouth, it's unlikely he had the diagnostic reasoning process in mind. But there is little doubt that they apply to an experienced clinician's ability to retain vast amounts of medical knowledge and to use it to find subtle patterns in a patient's medical history, physical exam, and lab data to reach an accurate diagnosis.

Medical and nursing students are trained to arrive at a diagnosis by exposure to numerous real-world cases and through tutorials on the appropriate thinking processes. Fast thinking, sometimes referred to as Type 1 or intuitive reasoning, is often used by experienced clinicians to arrive at a diagnosis, while Type 2 reasoning involves a slower, deliberate process of forming a hypothesis based on the available clues, testing that hutch using a series of well-documented if/then rules, and then retesting a tentative diagnosis as additional observations are made. Over time, with enough experience and exposure to enough cases, clinicians gradually build illness scripts that let them transition from Type 2 to Type 1 reasoning.

The process is not all that different from the if/then rules used by e-based CDSSs, but as any clinician who has used a computerized diagnostic aid knows, even the most advanced software programs can be woefully off base when dealing with the intricacies of human pathophysiology. The shortcomings of IBM Watson illustrate the point. IBM Watson had an impressive showing during the TV game show Jeopardy, defeating human champions. That success encouraged IBM managers to venture into medical diagnosis, developing partnerships with Memorial Sloan Kettering, MD Anderson Cancer Center and others. Those projects have not proven very successful.

An investigative report in *STAT*, produced by Boston Globe Media, found that IBM Watson for Oncology was still struggling to understand the basic differences between various types of cancer. "IBM hasn't published any scientific papers demonstrating how the technology affects physicians and patients. As a result, its flaws are getting exposed on the front lines of care by doctors and researchers who say that the system, while promising in some respects, remains undeveloped" according to the report [13]. The cloud-based supercomputer has been collecting physician notes and other components of patient records, inputting clinical guidelines, and analyzing all this data in the hope that it can supplement and even augment the diagnostic and treatment decisions made by oncologists. But the *Stat News* investigation concluded that "Perhaps the most stunning overreach is in the company's claim that Watson for Oncology, through artificial intelligence, can sift through reams of data to generate new insights and identify, as an IBM sales rep put it, 'even new approaches' to cancer care. STAT found that the system doesn't create new knowledge and is artificially intelligent only in the most rudimentary sense of the term."

The shortcomings of the IBM Watson project are only the proverbial tip of the iceberg. There are other cases in which data analytics have generated unreliable and almost laughable results. The adage about garbage in—garbage out certainly applies here. If the wrong kind of data is input into CDS tool, it will yield the wrong results, regardless of how sophisticated the computer system or the algorithms being employed. But the shortcomings of IBM Watson Health should not turn clinicians away from the field of electronic-based CDS. There are several software tools that have proven valuable as diagnostic assists, without making unrealistic claims. And these tools serve as a reminder that humans may be the "paragon of animals" but their cognitive skills are still limited. Those limitations include cognitive errors and limited memory—even clinicians with eidetic or photographic memory cannot keep up with the mountains of research findings published every year, computers can.

In the history of medicine, there have been several transformative milestones that improved a clinician's ability to decipher the underlying cause of a patient's signs and symptoms. There was a time when physicians were limited by their physical senses to arrive at a diagnosis. One could palpate the chest, hear a wheezing child's lungs, observe a rash, feel the temperature of the skin. But with the invention of the microscope, we could now see an invisible world of disease-causing microbes that were not previously on our list of potential culprits. The discovery of

X-rays likewise let us go beyond our physical senses to detect pathology, as have electrocardiogram (EKGs), and other advances. It required a certain degree of humility for clinicians to admit that their physical senses weren't enough and to embrace these technological tools. Today, we are at a similar crossroads, but now we have to recognize not only our physical limitations but our cognitive limitations as well. A more humbling realization.

We are all subject to reasoning mistakes from time to time. When those cognitive errors influence a clinician's diagnostic judgment, they can prove life-threatening. If you were a fan of the folk music duo Simon and Garfunkel, you will likely remember the lyrics to *The Boxer:* "All lies and jests, still a man hears what he wants to hear, and disregards the rest." Cognitive science has a term for that: affective error. The ability to convince ourselves that what we want to be true really is true. If a patient comes into the office with a persistent headache but is healthy in all other respects, one may be inclined to jump to the conclusion that it's nothing serious—probably stress related. Affective errors are often accompanied by confirmation bias, in which the clinician selectively picks clinical observations that confirm his or her suspicions.

Clinicians may also fall victim to anchoring, a second cognitive mistake, by favoring a specific diagnosis because of a few initial clinical findings. And once that bias sets in, one is then unwilling to alter the tentative conclusion in the light of new data. Availability bias, on the other hand, occurs if a physician sees numerous cases of a specific disorder. That exposure tends to prejudice the clinician's judgment in the direction of this common disorder. As the saying goes: If it looks like a duck and quacks like a duck, it probably is a duck. That kind of reasoning reduces the odds of detecting a rare condition.

*The Merck Manual* outlines a series of other cognitive errors that physicians need to be aware of, including representation error, which it explains [14]

*...occurs when clinicians judge the probability of disease based on how closely the patient's findings fit classic manifestations of a disease without taking into account disease prevalence. For example, although several hours of vague chest discomfort in a thin, athletic, healthy-appearing 60-yr-old man who has no known medical problems and who now looks and feels well does not match the typical profile of an MI, it would be unwise to dismiss that possibility because MI is common among men of that age and has highly variable manifestations. Conversely, a 20-yr-old healthy man with sudden onset of severe, sharp chest pain and back pain may be suspected of having a dissecting thoracic aortic aneurysm because those clinical features are common in aortic dissection. The cognitive error is not taking into account the fact that aortic dissections are exceptionally rare in a 20-yr-old, otherwise healthy patient; that disorder can be dismissed and other, more likely causes (e.g., pneumothorax, pleuritis) should be considered. Representation error also occurs when clinicians fail to recognize that positive test results in a population where the tested disease is rare are more likely to be false positive than true positive.*

## REVIEWING AVAILABLE CDS SYSTEMS

Although CDSSs may not address all the cognitive mistakes that clinicians encounter, they will often force providers to confront these shortcomings, which in the final analysis will improve patient outcomes. At Beth Israel Deaconess Medical Center, clinicians have access to three electronic tools that improve the diagnostic and therapeutic decision-making process: Informatics for Integrating Biology and the Bedside (i2b2), the Shared Health Research Information Network (SHRINE), and Clinical Query2. Also referred to as a software platform or infrastructure, i2b2 consists of a suite of digital tools or modules, including the following:

- A repository of patient records, which holds files of data such as radiological images and genetic sequences.
- A web workbench application and web-based application that let users perform searches.
- An analysis plug-in to detect correlations, which uses mutual information theory to calculate observed correlations within the data of the i2b2 hive.
- Plug-ins to analyze text, export, and import data.
- Software to perform natural language processing, manage projects, and manage ontology.
- An identity management cell, the purpose of which is to protect confidential patient information so that any data released to users are consistent with the Health Insurance Portability and Accountability Act of 1996 privacy rule.

The i2b2 software suite is an open-source platform, which means it is freely available to institutions outside of the Partners network. That has enabled over 90 research institutions and academic medical centers and more than 20 international organizations to use the infrastructure as a way to access and search its own EHR systems and other databases to facilitate clinical research and direct patient care.

The hospitals affiliated with Harvard Medical School, which include Massachusetts General Hospital, Brigham and Women's Hospital, Beth Israel Deaconess Medical Center, Children's Hospital Boston, and Dana Farber Cancer Center, each has i2b2 installed on their computers and each hospital has been able to use the software suite to search its respective HER system to inform patient care and generate hypotheses for clinical research. In 2009, a decision was made to link all the medical records from all five hospitals so that clinicians and researchers would have access to a much larger source of patient data. SHRINE, this combined source, is a federated web-based query system that allows qualified members of the Harvard community to cast a much wider net as it seeks to answer puzzling therapeutic and diagnostic questions and as it considers the formulation of new clinical research projects. SHRINE is available to members of the five hospitals and faculty at Harvard Medical School. However, since the

SHRINE software is freely available as open source, it can be used by other medical centers to establish similar data-sharing networks.

Kenneth Mandl, MD, MPH, Director, Computational Health Informatics Program and Donald AB Lindberg Professor of Pediatrics & Biomedical Informatics at Boston Children's Hospital, explained one function of SHRINE: "I use SHRINE to investigate personalized therapies for patients. Rather than relying on clinical trials data as a source of evidence, the approach is to examine the real-world experience of patients similar to ours. This is a shift toward using large-scale observational data sets to form the evidence base."

Clinical Query 2 is one of the highlights of Beth Israel Deaconess Medical Center's medical informatics platform. Like SHRINE, CQ2 is based on the i2b2 software suite. Each Harvard-affiliated hospital has a local query tool for its researchers. CQ2 is the name that BIDMC has given its local i2b2 implementation. CQ2 only accesses Beth Israel's patient population. The data in SHRINE start in 2001 and the data are always 6−12 months old. CQ2's data, on the other hand, start in 1997 and they are refreshed every 0−2 months. The depth of CQ2 also contributes to its value. SHRINE contains demographics, diagnoses, medications, and some lab tests. CQ2 includes all lab tests, procedures, and vital signs. In fact, the local systems of every hospital that are part of Harvard SHRINE have more data and are updated more often than Harvard SHRINE.

There are numerous other CDS tools available for clinicians who are not part of the Harvard community. A partial list includes UpToDate, Isabel Healthcare, VisualDx, ClinicalKey, and Interpreta. Each has its own unique features that will appeal to different workflow styles and clinician preferences.

*UpToDate.* The standard version of this CDS tool is a massive online, subscription-based medical textbook, with one important caveat: unlike traditional textbooks, which are usually revised every 4−5 years, UptoDate is revised every few months by experts in a long list of specialties, which justifies its name. Its mobile version is available from the Apple app store, Google Play and the Amazon Appstore for Android. The app gives subscribers access to more than 11,000 physician-relevant topics, 9500 graded recommendations, and 6000 drug monographs. There are also a variety of useful calculators and availability of CME credits.

As we have discussed earlier in the book, clinicians do not like to constantly jump from one application to another to input patient data or review useful information. They prefer to do all their work in one location, reducing the number of clicks necessary to accomplish their goal. UpToDate is cognizant of that preference and provides a way for its database to be directly accessed through several major EHR systems, including Allscripts, Epic, Cerner, NextGen, eClinicalWorks, MediTech, and others.

UpToDate recently introduced a more advanced version of its CDS tool. UptoDate Advanced allows providers to take a more patient-specific approach and includes interactive algorithms to create pathways that help personalize recommendations for individual patients. By way of example, if a patient presents for initial treatment of Type 2 diabetes, the pathway will discuss hemoglobin (Hgb) A1c goals, lifestyle modifications, required testing procedures, and contraindications for choosing the pathway, including pregnancy, breastfeeding, and a patient younger than 18 years. If the inclusion and exclusion criteria fit the individual patient, the clinician confirms this decision online, which then prompts the program to open up a series of targeted treatment options. A new decision tree lets the provider make yes/no decisions based on the patient's estimated glomerular filtration rate, contraindications to metformin, and other decision points. For patients who have abnormal lab results—hypoglycemia, for example—the CDS tool also offers customized interpretation to choose the best treatment choices, displayed visually in additional decision trees (Fig. 7.2).

ClinicalKey is a searchable database that relies heavily on content from the thousands of biomedical journals published by Elsevier, its parent company, among other sources (Fig. 7.3). The service also lets users browse its content in several categories, including books, journals, drug monographs, guidelines, and patient education. The database gives readers access to First Consult, which like UpToDate, provides expert reviews of numerous topics. These overviews are divided into several subsections: synopsis, terminology, diagnosis, treatment, complications and prognosis, screening and prevention, and references.

In addition to ClinicalKey, Elsevier offers STATdx for Radiology, and ExpertPath for Pathology. The radiology tool contains more than 4,300 common and complex diagnoses, 200,000 annotated image examples, and 20,000 patient cases, allowing radiologists to compare their patient's image to images in the Elsevier database. For example, if a physician is viewing an image he or she suspects points to mitral valve regurgitation, entering the term into the STATdx search engine will give sample images accompanied by detailed text on terminology, imaging, differential diagnoses, pathology, and diagnostic check lists.

ExpertPath for Pathology offers similar decision-making tools, helping pathologists make a differential diagnosis, and decide which molecular tests may help predict a response to a specific treatment protocol. It walks users through a list of relevant inherited clinical syndromes that may be responsible for the pathology findings.

Isabel Healthcare takes a somewhat different approach to clinical decision support by incorporating a patient-facing symptom checker in its software platform, as well as several functions designed specifically for health professionals. The symptom checker asks patients to input their age, gender, and a list of symptoms. Once these details are entered in the program, Isabel lists some of the common diagnoses, and recommendations on which health professionals are available to address these issues. Isabel Pro DDx Generator, illustrated in Fig. 7.4, is designed for clinicians and uses natural language processing to tap into its database of disease presentations. The clinician

(A)

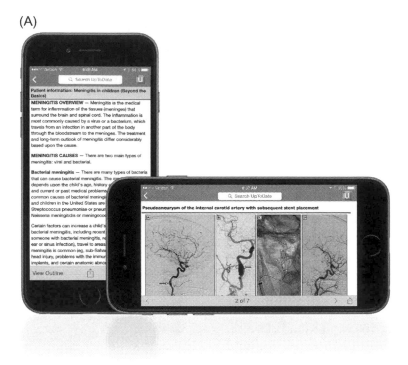

(B)

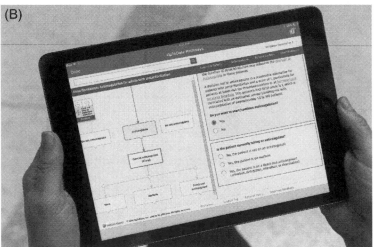

**Figure 7.2** (A) The standard version of UpToDate is a massive online, subscription-based medical textbook that is revised every few months by experts in a variety of specialties. (B) UpToDate Advanced takes a more patient-specific approach and includes interactive algorithms to create pathways that help personalize recommendations for individual patients. *(A) Used with permission of Wolters Kluwer.*

**Figure 7.3** *ClinicalKey* is a searchable database that relies heavily on content from the thousands of biomedical journals published by Elsevier.

enters lab values, vital signs, coexisting disorders, age, gender, and travel history, using free text or derived from an electronic medical record system. The software then displays possible diagnoses as well as medications that may be responsible for the symptoms. The list of potential disorders is linked to evidence-based databases to help clinicians make a differential diagnosis. Among the knowledge resources are Dynamed Plus, 5-minute Consult, and Best Practice from BMJ.

VisualDx. As the name suggests, this CDS tool places a great deal of emphasis on presenting clinicians with the visual clues that can help make an accurate diagnosis. VisualDx includes a symptom finder to help clinicians begin the diagnostic process and then walks the user through a series of decision tree branches to arrive at the correct diagnosis. The diagnostic reasoning begins when the physician chooses a chief complaint, medication, or diagnosis. The program then gives the user a series of differential diagnostic possibilities, as well as additional source material to explore these possibilities (Fig. 7.5).

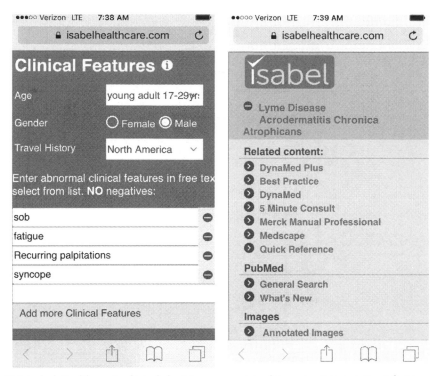

**Figure 7.4** Isabel Healthcare's clinical decision support tool incorporates a patient-facing symptom checker in its software platform, as well as several functions designed specifically for health professionals. *Used with permission of Isabel Healthcare.*

Interpreta takes a very different approach to CDS. While most vendors concentrate exclusively on diagnostic reasoning and treatment options, Interpreta focuses more on clinical risk analysis, patient compliance, personalized medicine, and population health management. The company provides several digital tools to meet these objectives. Its Continuous Member Prioritization platform uses an analytics engine to scan data on each patient to estimate their clinical acuity and severity to determine which are in greatest need of attention. This automated analysis, based on proprietary algorithms, is performed daily and generates a risk score that takes into account their disease burden, preventive needs, poor adherence to medication, and likelihood of requiring hospitalization. The scoring system is based on well-documented standards from the Centers for Medicare and Medicaid Services, the National Committee for Quality Assurance, the Centers for Disease Control and Prevention, among others. The Risk Adjustment and Inference module helps healthcare providers and insurers identify undocumented diagnoses and increased severity that may increase patients' risk of complications.

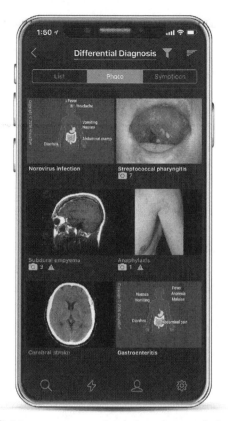

**Figure 7.5** VisualDx gives clinicians numerous visual clues that can help make an accurate diagnosis and includes a symptom finder. *Used with permission of VisualDx.*

## MEASURING THE IMPACT OF CLINICAL DECISION SUPPORT TOOLS

CDSSs like UpToDate, Isabel Healthcare, and VisualDx may be having an impact on patient care as evidenced by the research. For instance, Thomas Issac, MD, MBA, at Beth Israel Deaconess Medical Center and his associates compared length of stay, mortality rates, and quality performance among hospitals who did and did not use UpToDate over a 3-year period. In the 1017 hospitals using the CDSS, risk-adjusted length of stay was modestly improved, when compared to hospitals not using the tool (5.6 days compared to 5.7 days, $P < .001$). Realistically, however, it is hard to imagine any patient getting very excited about being discharged from the hospital about 2.5 hours earlier. On the other hand, Issac et al. found that hospitals using UpToDate experienced somewhat better mortality rates for six conditions—acute myocardial infarction, congestive heart failure, pneumonia, gastrointestinal hemorrhage, stroke, and hip fracture, suggesting that the CDS tool may save lives. Finally, the hospitals using UpToDate had better Hospital Quality Alliance metrics, with smaller hospitals and nonteaching hospitals seeing the largest gains [15].

Forrester Consulting was commissioned by Wolters Kluwer, UpToDate's parent company, to analyze the economic impact of its CDS tool in a Brazilian hospital. Forrester interviewed medical staff at a public and a private hospital, both of which had fixed or mobile access to UpToDate [16]. The analysis concluded that the service saves clinicians time finding and verifying information during the decision-making process, helps them avoid unnecessary referrals, and improves quality of care. Forrester's financial analysis stated: "The analysis points to quantifiable benefits of R $1.1 million versus total costs of R$270,000, adding up to a net present value (NPV) of approximately R$816,000 over the three years of the analysis." [R = risk adjusted.]

In an educational experiment, physician assistant students were asked to analyze standardized patient cases and submit diagnostic decisions and recommendations for further testing. The students were divided into two groups, with one group given access to Isabel Healthcare Pro while the other sought consultation with a resident physician. Investigators concluded: "In this study, the use of a diagnostic reminder system was more effective at improving diagnostic accuracy in PAS-1 students than case discussion with another provider. Interprofessional discussion while making diagnostic decisions may be helpful at improving diagnostic accuracy, but it should not be assumed that collaboration will correct for cognitive biases that are known to lead to diagnostic errors in individual providers (e.g. premature closure, anchoring bias, confirmation bias, overconfidence bias)." [17]

## WHAT WILL THE CDS SYSTEM OF THE FUTURE LOOK LIKE?

The CDS tools currently in use only scratch the surface in terms of what technology can offer providers. Many next generation systems are incorporating the latest innovations in AI, with application in primary care and a variety of specialties. For example, an application called Viz.Ai Contact, available on mobile phones and tablets, has been cleared by the FDA as CDS software to analyze CT images of the brain to help detect large vessel occlusions (LVOs) [18]. The system uses deep learning-based algorithms to assist neurologists as they triage patients suspected of having experienced an acute ischemic stroke. Viz.Ai sends text notifications to the attending neurovascular specialist while she is doing her own independent patient evaluation and may speed up the diagnostic process, according to a study presented at the 2018 International Stroke Conference [19].

Typically, the triage process for patients suspected of having an acute ischemic stroke proceeds from the patient's initial arrival in the hospital to a multimodal CT scan, manual image reading, ED examination, neurologist evaluation and when warranted, intravenous tPA and/or thrombectomy. The Viz.Ai tool is employed after the initial CT scan is performed and takes about 6 minutes, while the usual stroke workup takes about an hour. Barreira et al. compared the software to evaluation by an experienced stroke neurologist on 152 CT scans and found that "the algorithm obtained sensitivity of 0.97 and specificity of 0.52, with a PPV [positive predictive value] of 0.74 and NPV [negative predictive value] of 0.91, and overall accuracy of 0.78....The Viz.Ai-Algorithm performs remarkably well for proximal intracranial LVOs."

Another new program worth consideration is called IDx-DR. The neural network-enabled software, which is similar to that used in the diabetic retinopathy research cited earlier in this chapter, offers automated analysis of retinal scans. The operator uses a fundus camera—specifically the Topcon TRC-NW400 retinal camera—to take two photos of each eye, which are then sent to the IDx-DR client on a local computer, where it is analyzed using a diagnostic algorithm for signs of retinopathy in less than a minute. The software, which has received FDA clearance, is designed to work directly with EHR systems. Once the analysis is complete, the system generates jpeg, PDF, and XML files.

Machine learning—enabled algorithms are also finding their way into colorectal cancer screening. A large-scale study performed on data from Kaiser Permanente Northwest evaluated a colorectal cancer screening tool designed by Medial EarlySign, an Israel-based technology company [20]. Called ColonFlag, its screening algorithm more accurately identified patients at high risk of colorectal cancer, using readily available parameters, including a patient's age, gender, and complete blood count. The investigation analyzed more than 17,000 Kaiser Permanente patients, including 900 patients who already had colorectal cancer. The analysis generated a risk score for patients without the malignancy to gauge their likelihood of developing it. The researchers compared ColonFlag's ability to predict the cancer to that derived from looking at low Hgb levels. (Hgb declines when colorectal cancer causes gastrointestinal bleeding.) ColonFlag was 34% better at identifying the cancer within a 180—360-day period, when compared to low Hgb in patients between 50 and 75 years of age. The algorithms were more sensitive for detecting tumors in the cecum and ascending colon, versus the transverse and sigmoid colon and rectum. Put another way: "The study confirms the efficacy of Medial EarlySign's ColonFlag tool in identifying individuals with 10 times higher risk of harboring undiagnosed colorectal cancer (CRC) while still at curable stages. In many patients, ColonFlag was further able to identify risk for colorectal tumors up to 360 days earlier than its actual diagnosis using conventional practices." [21]

The results observed in this US population are consistent with the positive findings in studies of Israeli populations. The efficacy of tools like ColonFlag relies on the ability of the software to analyze massive databases, which is what Medial was able to do to create its algorithms. It initially analyzed data from more than 605,000 patients in Maccabi Healthcare Services, a large HMO located in Israel. The dataset included more than 3000 cases of colorectal cancer, which was divided into training and validation sets. The model upon which the algorithms were based was also validated using deidentified records of patients in Great Britain's Health Improvement Network, including 25,610 individuals over age 40, of which 5061 had colorectal cancer [22].

Medial has developed a similar predictive tool to help clinicians determine which prediabetic patients will develop diabetes. The database initially analyzed 645,000 prediabetics. Using its AI-based algorithm, the software identified 64% who would become diabetic within a year. Like the colorectal cancer screening tool, this one has the advantage of using routine, preexisting parameters so there was no need to do additional testing. The algorithm used 14 features stored in EHRs [23]. (The results of the analysis have yet to be published in a scientific journal as we go to press.)

Medial is by no means the only innovative company interested in applying machine-learning technology to diabetes care. DreaMed, also an Israeli vendor, has created DreaMed Diabetes to provide clinical decision assistance to clinicians managing Type 1 diabetes for patients who are using an insulin pump and continuous glucose monitoring. It Advisor Pro algorithms collect several types of data, including the patient's daily blood glucose readings, meal carbohydrate data, insulin dosing records, and physical activity level. The software then uses event-driven machine learning and adaptive technology to create a more individualized regimen, adjusting its recommendations on insulin dosing and offering behavior-modification recommendations accordingly.

DreaMed Diabetes relies on a clinical AI program called MD-Logic. It uses fuzzy logic and adaptive learning algorithms to approximate the way diabetes specialists reason as they adjust an individual's insulin regimen. However, the company claims that the software provides "faster analysis and deeper insights" than would normally be available with routine endocrinologist care. There is research support for this automated approach to Type 1 diabetes management.

MD-Logic has been used to drive a wireless artificial pancreas that has been tested in Slovenia, Germany, and Israel. The goal is to maintain blood glucose within the normal range while reducing the risk of hypoglycemia, which is always a risk in patients on insulin. Revital Nimri, with the Jesse Z. and Sara Lea Shafer Institute for Endocrinology and Diabetes, National Center for Childhood Diabetes, Schneider Children's Medical Center of Israel, Petah Tikva, Israel, and associates used the software platform on 24 Type 1 patients with diabetes ages 12–43 years for 6 weeks of home treatment in a randomized crossover trial. The program was used in conjunction with a Medtronic insulin pump and real time sensor, along with a glucose meter from Bayer Healthcare. By the end of the trial, MD-Logic reduced the amount of time patients experienced hypoglycemia and increased the percentage of time they remained in the target blood glucose range (70—140 mg/dL)—when compared to readings generated in patients on standard sensor-augmented insulin pump therapy [24]. Nimri et al. also found the AI-enabled system reduced overnight insulin doses and the average daytime glucose levels. None of the patients experienced any severe adverse reaction to the artificial pancreas system and only one case of severe hypoglycemia was observed, and that happened during the control phase of the experiment. In a separate study that looked at the psychological impact of the artificial pancreas system, Claudia Zeigler, with the Diabetes Centre for Children and Adolescents in Hannover, Germany, and associates found that patients reported fewer worries about hypoglycemia, said the system was easy to use, and gave it high scores on a questionnaire that measured overall satisfaction [25].

Evidence-based medicine purists may reject some of these findings out of hand because they have yet to be published in a peer-reviewed journal or have not been replicated in independent studies by other investigators. But at this junction, it is important to remember that innovation is usually the early phase in the development of a technology, a phase that rarely comes with all the supporting evidence associated with a mature product or service.

## INCORPORATING SYSTEMS BIOLOGY/NETWORK MEDICINE INTO CDS

Folding the latest machine-learning technology into clinical decision support systems will no doubt improve the screening and diagnostic processes, but these advances pale in comparison to what will eventually be achieved by incorporating the findings of systems biology into CDS. Imagine it is the year 2040. The Precision Medicine Initiative's All of Us project has been completed for more than 10 years, and the data collected on 1 million Americans have been analyzed to yield new insights on health and disease. Furthermore, society has come to the realization that if an ounce of prevention is worth a pound of cure, a pound of prevention will eliminate even more human suffering. Unfortunately, as of 2019, we have yet to achieve that level of enlightenment: "... treatments determined by the Food and Drug Administration (FDA) to be safe and effective are usually covered by insurers regardless of their cost, but preventive services have been held to a higher standard: they are often assessed on the basis of whether they generate a positive return on investment and save money in the short term. This disparity leads to overprovision of treatments and under-provision of preventive services, a trend that is exacerbated by high turnover in many health insurance markets. Because insurance contracts tend to be only 1 year long, insurers don't want to spend money to prevent disease in members who may be covered by a different insurer in the near future." [26].

In Chapter 2, Innovations in mHealth, Part 2: EHR-Linked Apps, Remote Patient Monitoring, and the Internet of Things, we discussed the basic concepts behind systems biology. Most medical hypothesis testing is built on a reductionistic approach, a divide and conquer methodology that's "rooted in the assumption that complex problems are solvable by dividing them into smaller, simpler, and thus more tractable units." [27]. As the name implies, systems biology looks at entire biological or pathologic systems, rather than trying to decipher the cause of a disorder by analyzing one variable at a time. Systems biology can also use sophisticated data analytics to tease out numerous interacting contributors, rather than rely on traditional statistical methods that compare single causes for each phenomenon being studied.

Using systems biology to inform clinical decision support in this futuristic scenario involves expanding the patient assessment process to include a long list of potential contributing causes and risk factors that in the past have not been fully understood or appreciated. That list, summarized in Table 7.1, includes the results of a patient's whole genome sequencing, a variety of lifestyle and behavioral measures, sensor-derived physiological data from mobile health apps, prescription and over-the-counter medication usage, psychosocial stress, routine lab data, and so on. Equally important, it requires a CDSS programed to detect complex patterns that result from the interplay of contributing causes that only have clinical consequences when combined with *other* contributing causes. This CDSS will also have the ability to detect the varying strengths of each contributing cause and factor that into its recommendations.

By way of illustration, consider the whole genome report for patient X depicted in Table 7.2. It indicates that this patient has an increased risk of prostate cancer. The predictive analytics engine in our futuristic CDS tool will likely send an alert to his physician recommending annual prostate specific antigen (PSA) testing. Although universal PSA screening is no longer recommended, that advice only applies to the general public, not individual patients at increased risks of the cancer. The same genome report also detected a gene variant called CYP2C9★2, which affects one's ability to metabolize warfarin. By reducing the liver's ability to break down the anticoagulant, it increases the risk of bleeding and warrants a reduction in dosage. A futuristic CDSS would no doubt insert a reminder in patient X's electronic medical record about this potential danger. Given the current insurance scenario in the United States, it is unlikely most patients will ever learn of such susceptibilities because pharmacogenomic testing is rarely covered, and most physicians do not order such tests because few clinical guidelines support their use. This despite the fact that FDA has approved the use of pharmacogenomic testing for more than 150 drugs. (Details on the value of pharmacogenomic testing and initiatives underway to incorporate it into clinical decision support systems are available in Box 7.1.)

**Table 7.1** Data Sources to Inform a Systems Biology Approach to Clinical Decision Support

| Data Category | Examples |
|---|---|
| Behavioral and lifestyle measures | Diet, physical activity, alternative therapies, smoking, alcohol, assessment of known risk factors (e.g., guns, illicit drug use) |
| Sensor-based observations through phones, wearables, home-based devices | Location, activity monitors, cardiac rate and rhythm monitoring, respiratory rate obtained from Smartphone sensors, commercial and research-grade physiologic monitors |
| Structured clinical data derived from EHRs | ICD/CPT billing codes, clinical lab values, medications, problem lists |
| Unstructured and specialized types of clinical data derived from EHRs | Narrative documents, images, EKG and EEG waveform data |
| Healthcare claims data | Periods of coverage, charges and associated billing codes as received by public and private payers, outpatient pharmacy dispensing (product, dose, amount) |
| Biospecimen-derived laboratory data | Genomics, proteomics, metabolites, cell-free DNA, single cell studies, infectious exposures, standard clinical chemistries, histopathology |
| Geospatial and environmental data | Weather, air quality, environmental pollutant levels, food deserts, walkability, population density, climate change |
| Misc | OTC medication purchases |

*EHRs*, Electronic health records; *ICD*, International classification of diseases; *CPT*, Current procedural terminology; *EEG*, Electroencephalogram; *OTC*, Over the counter.
Adapted from The Precision Medicine Initiative Cohort Program—Building a Research. Foundation for 21st Century Medicine. Precision Medicine Initiative (PMI) Working Group Report to the Advisory Committee to the Director, NIH. 2015 https://acd.od.nih.gov/documents/reports/DRAFT-PMI-WG-Report-9-11-2015-508.pdf.

For sake of this discussion on futuristic CDS tools, let's also assume that some of patient X's routine lab results are suspicious for Type 2 diabetes. His fasting blood glucose is 115 mg/dL, suggesting the possibility of prediabetes. That would automatically trigger a recommendation to perform a diabetes risk assessment with a diabetes risk prediction similar to the one developed by Jeremy Sussman from the University of Michigan. [28]. That tool, illustrated in our book on precision medicine, asks clinicians to insert data on seven key parameters:

- Fasting blood glucose
- Hgb A1c
- Family history of elevated blood glucose
- Blood triglyceride level
- Waist measurement in centimeters
- Waist-to-hip ratio
- Height

**Table 7.2** Gene Report Excerpt

| Variant | Phase/Zygosity | Allele Freq | Impact | Evaluation | Summary |
|---|---|---|---|---|---|
| ELAC2-S2171 | Het unknown | 0.209 | Complex/Other pathogenic | Low clinical importance, uncertain | Reported to be associated with increased susceptibility to prostate cancer, but later studies weaken the hypothesis. Xu et al.'s metaanalysis concludes that there is a small but significant increased risk (OR = 1.13). Assuming a lifetime risk of 16% for prostate cancer, we calculate this leads to an increased risk of ~ 1.5% (17.5% total) |
| SLC22A1-R61C | Het unknown | 0.024 | Unknown pharmacogenetic | Insufficiently evaluated | Prioritization score: 3; PolyPhen 2: 1.0 (probably damaging) |
| SLC22A1-L160F | Het unknown | 0.892 | Unknown not reviewed | Insufficiently evaluated | Prioritization score: 0; PolyPhen 2: unknown |
| SLC22A1-M408V | Het unknown | 0.715 | Unknown not reviewed | Insufficiently evaluated | Prioritization score: 0; PolyPhen 2: unknown |
| SSX7-D182E | Homozygous | 0.023 | Unknown not reviewed | Insufficiently evaluated | Prioritization score: 2; PolyPhen 2: 0.994 (probably) |
| ITGAM-P1147S | Het unknown | 0.141 | Unknown not reviewed | Insufficiently evaluated | Prioritization score: 0; PolyPhen 2: unknown |
| CYP2C9-R144C | Het unknown | 0.027 | Unknown pharmacogenetic | Moderate clinical importance, well established | This variant, also called CYP2C9*2, is a pharmacogenetic variant that modulates sensitivity for warfarin (due to reduced metabolism). This variant is associated with Caucasians. The FDA has approved reduced recommended warfarin dosage based on the presence of this variant |

Derived from analysis of John Halamka's genome.

## BOX 7.1 Making a Case for Pharmacogenomic Testing

Although the US Food and Drug Administration has approved pharmacogenomic testing for over 150 drugs, the Centers for Disease Control and Prevention doesn't believe there is enough outcomes data to justify routine testing outside a research setting [29]. Similarly, the US Centers for Medicare and Medicaid Services has refused to pay for almost all such testing. Several thought leaders in genomics question this policy and believe it's time to implement testing for several gene/drug interactions in clinical practice.

For example, MV Relling and WE Evans, with the Department of Pharmaceutical Sciences at St Jude Children's Research Hospital in Memphis, TN, point out that 7% of FDA-approved drugs would yield actionable insights if pharmacogenomic testing were performed, which translates into 18% of all US outpatient prescriptions [29,30]. The Clinical Pharmacogenetics Implementation Consortium (CPIC) has also been writing guidelines to help clinicians put these actionable insights into practice at the bedside. The nonprofit group believes there is enough evidence from randomized clinical trials and other clinical studies to justify gene testing. CPIC has documented about 150 gene-drug interactions that are actionable. To date: "the group, which focuses on inherited genomic variations, has released clinical practice guidelines for 13 genes affecting the response to more than 30 drugs."

Finally, an NIH-funded group called Implementing Genomics in Practice (IGNITE) has created a toolbox to help clinicians and healthcare systems to help foster the uptake of pharmacogenetic testing (PGx), including CDS alerts that can be added to an EHR system. Geoffrey Ginsburg, MD, PhD, director of the Center for Applied Genomics and Precision Medicine at Duke University Medical Center, sums up the future this way: "PGx is the leading edge of genomic medicine… Providers who are not at least thinking about how to incorporate PGx into their practices might find themselves behind the curve in the next 3 to 5 years as the evidence accumulates and practice guidelines adopt this area [of] genetics in the clinic."

Patients who have a high score are more likely to develop full-blown diabetes than the general public. But it is still possible for patient X to get a low score on the diabetes risk prediction tool since it is not 100% accurate. That is where systems biology comes into play. The Sussman tool assumes that Type 2 diabetes is primarily a pancreatic disease and one affected by body weight; systems biology requires we take a far more holistic approach and assume it is a systemic disorder that may emerge from genetic predisposition, a lifetime of overconsumption of added sugars, psychosocial stress, inflammation, elevated cortisol levels, intestinal dysbiosis, sleeping habits, social determinants such as domestic abuse and lack of fresh fruits and vegetables in local markets, and a variety of other risk factors not accounted for by the Sussman risk assessment. Our futuristic CDSS would have specific tools in place to measure each of these parameters. Put another way, Type 2 diabetes may be *many* different diseases, requiring many different approaches and more focus on the individual rather than the most obvious manifestations of the disorder. Focusing all our attention on managing hyperglycemia overlooks all the other underlying causes and the therapies that can address them.

## REFERENCES

[1] Obermeyer Z, Lee TH. Lost in thought—the limits of the human mind and the future of medicine. N Engl J Med. 2017;377:1209—11.

[2] Institute of Medicine. Improving diagnosis in health care quality chasm series. National Academies of Sciences, Engineering, and Medicine, <http://www.nationalacademies.org/hmd/Activities/Quality/DiagnosticErrorHealthCare.aspx>; 2015.

[3] Gulshan V, Peng L, Coram M, et al. Development and validation of a deep learning algorithm for detection of diabetic retinopathy in retinal fundus photographs. JAMA. 2016;316:2402—10.

[4] Esteva A, Kuprel B, Novoa RA, et al. Dermatologist-level classification of skin cancer with deep neural networks. Nature. 2017;542:115—18.

[5] Somers J, Is AI. Riding a one-trick pony?. MIT Technol Rev. 2017; Available from: https://www.technologyreview.com/s/608911/is-ai-riding-a-one-trick-pony/.

[6] Kharbanda EO, Asche SE, Sinaiko AR, et al. Clinical decision support for recognition and management of hypertension: a randomized trial. Pediatrics. 2018;141. Available from: https://doi.org/10.1542/peds.2017-2954.

[7] Meador M, Osheroff JA, Reisler B. Improving identification and diagnosis of hypertensive patients hiding in plain sight (HIPS) in health centers. Joint Commission J Qual Patient Saf. 2018;44:117—29.

[8] Wang X, Janowczyk A, Zhou Y, et al. Prediction of recurrence in early stage non-small cell lung cancer using computer extracted nuclear features from digital H&E images. Sci Rep. 2017;7:13543. Available from: https://doi.org/10.1038/s41598-017-13773-7.

[9] Shimabukuro DW, Barton CW, Feldman MD, et al. Effect of a machine learning-based severe sepsis prediction algorithm on patient survival and hospital length of stay: a randomised clinical trial. BMJ Open Respir Res. 2017;4:e000234. Available from: https://doi.org/10.1136/bmjresp-2017-000234.

[10] Desautels T, Calvert J, Hoffman J, et al. Prediction of sepsis in the intensive care unit with minimal electronic health record data: a machine learning approach. JMIR Med Inform. 2016;4:e28. Available from: https://asset.jmir.pub/assets/6c99f055bbe6a640050163061c3f1b2b.pd.

[11] Beckett J. Hidden figures: how AI could spot a silent cancer in time to save lives. Nvidia, <https://blogs.nvidia.com/blog/2018/05/21/ai-pancreatic-cancer/>; 2018.

[12] Yu Q, Xie L, Wang Y et al. Recurrent saliency transformation network: incorporating multi-stage visual cues for small organ segmentation. ArXiv, <https://arxiv.org/pdf/1709.04518.pdf>; 2018.

[13] Ross C, Swetlitz I. IBM pitched its Watson supercomputer as a revolution in cancer care. It's nowhere close. Stat News September 5, 2017.

[14] McGee DL. Cognitive errors in clinical decision making. Merck Manual, Professional Version, <https://www.merckmanuals.com/professional/special-subjects/clinical-decision-making/cognitive-errors-in-clinical-decision-making>; 2015.

[15] Issac T, Zheng J, Jha A. Use of UpToDate and outcomes in US hospitals. J Hosp Med. 2012;7:85—90.

[16] Selhorst S. The total economic impact of UpToDate: a case study based on the experience of a public and a private hospital in Brazil. Forrester Consulting; 2016.

[17] Carlson J, Tomkowiak J, Morrison J, Rheault W. Does collaboration lead to fewer diagnostic errors? AAMC poster 5/20/2014, <https://www.isabelhealthcare.com/pdf/collaboration_poster_AAMC_5-28-13.pdf?hsCtaTracking = 37068d3b-6319-4e7d-8ff3-49c700689211%257C1a1879b6-a061-4e23-9fde-cbca511abf3c>

[18] Food and Drug Administration. FDA permits marketing of clinical decision support software for alerting providers of a potential stroke in patients, <https://www.fda.gov/NewsEvents/Newsroom/PressAnnouncements/ucm596575.htm>; 2018.

[19] Barreira CM, Bouslama M, Haussen DC, et al. Abstract WP61: Automated Large Artery Occlusion Detection IN Stroke Imaging—ALADIN Study Stroke. 2018;49(Suppl. 1) WP61. Available from: http://stroke.ahajournals.org/content/49/Suppl_1/AWP61.

[20] Hornbrook MC, Goshen R, Choman E, et al. Early colorectal cancer detected by machine learning model using gender, age, and complete blood count data. Dig Dis Sci. 2017;62:2719—27.

[21] Medial Early Sign. New clinical data research confirms medial EarlySign's machine learning platform can identify patients at high-risk for colorectal cancer. News release, <http://earlysign.com/news-and-events/1711/>; 2017

[22] Medial Early Sign. Colorectal cancer (CRC): early detection of colorectal cancer is vital to saving lives, <http://us.earlysign.com/clinical-research/colorectal-cancer/> [accessed 20.06.18].

[23] Medial EarlySign. Medial EarlySign machine learning algorithm predicts risk for prediabetics becoming diabetic within 1 year. Press release, <http://us.earlysign.com/news-and-events/medial-earlysign-machine-learning-algorithm-predicts-risk-prediabetics-becoming-diabetic-within-1-year/>; 2017.

[24] Nimri R, Muller I, Atlas E, et al. MD-logic overnight control for 6 weeks of home use in patients with type 1 diabetes: randomized crossover trial. Diabetes Care. 2014;37:3025—32.

[25] Ziegler C, Liberman A, Nimri R, et al. Reduced worries of hypoglycaemia, high satisfaction, and increased perceived ease of use after experiencing four nights of MD-logic artificial pancreas at home (DREAM4). J Diab Res. 2015; Article ID590308, https://doi.org/10.1155/2015/590308.

[26] Pryor K, Volpp K. Deployment of preventive interventions—time for a paradigm shift. N Engl J Med. 2018;378:1761—3.

[27] Ahn AC, Tewari M, Poon C-S, Phillips RS. The limits of reductionism in medicine: could systems biology offer an alternative? PLoS Med. 2006;3:e208.

[28] Cerrato P, Halamka J. Realizing the promise of precision medicine: The role of patient data, mobile technology, and consumer engagement. Cambridge, MA: Elsevier/Academic Press; 2018.

[29] Abbasi J. Getting pharmacogenomics into the clinic. JAMA. 2016;316:1533—5.

[30] Relling MV, Evans WE. Pharmacogenomics in the clinic. Nature. 2015;526:343—50.

CHAPTER EIGHT

# Telemedicine: Is It Good Patient Care?

Like all innovations throughout the history of medicine, telemedicine has its detractors and its champions. Our purpose in this chapter is to discuss its benefits and limitations, including evidence that demonstrates its clinical effectiveness and cost savings, the regulatory roadblocks that prevent its full implementation, and legitimate criticisms about its misuse.

## WHAT DOES TELEMEDICINE INCLUDE?

There are many "ingredients" that make up telemedicine that need to be kept in mind when evaluating the value of a specific system or when considering a vendor that offers these services. At its most basic level, telemedicine is a way to let clinicians and patients communicate at a distance, or allow clinicians to digitally communicate with others. That communication can include audio and video, data file delivery, and remote patient monitoring with a variety of data recording devices. It may also allow the exchange of images, downloading capabilities, and streaming. Telemedicine platforms allow direct real-time interactive communication (synchronous) or asynchronous, store, and forward communication, in which a patient or clinician sends information to a clinician and he or she responds at a later time. By way of example, it can include an image of a potentially poisonous mushroom to confirm its safety (John Halamka is an expert on the subject), or a conference call conducted by a tumor board. It also can include sending blood pressure readings from a home device to a doctor's office for analysis.

Telemedicine vendors offer a wide variety of options, with some providing their own clinicians to handle a health system's patients and others only offering the technological infrastructure that is then used by the health system's own clinicians. Some vendors contract with clinicians from established health systems as part of their package. Some boast about their ability to deliver instantaneous access to patients who need a physician while others require patients to request a consult and wait to be contacted once the physician becomes available. Many telemedicine vendors also have the technology available to tap into patients' electronic health records and make that information quickly available to the provider during the eVisit. Certain vendors have expertise in critical care medicine, offering state-of-the-art tele-intensive care unit

*The Transformative Power of Mobile Medicine.*
DOI: https://doi.org/10.1016/B978-0-12-814923-2.00008-8

(ICU) services, while others cater more to the ambulatory market. Some emphasize their exceptionally high-quality audio and video capability, which is of value to hear the subtleties of certain heart sounds and the small changes in blood vessels during a diagnostic procedure. Health-care systems may also operationally execute their own telehealth programs via already existing infrastructure. Regardless of what type of service the vendor offers, it must ensure that communication between clinician and patient is Health Insurance Portability and Accountability Act (HIPAA) compliant, which means the platform must have security protocols in place to reduce the risk of a data breach. (A more detailed discussion of privacy and security of mobile health systems will be discussed in Chapter 10). A recent summary of 10 well-established telemedicine vendors, available from Healthcare IT News, includes American Well, Doctor on Demand, MDLive, TelaDoc, Philips, Polycom, and SnapMD. SnapMD, for example, was recently selected by the American Academy of Pediatrics (AAP) as its telemedicine provider. The Academy will use the vendor's Virtual Care Management platform as part of its AAP Member Advantage Program. The platform lets pediatricians launch virtual visits using their own clinicians and under their own brand. The platform also provides AAP members with consulting services to help them get started in telemedicine, establish a continuity of care model that engages patients with "educational content creation/delivery, personalized patient interaction, remote patient monitoring, Wellcare messaging programs and other community outreach strategies," and lastly helps them with marketing and advertising [1].

## WHAT ARE THE ADVANTAGES OF TELEMEDICINE?

Cost savings, better quality of care, clinical efficacy, and efficiency are among the potential benefits to be reviewed when deciding to adopt a telemedicine program. The research on costs is mixed and is dependent in part on which financial markers are measured. While many analyses look solely at expenditures and revenue generated by health plans and employers, there are other metrics worth considering, including patients' transportation costs. Navjit Dullet from the Touro University College of Medicine in Vallejo, CA, and associates from the University of California, Davis, evaluated a telemedicine consultation database, calculating travel distances and travel times between a patient's home, the telemedicine clinic, and the UC Davis in-person clinic. They then estimated travel cost savings and the environmental impact of letting patients avoid driving to the in-person clinic. The analysis included more than 19,000 consultations and over 11,000 patients [2]. The remote visits saved over 5 million miles in travel, more than 4.5 million minutes in travel times—equivalent to almost

9 years. The average patient saved about 278 miles round trip for each eVisit and about $156. Finally, Dullet et al. found that "Telemedicine consultations resulted in a total emissions savings of 1969 metric tons of $CO_2$, 50 metric tons of CO, 3.7 metric tons of NOx, and 5.5 metric tons of volatile organic compounds."

On the other hand, there is evidence to suggest that virtual visits don't always replace in-person visits but may actually increase health-care utilization, which would increase overall health-care costs. For example, patients who belong to Kaiser Permanente Northern California (KPNC) have for years had access to telemedicine services and have expressed satisfaction with the program. While these video conferencing visits are less expensive than office visits, "To date, the increasing use of Internet, mobile, and video alternatives has apparently not had an impact on the number of traditional office visits," according to Robert Pearl, CEO and executive director of the Permanente Medical Group in Oakland, CA [3] (Fig. 8.1).

A Rand Corporation study that analyzed over 300,000 patients has come to the same conclusion. J Scott Ashwood, a policy researcher with RAND, and associates, analyzed commercial insurance claims for beneficiaries who had medical benefits that included direct-to-consumer (DTC) telemedicine. They found that only 12% of the telemedicine visits had actually replaced office visits or trips to the emergency

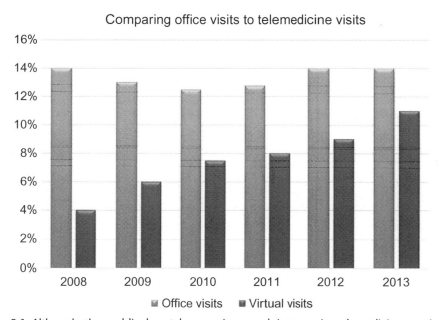

**Figure 8.1** Although the public has taken an increased interest in telemedicine services, the increase in virtual visits is not necessarily accompanied by a drop in office visits. *Adapted from Pearl R. Kaiser Permanente Northern California: current experiences with internet, mobile, and video technologies. Health Affairs 2014;33:251−7.*

department (ED), which means 88% of visits represented new utilization. That translated into an increase in net annual spending on acute respiratory illness of $45 per telemedicine user [4]. The analysis was based on claims and enrollment data from 2011 to 2013 among patients who were enrolled in CalPERS Blue Cross of California's health maintenance organization plan and only included claims for acute respiratory infections. On a more positive note, Ashwood et al. tried to determine if a virtual visit was more likely to result in follow-up appointments, testing, or prescriptions, when compared to office visits. When all these variables were taken into account, virtual visits were still about 50% less expensive than a trip to the doctor's office and less than 5% of the cost of an ED visit.

By way of contrast, telemedicine companies such as Teledoc and American Well claim that about 10% of telemedicine visits are the result of new utilization, compared to 88% in the *Health Affairs* analysis. Ashwood et al. point out that the vendor's estimate is based on retrospectively obtained patient surveys, which can be notoriously imprecise, because they are often influenced by recall bias, social desirability bias, and a variety of other psychological factors. The *Health Affairs* analysis, on the other hand, was based on actual observed use of telemed users.

Of course, cost is not the only factor that employers and policy makers should keep in mind when evaluating the benefits of DTC telemedicine services. Ashwood et al. conclude "Even if direct-to-consumer telehealth services do not save money, telehealth is clearly a service of value to customers and may yield benefits in other metrics, such as employee satisfaction. Furthermore, as direct-to-consumer telehealth services grow in popularity and become a standard offering, employees may come to expect the services to be part of their benefits package. If this becomes the case, the strategy of cost conscious employers and health plans should be to offer the services while simultaneously, attempting to limit overuse." For health-care employers, telemedicine is advantageous as it reduces time missed from work.

A cost analysis of telemedicine used by US veterans, on the other hand, paints a different picture. The Veterans Health Administration (VHA) launched its telehealth programs in the 1990s and has been leading the way ever since, addressing the needs of veterans with diabetes, congestive heart disease, hypertension, chronic obstructive pulmonary disease, posttraumatic stress syndrome, and depression. These initiatives have also generated cost savings. For instance, traditional home care cost over $13,000 per patient per year in 2012 and more than $77,000 for nursing home care. The annual cost of a telemed program was only $1600 per patient per year [5]. VHA's telehealth programs have also resulted in a 25% drop in the number of bed days and a 19% drop in hospital admissions. More specifically, the program cut hospitalization among patients with mental health problems by more than 40% while patients with heart failure and hypertension experienced a 25%—30% reduction. It is estimated that the entire VHA telemedicine program saved $6500 per patient annually in 2012 [6].

There is mounting evidence to suggest that telemedicine services reduce the cost of care for pediatric patients who have sustained sports injuries. A presentation given at the AAP National Conference in 2017 reported on the results of a study conducted by the Nemours Health System. Alfred Atanda, MD, evaluated 120 patients ages 17 years and younger who had at least one telemedicine visit in a 1-year period and compared them to patients receiving in-person care. The study found that patients saved about $50 in travel costs and 51 minutes in waiting and visit time using the telemed service. The health system saved $24 per patient [7].

Byung-Kwang Yoo, MD, PhD, with the University of California, Davis, and associates have performed a cost analysis to evaluate the value of telemedicine in an ICU by creating a hypothetical scenario [8]. Yoo et al. used decision modeling to simulate the impact of telemedicine on an ICU. Their economic analysis took into account telemed equipment installation (start-up costs), the cost of 5 year depreciation, maintenance costs, and clinician staffing. To do their cost–effectiveness analysis, they measured the cumulative quality-adjusted life years 5 years after discharge from the ICU, comparing ICU scenarios with and without telemedicine capabilities. Their analysis concluded

> The base case cost-effectiveness analysis estimated telemedicine in the ICU to extend 0.011 quality-adjusted life years with an incremental cost of $516 per patient compared with ICU without telemedicine, resulting in an incremental cost-effectiveness ratio of $45,320 per additional quality-adjusted life year (=$516/0.011). The probabilistic cost-effectiveness analysis estimated an incremental cost-effectiveness ratio of $50,265 with a wide 95% CI from a negative value (suggesting cost savings) to $375,870. These probabilistic analyses projected that cost saving is achieved 37% of 1,000 iterations. Cost saving is also feasible if the per-patient per-hospital-stay operational cost and physician cost were less than $422 and less than $155, respectively, based on break-even analyses.

The wide 95% confidence interval detected during the analysis indicates that the cost effectiveness of telemedicine in the ICU varies considerably, depending on start-up costs, maintenance, and staffing expenditures, among other variables.

Geisinger Health Plan (GHP) launched a telemonitoring service in March 2008 that serves patients with heart failure in rural central Pennsylvania. The program includes a Bluetooth-enabled body weight scale for patients to use in their home. Sudden changes in body weight can signal a worsening in a patient's heart condition. An increase of 2–3 lb in 24 hours suggests that the body is retaining fluid, which may indicate that heart failure is worsening.

The program also included an interactive voice response system that allowed patients to ask several questions about their condition, including the onset of shortness of breath, changes in leg swelling and appetite, and how well they were managing their prescription.

It is important to stress that this telemedicine initiative was *not* a one-off intervention, as is often the case with consumers who have a single eVisit with a physician working for a popular telemedicine service. It is part of a long-term case management program that monitors patients over time and emphasizes continuity of care. This approach paid measurable dividends. Over 4.5 years, the telemedicine initiative resulted in a significant drop in all-cause hospital admissions, 30- and 90-day readmissions, and cost of care. A summary of the initiative described in the American Hospital Association's report on telemedicine provided more details: "In a given month of the study, patients enrolled in the program were 23 percent less likely to experience a hospital admission. The odds of experiencing a 30-day readmission were 44 percent lower and the odds of experiencing a 90-day readmission were 38 percent lower than patients not enrolled in the telemonitoring program. . . . The estimated return on investment associated with the telemonitoring program was approximately $3.30 return in terms of cost savings accrued to GHP for every $1 spent to implement the program." [9,10].

## PHYSICIANS REMAIN SKEPTICAL

Despite encouraging reports from organizations such as Geisinger, many healthcare providers remain skeptical about the cost effectiveness of telemedicine. A 2017 report from KLAS and The College of Healthcare Information Management Executives (CHIME) included interviews with over 100 healthcare organizations, asking about the use of virtual care platforms for scheduled patient visits, on-demand consumer-focused visits, and telespecialty consultations. It concluded that "Reimbursements are the biggest constraint on the successful expansion of telehealth technologies, and insurance companies, Medicare/Medicaid, and Accountable Care Organizations (ACOs) have been slow to reimburse virtual visits. Though some provider organizations have received reimbursements, these often amount to less than is needed to cover the cost of the services provided. Unincentivized providers are a natural consequence of this since providers can earn more for in-person visits. The lack of reimbursement has made it difficult for organizations to make a business case for expanding telehealth solutions." [11].

On a more positive note, executives responding to KLAS/CHIME also opined that scheduled patient visits increased patient satisfaction while on-demand consumer visits improved brand awareness and increased their organization's market share. Telespecialty consults generated "better clinical outcomes driven primarily by telestroke technology." It is important to keep in mind, however, that these conclusions were not supported by detailed statistics; the report was not intended to gather and interpret this kind of evidence. Instead, its goal was to collect the strong opinions of its interviewees.

The KLAS/CHIME report also suggested that telemedicine services help reduces ED and urgent care visits, making it cost effective. One CEO summed up his organization's opinion this way:

*The telehealth program has been cost effective for a lot of self-insured businesses, so it increases access to care immensely, even for our employees who are using it quite a bit now. Telehealth is reducing ED and urgent care visits, so it is a very cost effective way to get care. I also like that [our telehealth vendor] follows very specific protocols so that we don't have antibiotics and narcotics spewing out of the phones. [Our vendor] has very specific criteria in terms of patients getting the appropriate treatment. Telehealth is also a good marketing tool for us. [Our vendor] has advertisements for the virtual-care service on kiosks and elevator doors at the mall, and we have it on some buses. That is a way to advertise our name and a service that stands out that other organizations don't have.*

The KLAS report suggested that telemedicine may not offer much financial benefit in a fee-for-service world, but in a value-based system in which providers take on more risk and are responsible for long-term population health, including ACOs, it looks more appealing. Anecdotal evidence also suggests that on demand consumer-oriented telemed services may be more cost effective than scheduled telemed, because they attract new patients and serve as a marketing tool to promote the organization. One healthcare executive expressed this sentiment: "We have been tracking things like new patients and patient demographics. Because of Virtual Care, we are getting new patients, and these patients are able to access many of the levels of care that we provide. Also, a few months after implementing Virtual Care, we started getting new patients who had no immediate connection to our facility. We feel that Virtual Care has helped us advertise and network. We were able to be one of the first services delivering virtual care in our area. Virtual care is really new and helped us differentiate ourselves for a few years. Then the other local competitors started offering virtual care, too."

## REGULATIONS GOVERNING TELEMEDICINE REIMBURSEMENT

One of the roadblocks to cost savings in telemedicine has been the archaic, confusing federal regulations that govern Medicare reimbursement. Those regulations are slowly entering the 21st century. The Centers for Medicare and Medicaid Services has proposed a new set of regulations for the 2019 Medicare Physician Fee Schedule (PFS) and Quality Payment Program that should improve payment for remote patient monitoring and telehealth programs [12]. Centers for Medicare and Medicaid Services (CMS) has proposed three new codes to cover remote patient monitoring; it is now calling this type of telemedicine service "chronic remote physiological monitoring." The new codes are CPT 990X0, 990X1, and 994X9. These codes will supplement and improve on the existing billing code CPT 99091 used for remote monitoring. Currently, 99091 covers the collection and interpretation of data such as ECG, blood pressure, and glucose monitoring. The existing code takes into account digitally stored and/or transmitted data by a patient and/or a caregiver to a clinician. The telemed action requires at least 30 minutes of time.

CPT 994X9 differs from 99091, because it only requires 20 minutes per calendar month, while 99091 calls for 30 minutes per 30-day period. The former is easier to keep track of and requires 33% less time. The newly proposed codes also take into account the expenditures that healthcare providers must cope with during initial setup. For instance, the new codes will let organizations bill for the work of setting up remote patient monitoring hardware and patient training in using the equipment. Nathaniel Lacktman, a lawyer with expertise in the subject, explains "…this separate payment is different from how Medicare reimburses Durable Medical Equipment (DME) suppliers (e.g., CPAP, oxygen, etc.). CMS requires the DME supplier to set up the equipment at the patient's home and educate the patient on how to use the equipment but does not offer separate payment for that work." [12].

There are other more subtle differences in the old and new CPT codes that will likely lift some of the financial burden off healthcare providers trying to develop and maintain a viable telemedicine service. For instance, CPT 99091 requires remote patient monitoring to be performed by "physicians and qualified healthcare professionals" which does not expressly include RNs, medical assistants, and others that would fall into the category of "clinical staff." The new codes would allow the latter group, which is paid at a lower salary, to perform these tasks.

CMS is also proposing new regulations that would cover virtual check ins, what they called "brief communication technology-based service," asynchronous images and video, which the agency has labeled "remote evaluation of pre-recorded patient information," and peer-to-peer internet consults or "Interprofessional internet consultation." The good news about these new standards, if approved, is that they do not require the patient be located at qualified originating site or rural area, which is the case currently.

While the aforementioned proposed billing codes will likely take effect in 2019, CMS has already implemented new telemedicine rules based on the Medicare Access and CHIP Reauthorization Act of 2015 (MACRA), which established the Quality Payment Program for eligible clinicians. The final updated rules were published by the US Department of Health and Human Services on November 2, 2017 and can be accessed online in the Federal Register [13]. The full depth and breadth of the new rules are beyond the scope of this book, but it is worth mentioning that they provide new payment options for telemedicine, expanding access to patients in underserved areas and making it easier for clinicians to bill for them. Excerpts from the new HHS final rule are available in Box 8.1.

## BOX 8.1 CMS Position on Telemedicine

Excerpts from the Centers for Medicare and Medicaid Services Final Rule

*CY 2018 Updates to the Quality Payment Program; and Quality Payment Program: Extreme and Uncontrollable Circumstance Policy for the Transition Year [13]*

After consideration of the public comments, we are finalizing for performance periods occurring in 2018 and future years that at §414.1305 nonpatient facing MIPS eligible clinician means an individual MIPS (Merit-based Incentive Payment System) eligible clinician that bills 100 or fewer patient-facing encounters (including Medicare telehealth services defined in section 1834(m) of the Act) during the nonpatient facing determination period, and a group or virtual group provided that more than 75 percent of the NPIs (National Provider Identifier) billing under the group's TIN (Tax Identification Number) or within a virtual group, as applicable, meet the definition of a nonpatient facing individual MIPS eligible clinician during the nonpatient facing determination period. In addition, we are finalizing that for performance periods occurring in 2018 and future years that for purposes of nonpatient facing MIPS eligible clinicians, we will utilize E&M codes and Surgical and Procedural codes for accurate identification of patient-facing encounters, and thus, accurate eligibility determinations regarding nonpatient facing status. Further, we are finalizing that a patient-facing encounter is considered to be an instance in which the individual MIPS eligible clinician or group billed for items and services furnished such as general office visits, outpatient visits, and procedure codes under the PFS. Finally, we are finalizing that for performance periods occurring in 2018 and future years, that for the nonpatient facing determination period, in which the initial 12-month segment of the nonpatient facing determination period would span from the last 4 months of a calendar year 2 years prior to the performance period followed by the first 8 months of the next calendar year and include a 30-day claims run out; and the second 12-month segment of the nonpatient facing determination period would span from the last 4 months of a calendar year 1-year prior to the performance period followed by the first 8 months of the performance period in the next calendar year and include a 30-day claims run out. f. [facing] MIPS Eligible Clinicians Who Practice in Critical Access Hospitals Billing under Method II (Method II CAHs).

After consideration of the public comments received, we are finalizing our proposal that each MIPS eligible clinician who is part of a virtual group will be identified by a unique virtual group participant identifier, which will be a combination of three identifiers: (1) virtual group identifier (established by CMS; e.g., XXXXXX); (2) TIN (9 numeric characters; e.g., XXXXXXXXX); and (3) NPI (10 numeric characters; e.g., 1111111111). For example, a virtual group participant identifier could be VG-XXXXXX, TINXXXXXXXXX, NPI-11111111111.

d. Application of group-related policies to virtual groups

1. Generally in the CY 2017 Quality Payment Program final rule (81 FR 77070 through 77072), we finalized various requirements for groups under MIPS at §414.1310(e), under which groups electing to report at the group level are assessed and scored across the TIN for all four performance categories. In the CY 2018 Quality Payment Program proposed rule (82 FR 30029), we proposed to apply our previously finalized and proposed group-related policies to virtual groups, unless otherwise specified. We recognized that

there are instances in which we may need to clarify or modify the application of certain previously finalized or proposed group-related policies to virtual groups, such as the definition of a nonpatient facing MIPS eligible clinician; small practice, rural area, and HPSA designations; and groups that contain participants in a MIPS APM or an Advanced APM [Alternative Payment Model] (see Section II.C.4.b. of this final rule with comment period). More generally, such policies may include, but are not limited to, those that require a calculation of the number of NPIs across a TIN (given that a virtual group is a combination of TINs), the application of any virtual group participant's status or designation to the entire virtual group, and the applicability and availability of certain measures and activities to any virtual group participant and to the entire virtual group.

We refer readers to Section II.C.4.d.(5) of this final rule with comment period for a summary of the public comments we received on these proposals and our responses.

2. Application of Nonpatient Facing Status to Virtual Groups

With regard to the applicability of the nonpatient facing MIPS eligible clinician-related policies to virtual groups, in the CY 2017 Quality Payment Program final rule (81 FR 77048–77049), we defined the term nonpatient facing MIPS eligible clinician at §414.1305 as an individual MIPS eligible clinician that bills 100 or fewer patient-facing encounters (including Medicare telehealth services defined in section 1834(m) of the Act) during the nonpatient facing determination period, and a group provided that more than 75% of the NPIs billing under the group's TIN meet the definition of a nonpatient facing individual MIPS eligible clinician during the nonpatient facing determination period. In the CY 2018 Quality Payment Program proposed rule (82 FR 30021, 30029), we proposed to modify the definition of a nonpatient facing MIPS eligible clinician to include clinicians in a virtual group, provided that more than 75% of the NPIs billing under the virtual group's TINs meet the definition of a nonpatient facing individual MIPS eligible clinician during the nonpatient facing determination period. We noted that other policies previously established and proposed in the proposed rule for nonpatient facing groups would apply to virtual groups (82 FR 30029). For example, as discussed in Section II.C.1.e. of this final rule with comment period, virtual groups determined to be nonpatient facing would have their advancing care information performance category automatically reweighted to zero.

With regard to the application of small practice status to virtual groups, in the CY 2017 Quality Payment Program final rule (81 FR 77188), we defined the term small practices at §414.1305 as practices consisting of 15 or fewer clinicians and solo practitioners. In the CY 2018 Quality Payment Program proposed rule (82 FR 30019, 30029), we proposed that a virtual group would be identified as a small practice if the virtual group does not have 16 or more eligible clinicians. In addition, we proposed for performance periods occurring in 2018 and future years to identify small practices by utilizing claims data; for performance periods occurring in 2018, we would identify small practices based on 12 months of data starting from September 1, 2016 to August 31, 2017 (82 FR 30019–30020). We refer readers to Section II.C.1.c. of this final rule with comment period for the discussion of our proposal to identify small practices by utilizing claims data. We refer readers to Section II.C.4.d.(3) of this final rule with comment period for the discussion regarding how small practice status would apply to virtual groups for scoring under MIPS.

In the CY 2018 Quality Payment Program proposed rule (82 FR 30020–30021), we proposed to determine rural area and HPSA practice designations at the individual, group, and virtual group level. Specifically, for performance periods occurring in 2018 and future years, we proposed that an individual MIPS eligible clinician, a group, or a virtual group with multiple practices under its TIN or TINs within a virtual group would be designated as a rural area or HPSA practice if more than 75% of NPIs billing under the individual MIPS eligible clinician or group's TIN or within a virtual group, as applicable, are designated in a ZIP code as a rural area or HPSA. We noted that other policies previously established and proposed in the proposed rule for rural area and HPSA groups would apply to virtual groups (82 FR 30029). We note that in Section II.C.7.b.(1)(b) of this final rule with comment period, we describe our scoring proposals for practices that are in a rural area.

As noted above, we proposed to apply our previously finalized and proposed group-related policies to virtual groups, unless otherwise specified (82 FR 30029). In particular, we recognized that the measures and activities applicable and available to groups would also be applicable and available to virtual groups. Virtual groups would be required to meet the reporting requirements for each measure and activity, and the virtual group would be responsible for ensuring that their measure and activity data are aggregated across the virtual group (e.g., across their TINs). We noted that other previously finalized and proposed group-related policies pertaining to the four performance categories would apply to virtual groups.

There are still limitations to telemedicine coverage by CMS; often, only regions in rural Metropolitan Statistical Areas are covered under fee-for-service. Urban hospitals, therefore, may not be able to reduce visits into their tertiary care centers. Furthermore, chronic care management CPT code modifiers are often only billable once per month per patient. Most patients with comorbidities could benefit from telemedicine to avoid the burden of their illnesses; however, only one physician for each patient—either the primary care provider, diabetes specialist (endocrinologist), or congestive heart failure (cardiologist)—may benefit from the monthly telemedicine reimbursement.

## EVIDENCE OF CLINICAL EFFECTIVENESS

The decision to implement telemedicine cannot be dictated by cost considerations alone. There is a large collection of research on its effectiveness that must be weighed as well. Robert Pearl, executive director and CEO of the Permanente Medical Group in Oakland, CA, has summarized the experience that his organization has had using such services [3]. Patients who belong to KPNC have had access to telemedicine services for many years. They can send secure email messages to primary care providers and specialists who are treating them, including nonurgent requests for information and attachments of images. Dermatologists in the group often make a definitive diagnosis of a rash based on those attachments. Doctors working for the system are expected to respond to emails in 2 business days and have managed to do so 98% of the time. KPNC also offers telephone visits those last 10—15 minutes, as an alternative to office visits. The group has offered support for pregnant women with substance abuse disorders as well. Its Early Start program screens patients for alcohol and drug abuse. One study has found a rate of fetal demise of 0.5% in women involved in the program, compared to 7.1% in a control group. The rate of preterm birth in the control group was more than twice the rate observed in the Early Start Program [14].

The emergency department may seem like an unlikely place to implement a tele-medicine service. After all, mending a broken leg or administering clot-busting drugs such as tissue plasminogen activator can hardly be performed over the Internet. But inno-vative clinicians at Georgetown University Hospital have devised a protocol that lets phy-sicians do intake assessments via telemedicine. Izzo et al. compared the tele-intake approach, which included ordering labs, X-rays, CT scans, MRI, and medication [15]. Their retrospective analysis included over 6500 in-person evaluations and over 6000 tele-intake assessments. The assessments were followed up by another ED clinician to com-plete each patient's care. When the researchers compared the number of orders added by the second provider, they found no significant difference. Similarly, fewer than 1% of ini-tial orders were canceled by the second clinician, also an insignificant difference.

A randomized trial conducted in Norway has likewise supported the benefits of telemedicine [16]. Kai Muller, MD, with the Arctic University of Norway and associ-ates randomized patients with nonacute headache to either telemedicine ($n = 200$) or in-person care ($n = 202$) over a 12-month period and found no difference in clinical outcomes. Outcomes were measured using the Headache Impact Test-6 and a pain intensity visual analog scale.

An exhaustive review of the medical literature published by the Cochrane Library provides a generally positive take on telemedicine [17]. The analysis, which included 93 trials and over 22,000 participants, evaluated the effectiveness of inter-active telemedicine. Among 16 studies that looked at patients with heart failure, Flodgren et al. found no difference in all-cause mortality between patients who received telemedicine care and those assigned to traditional care after 6 months of follow-up. Among the 11 studies that looked at hospital admissions, there was a wide range of findings, from a 64% decrease to an increase of 60% at median 6 months follow-up.

Additional findings gleaned from the Cochrane review include the following:

- Improved quality of life (five studies) for patients assigned to telemedicine, com-pared to usual care at 3 months follow-up.
- Lower glycated hemoglobin among patients with diabetes, compared to controls, as 9 months follow-up.
- Decreased LDL cholesterol and blood pressure readings, compared to usual care.
- No differences in the effects of therapy among patients with mental health and sub-stance abuse problems, when comparing video conferencing to face-to-face care.

As you might expect, improvements and noninferiority varied among the studies evaluated depending on several variables, including "those related to the study population e.g. the severity of the condition and the disease trajectory of the participants, the function of the intervention e.g., if it is used for monitoring a chronic condition, or to provide access to diagnostic services, as well as the healthcare provider and healthcare system involved in delivering the intervention."

An independent multicenter study of ICU telemedicine conducted by the University of Massachusetts Medical School in Worcester, MA, has generated positive results as well. Lilly et al. evaluated nearly 119,000 adult patients from 56 ICUs in 32 hospitals from 19 US healthcare systems and found reduced ICU mortality (hazard ratio 0.74) in the ICU telemedicine group, when compared to controls. Similarly the hospital length of stay was lower on average. Improved mortality and reduced length of stay (LOS) was associated with "(1) intensivist case review within 1 h of admission, (2) timely use of performance data, (3) adherence to ICU best practices, and (4) quicker alert response times." [18].

There is also evidence to support the use of telemedicine services among children in need of critical care. Dayal et al. with the Department of Pediatrics, University of California, Davis, examined the transfer records of 584 patients from 15 emergency departments who were receiving telemedicine to 524 patients from 60 EDs without telemedicine. Both cohorts were transferred to pediatrics ICUs. Children who had received telemedicine services reached the PICU less sick; observed-to-expected mortality ratios were better in the telemedicine group [19].

The Agency for Healthcare Research and Quality, a division of the US Department of Health and Human Services, has published an exhaustive review of the evidence on the strengths and weaknesses of telemedicine, entitled: *Telehealth: Mapping the Evidence for Patient Outcomes From Systematic Reviews* [20]. The AHRQ team evaluated over 200 systematic reviews and hundreds of published papers, narrowing down its analysis to 58 reviews meeting its evidential criteria. The overall conclusion stated that "The largest volume of research reported that telehealth interventions have produced positive results when used in the clinical areas of chronic conditions and behavioral health and when telehealth is used for providing communication/counseling and monitoring/management. Considering both clinical areas and the functions of telehealth allowed us to create more specific subgroups and look at the variation and consistency within these as well." The analysis also found that there was limited evidence to support the use of telehealth to perform triage in urgent/primary care, manage serious pediatric disorders, and integrate behavioral and physical health.

One of the charts generated by the AHRQ analysts rates the strength of the clinical evidence on the benefits of telemedicine. In Fig. 8.2, it uses the horizontal axis for that purpose, ranging from 0, indicating no benefit through 3, positive

Telehealth literature map by clinical focus

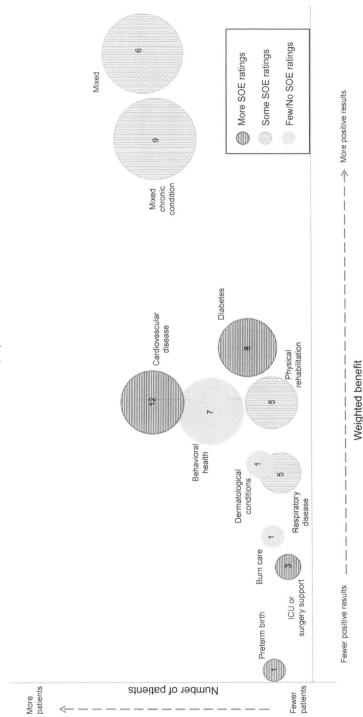

**Figure 8.2** Telehealth literature map of systematic reviews by clinical focus.

1. Bubble size reflects the unduplicated number of individual studies included in the systematic reviews about that clinical focus. The number label on each bubble is the number of systematic reviews. Smaller bubbles indicate fewer studies, larger bubbles indicate more studies. The color of the bubble represents how many of systematic reviews included strength of evidence assessment.

2. Weighted relative benefit is calculated by weighting the overall conclusion of each review by the number of studies in the review. Bubbles to the right indicate more positive findings while bubbles to the left represent findings that are unclear or found no benefit.

*ICU, Intensive care unit; SOE, strength of evidence. Telehealth: mapping the evidence for patient outcomes from systematic reviews June 2016 AHRQ. Totten AM, Womack DM, Eden KB, McDonagh MS, Griffin JC, Grusing S, Hersh WR. Telehealth: mapping the evidence for patient outcomes from systematic reviews. In: Technical brief no. 26. (Prepared by the Pacific Northwest evidence-based practice center under contract no. 290-2015-00009-I.) AHRQ publication no. 16-EHC034-EF. Rockville, MD: Agency for Healthcare Research and Quality; 2016. www.effectivehealthcare. ahrq.gov/reports/final.cfm.*

benefit. The number within each bubble—from 1 to 12—indicates the number of reviews that were included for each disease category. The vertical position of each category indicates the relative number of patients reviewed in that category. The size of the bubble that represents each disease group represents the number of studies that were reviewed. For instance, the bubble representing cardiovascular disease is located about midway on the horizontal axis, showing that the evidence indicates

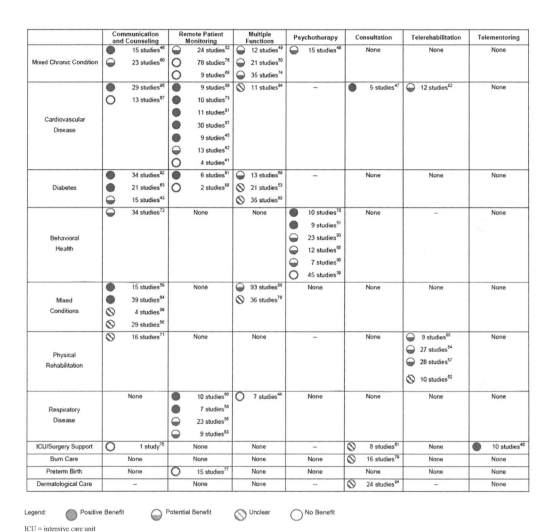

| | Communication and Counseling | Remote Patient Monitoring | Multiple Functions | Psychotherapy | Consultation | Telerehabilitation | Telementoring |
|---|---|---|---|---|---|---|---|
| Mixed Chronic Condition | 15 studies[46] <br> 23 studies[60] | 24 studies[52] <br> 78 studies[76] <br> 9 studies[68] | 12 studies[49] <br> 21 studies[50] <br> 35 studies[74] | 15 studies[48] | None | None | None |
| Cardiovascular Disease | 29 studies[95] <br> 13 studies[87] | 9 studies[89] <br> 10 studies[73] <br> 11 studies[91] <br> 30 studies[87] <br> 9 studies[45] <br> 13 studies[42] <br> 4 studies[41] | 11 studies[84] | – | 5 studies[47] | 12 studies[82] | None |
| Diabetes | 34 studies[92] <br> 21 studies[63] <br> 15 studies[43] | 6 studies[91] <br> 2 studies[88] | 13 studies[69] <br> 21 studies[53] <br> 35 studies[80] | – | None | None | None |
| Behavioral Health | 34 studies[72] | None | None | 10 studies[70] <br> 9 studies[51] <br> 23 studies[93] <br> 12 studies[65] <br> 7 studies[90] <br> 45 studies[39] | None | – | None |
| Mixed Conditions | 15 studies[59] <br> 39 studies[64] <br> 4 studies[38] <br> 29 studies[56] | None | 93 studies[86] <br> 36 studies[78] | None | None | None | None |
| Physical Rehabilitation | 16 studies[71] | None | None | – | None | 9 studies[85] <br> 27 studies[54] <br> 28 studies[57] <br> 10 studies[62] | None |
| Respiratory Disease | None | 10 studies[66] <br> 7 studies[58] <br> 23 studies[55] <br> 9 studies[83] | 7 studies[44] | None | None | None | None |
| ICU/Surgery Support | 1 study[75] | None | None | – | 8 studies[61] | None | 10 studies[40] |
| Burn Care | None | None | None | None | 16 studies[79] | None | None |
| Preterm Birth | None | 15 studies[77] | None | None | None | None | None |
| Dermatological Care | – | None | None | – | 24 studies[64] | – | None |

Legend: ● Positive Benefit   ◐ Potential Benefit   ⦸ Unclear   ○ No Benefit

ICU = intensive care unit

**Figure 8.3** Evidence from systematic reviews: the intersection of clinical focus and telehealth function. *Telehealth: mapping the evidence for patient outcomes from systematic reviews June 2016 AHRQ. Totten AM, Womack DM, Eden KB, McDonagh MS, Griffin JC, Grusing S, Hersh WR. Telehealth: mapping the evidence for patient outcomes from systematic reviews [20].*

telemedicine services offer potential benefit; there were 12 reviewed studied to reach that conclusion.

The AHRQ report not only evaluated the clinical focus of the systematic reviews, it categorized the telemedicine services by function, grouping them into seven broad functional groups:

- Consultation
- Remote patient monitoring
- Psychotherapy
- Telementoring, defined as the use of technology to allow a remote provider to view and advise on a procedure being conducted in another location in real time.
- Telerehabilitation
- Communication and counseling
- Multiple function

The analysis found that telemedicine services produced the most positive benefits in the area of communication and counseling. Remote patient monitoring also received a high grade. Fig. 8.3 shows the benefits of telemedicine for each clinical area, breaking down the evidence by functional group. For instance, in the cardiovascular disease area, there are five systematic reviews that concluded that remote patient monitoring provides positive benefit, illustrated by a solid green circle. On the other hand, there are no reviews to suggest that telementoring is of any value in cardiovascular disease. In the clinical area of preterm birth, a systematic review of 15 studies found no benefit to remote patient monitoring.

## LIMITATIONS, CONCERNS, AND CRITICISMS

As we discussed earlier, many physicians remain highly skeptical of telemedicine, especially the way it is used to provide direct one-on-one services to consumers who do not have an established in person relationship with their clinician. Although there is a growing number of mobile devices available to remotely measure various physiological parameters, including body weight, blood pressure, and the heart's electrical signaling, there is still no substitute for an experienced clinician's touch and an in-person physical examination. Their ability to palpate a sprained ankle or evaluate bowel sounds through a stethoscope, for instance, has no digital substitute.

Licensing requirements for the synchronous (direct real-time) care of patients are incredibly limited for telemedicine. Such laws follow traditional medical licensing laws, with very few state-specific exceptions. The Interstate Telemedicine Licensing Contract, founded in 2017, is aimed at improving health care access by providing licenses to physicians already (medically) licensed in the designated states. At the time of this writing, there are 24 member-states. To apply, physicians must pay a $700 application fee followed by an average $400 application fee for *each* state desiring a telemedicine application. For the other 26 states in the union without telemedicine laws, licensure in the state (such as Massachusetts) denotes the ability to practice *only* in that particular state.

Malpractice risks are another concern of physicians. There are many "landmines" that justify this concern. If a patient is injured as a result of the advice provided online and the clinician does not have a license to practice in the state in which the patient resides, there may be grounds for legal action. Similarly, the standards of care for telemedicine have not been clearly spelled out in many states, making it more difficult for a clinician to defend their actions in a lawsuit. And if an incorrect diagnosis is made based on a transmitted visual image of a lesion, there are additional legal issues to resolve about who was responsible for the quality of the image and its interpretation. There are also privacy and security concerns to contend with in the event of a data breach since HIPAA regulations apply in most telemedicine scenarios.

Prescribing medication through a virtual visit can be problematic depending on how the service has been set up and the business agreements among all concerned parties. Although malpractice suits involving telemedicine are few and far between, those that have occurred have centered on clinicians prescribing medication over the internet. "Major concerns related to online prescribing include whether an appropriate provider–patient relationship has been established, whether the doctor has been able to adequately assess the patient, and whether the patient has provided an accurate health history," according to the Medpro Group, which provides risk consulting services. In one case that resulted in jail time and a fine, a physician prescribed an antidepressant to a patient in a different state after the patient made the request through an off-shore website after filling out a questionnaire. The physician never met or communicated directly with the patient, who committed suicide shortly after the incident [21].

These landmines make it all the more urgent for clinicians and healthcare systems to know all the relevant federal and state laws and regulations governing telemedicine.

The Center for Connected Health Policy [22] maintains a database that monitors state laws on online prescribing, along with a long list of other relevant rules and regulations that impact mobile medicine. For example, "The Alabama Board of Medical Examiners holds the position that, when prescribing medications to an individual, the prescriber, when possible, should personally examine the patient. Prescribing medications for patients the physician has not personally examined may be suitable for certain circumstances, including telemedicine." The Colorado regulations address the problem that led to conviction of the physician discussed above: "Pharmacists are prohibited from dispensing prescription drugs if they know, or should have known, that it was on the basis of an internet-based questionnaire, an Internet-based consult, or a telephone consultation, all without a valid pre-existing patient-practitioner relationship."

Another legally risky area for clinicians working in telemedicine is the prescription of controlled substances. The Ryan Haight Act, which amended the Controlled Substances Act, prohibits the dispensing of controlled substances over the internet unless the patient has received what it defines as a valid prescription [23]. That definition requires a clinician to conduct an in-person evaluation before writing the prescription. While the law has helped to reduce access to addictive pain killers to those who would abuse them, it has also restricted online access to other Schedule II–V drugs that have legitimate use and that are not pain killers. Some states have stepped in to rectify this problem. For instance, Indiana allows the telemedicine prescription on opioids that are partial agonists, which are used to manage opioid dependence. Hawaii and Florida have also enacted laws to help address the shortcomings of the federal Ryan Haight Act. But according to an analysis from the law firm Epstein Becker and Green, clinicians and administrators must keep in mind that "Prescribers should therefore be cautious and understand that remote prescribing of controlled substances, even within the confines of a state law, still could be considered a violation of federal law with penalties including prison, fines, and temporary or permanent loss of the prescriber's DEA Registration." [23]

Earlier in this chapter, we discussed the marketing value of on-demand telemedicine services and how it has helped some health systems attract new patients. But on-demand virtual medicine can also be a trap for providers, patients, and vendors who rush into this arena too quickly. A disturbing report published in *JAMA Dermatology* illustrates the dangers [24].

Jack Resnick, MD, with the department of dermatology at the University of California, San Francisco School of Medicine, and his associates created simulated case reports for imaginary patients with skin disorders and sent them to several regional and national DTC telemedicine web sites and smartphone apps that were offering services in California. The DTC web services studied in this experiment included DermatologistOnCall, Dermcheck, DermLink, Direct Dermatology, First Derm, SkyMD, Spruce, Virtual Acne, YoDerm, Amwell, First Opinion, HealthTap Prime, MDLive, MeMD, Teladoc, and Virtuwell.

They heard back from 17 DTC services and recorded 62 clinical encounters. Many of the responses fell short of accepted medical standards for dermatological care. For example, only 26% of the telemedicine services informed simulated patients that they used licensed clinicians, and some used clinicians outside the United States who did not have a license to practice in the state of California. Only 10% offered to send the patient's records to their primary care physician.

A diagnosis or likely diagnosis was made in 48 patients and the researchers found that many of the diagnoses were correct when photographs alone were adequate to arrive at that diagnosis. However, if the correct diagnosis required additional information, including details on fever, oligomenorrhea, and excess hair growth, the clinicians "regularly failed to ask simple relevant questions and diagnostic performance was poor. Major diagnoses were repeatedly missed, including secondary syphilis, eczema herpeticum, gram-negative folliculitis, and polycystic ovarian syndrome." Equally important was the discovery that some of the prescribed treatments did not conform to clinical guidelines.

A RAND Corporation analysis of DTC telemedicine also revealed some short-comings to this approach to virtual care [25]. Uscher-Pines et al. evaluated medical claims data from patients enrolled in the California Public Health Employees' Retirement System's HMO, comparing the performance of Teledoc to visits to physicians' offices. Over 3000 adults logged more than 4600 televisits. The investigators found the clinicians manning the telemedicine service fell short on following quality of care standards for managing pharyngitis, ordering a strep test only 3% of the time, compared to 50% in the in-person group. Protocols for managing bronchitis also were less than optimal. Antibiotics should usually be avoided in adults with acute bronchitis but were overprescribed among patients on telemedicine care.

Diagnostic accuracy remains a challenge for all clinicians, regardless of the setting, and several studies have documented misdiagnosis as a significant problem among patients who are being cared for in person. Adding long-distance virtual care into the mix can certainly complicate matters. Several researchers have addressed this issue of diagnostic accuracy in a controlled setting. Daniel M. O'Connor, MD, Section of Dermatology, Division of General Pediatrics, Children's Hospital of Philadelphia, and his colleagues have compared photos of pediatric skin lesions submitted by parents through parent-to-clinician telemedicine to in-person evaluation by a pediatric dermatologist [26]. Forty parent/child pairs participated in the study, and a secondary analysis was performed to compare parents who took photos after receiving instructions on the best way to take the pictures to parents who received no instructions. There were few differences between in-person diagnoses and diagnoses based on parent-submitted photos, with a concordance of 83%. There were also no significant differences between photos from parents who were given special instructions, when compared to those who had not been instructed (85% vs 80%). Despite their positive findings, O'Connor et al. still concluded

*We agree with recent recommendations that telemedicine is best performed by physicians who are part of a patient's medical home or health system.... When a teledermatology diagnosis is uncertain or requires further management, there must be a system in place to facilitate appropriate follow-up with the patient's primary clinician, dermatologist, or other specialists. Without the opportunity for in-person follow-up, patients may not receive accurate diagnoses when teledermatology is insufficient, may be sent to emergency departments, or may not receive further care at all.*

*Providing care integrated into local health networks also enables clinicians practicing telemedicine to view a patient's existing medical record and readily communicate with the patient's established medical professionals. In our study, additional history that could have been gleaned from the electronic health record may have allowed for more accurate diagnoses. Being part of a local network would also allow telemedicine clinicians to order diagnostic studies or laboratory tests and prescribe medications while preventing siloed or fragmented care by integrating directly into patient records.*

## THE FUTURE BELONGS TO MEDICAL SELF-CARE

One of the problems in today's health-care delivery system is that the disease burden in most wealthy countries has shifted. Acute infection and broken bones have been largely replaced with far more complex disorders such as diabetes, heart disease, obesity, depression, and cancer, all of which require more labor intensive patient education and self-management. Unfortunately, there is little time built into the health-care system for such a shift. With the average office visit limited to 15 minutes or less, most patients get shortchanged. In Chapter 1, we quoted Joseph Kvedar, MD, on this dilemma: "The usual practice of writing a prescription for a drug, advising a patient to 'lose weight and get more exercise,' or expecting an individual to successfully follow a recommended diet plan just doesn't work. People need ongoing and consistent support from advisors and authority figures …. The right text at the right time, a thoughtful email or televisit from a doctor or medical coach, or a phone call from a nurse monitoring personal health data recorded by the patient sitting at home can prevent a potential problem from spiraling into an expensive and potentially dangerous medical issue." [27].

There are three potential solutions to the problem: Physicians can double or triple the amount of time they spend with each patient and agree to a significant drop in their income; they can hire so-called physician extenders—nurses, medical assistants, and physician assistants—to provide more extensive patient education and coaching, or they can provide patients with the digital tools to optimize medical self-care. Few physicians will choose option one; option two is already in place in many practices and health systems with some success. Option three is slowly gathering momentum as clinicians make better use of telehealth services and patient portals. But there is so much more that can be done—and must be done—in order to bring these chronic diseases under control.

Although telemedicine has the potential to improve healthcare worldwide, it should concentrate more on encouraging medical self-care and providing patients with the intellectual tools they need to tell the difference between good and bad self-care interventions. The real power of mobile health is its ability to teach patient self-empowerment, critical thinking, and the ability to differentiate between voodoo science and health science. Teaching self-empowerment means encouraging shared decision-making and discouraging dependent thinking. It also requires clinicians to have the humility to recognize that, despite their years of scientific training, they do not always have the answers. Letting patients see that fact does not diminish their respect for their provider, it *strengthens* it.

One of the mistakes clinicians sometimes make is they assume that patient self-empowerment and a willingness to become active is an inherent personality trait. "Some patients are 'built' that way and some are not." But in fact, self-empowerment can be learned, and clinicians can facilitate that learning process by encouraging them to educate themselves about their condition, or how to prevent a disease they are at risk for. Of course, self-education can send gullible patients down the wrong path. With so much misinformation available on the internet and in print, choosing *evidence*-based information can be challenging. That can be partially remedied by developing a simple database of educational resources that can be prescribed to patients. One approach is to make a list of the 20 most frequently asked questions raised by your unique patient population and putting together a collection of online materials that directly address them. Your patient panel may often ask: "Is this pediatric vaccine safe? I'm worried about the risk of autism if my child is given the vaccine." Or "I don't want to take this statin, it causes muscle disease." Another common issue: "I don't want this diagnostic test. My friend had the procedure done and it caused complication XX." Every clinician faces a specific set of concerns and questions. Creating a list of answers to these issues and sending them to patients personalizes their care and at the same time saves you the time required to provide a detailed explanation each time the issue arises. Among the many professional resources that clinicians can choose from as they develop their own database of patient education materials: Elsevier's patient engagement materials and UpToDate, which has a large collection of online handouts.

But the challenge of teaching patients self-management goes much deeper than this. Many patients don't even grasp the notion of *evidence* itself! It is enough for them to hear a friend's testimony about a new herbal supplement to convince them it has merit, or to avoid a well-documented treatment because their neighbor developed an adverse reaction, or to refuse transport to hospital X in an emergency because their sister died there last month. Clinicians obviously cannot spend an inordinate amount of time teaching patients critical thinking skills. That's a societal problem that requires systemic solutions. But taking a few minutes to gently debunk a misconception that prevents a patient from taking advantage of a well-documented treatment may be just enough to convince them to change their mind.

When Ms. Jones insists that a cystoscopy is going to cause urinary incontinence because that's what happened to her mother several years ago, a simple response might be "How many people do you know who have developed incontinence after the procedure? There are about 50,000 people each year who have a cystoscopy. Is it reasonable to conclude that a person will become incontinent based on one person's experience?" A plain English explanation of health risks might also help her understand such faulty reasoning. There are many excellent online resources for those willing to listen. Similarly, gentle persuasion might convince Mr. Smith that he is not allergic to his antibiotic just because an applied kinesiologist found his arm muscle gets weaker when he holds the drug in his hand. But immediately reacting to his claim with comments such as "The guy who told you that is a quack" is likely to alienate a patient. A more persuasive response would be I know a lot of people believe in this diagnostic technique, but I haven't seen much evidence to support applied kinesiology.

Explaining the varying levels of evidence used to judge a treatment option may also help some patients see that not all claims carry equal weight. A series of carefully documented case reports from a medical center may not be definitive proof of the value of a treatment, but it is certainly stronger evidence than a single person testimonial from a relative. And a series of test-tube experiments that demonstrate a biologically plausible mechanism of action underpinning a treatment adds more credibility to that treatment option. The next rung on this evidence ladder would be an observational study that found a significant correlation. For instance, researchers may look at the diets of 500 middle-aged men at risk for benign prostate hyperplasia (BPH) and discover that those with a zinc-rich diet were far less likely to develop the condition. An open-label interventional study would carry even more weight if it found that giving 50 mg of zinc to those at risk reduced the incidence of BPH, while a study in which clinicians and patients were both kept in the dark about who received the mineral and who received a placebo would rate close to the top of the evidence ladder.

No discussion about teaching the public to think critically would be complete without an exposé on the many tricksters, paid consultants, and public relations firms willing to bend statistics and cast doubt on well-established science. Naomi Oreskes, PhD, professor of the History of Science at Harvard University, refers to these con-men as *merchants of doubt* [28]. Over the last several decades, they have challenged the role of tobacco as a cause of lung cancer, downplayed the effect of acid rain on the environment, ridiculed the causative role of chlorofluorocarbons in creating an ozone hole in the atmosphere and continue to question the science behind global warming. All this despite the preponderance of evidence supporting these links. Oreskes summarized this "merchandizing" this way: "Doubt is crucial in science—in the version we call curiosity or healthy skepticism, it drives science forward—but it also makes science vulnerable to misrepresentation, because it is easy to take uncertainties out of context and create the impression that *everything* is unresolved. This was the tobacco industry's key insight: that you could used[use] normal scientific uncertainty to undermine the status of actual scientific knowledge." As one industry memo put it: "Doubt is our product."

Individual clinicians cannot single-handedly combat this kind of antiscience, a climate that has only been fostered by some political and religious leaders and by the social media. But at the very least, we can make our patients aware of the forces at play and the mind games such merchants of doubt employ.

## REFERENCES

[1] SNAPMD. Telemedicine professional services, <https://snap.md/services/> 2018.
[2] Dullet NW, Geraghty EM, Kaufman T, et al. Impact of a university-based outpatient telemedicine program on time savings, travel costs, and environmental pollutants. Value Health 2017;20:542—6. Available from: https://www.valueinhealthjournal.com/article/S1098-3015(17)30083-9/pdf.
[3] Pearl R. Kaiser Permanente Northern California: current experiences with internet, mobile, and video technologies. Health Affairs. 2014;33:251—7.
[4] Ashwood JS, Mehrotra A, Cowling D, et al. Direct-to-consumer telehealth may increase access to care but does not decrease spending. Health Affairs. 2017;36:485—91.
[5] American Hospital Association. TrendWatch: the promise of telehealth for hospitals, health systems and their communities, <https://www.aha.org/system/files/research/reports/tw/15jan-tw-telehealth.pdf>; 2015.
[6] Healthcare Information and Management Systems Society. The Department of Veterans Affairs #mHealth Case Study, <https://www.himss.org/department-veterans-affairs-mhealth-case-study?ItemNumber = 30310> 2014 [accessed 07.03.16].
[7] Comstock J. Nemours finds that pediatric telemedicine saved money and time for patients, health system. Mobihealth News. September 18, 2017. https://www.mobihealthnews.com/content/nemours-finds-pediatric-telemedicine-saved-money-and-time-patients-health-system.
[8] Yoo B-Y, Kim M, Sasaki T, et al. Economic evaluation of telemedicine for patients in ICUs. Crit Care Med. 2016;44:265—74.
[9] American Hospital Association. Issue Brief: Telehealth: helping hospitals deliver cost-effective care. American Hospital Association, <https://www.aha.org/system/files/content/16/16telehealthissuebrief.pdf>; 2016.
[10] Maeng D, Starr AE, Tomcavage JF, et al. Can telemonitoring reduce hospitalization and cost of care? A health plan's experience in managing patients with heart failure. Popul Health Manage 2014;17:340—4.
[11] KLAS. Telehealth virtual care platforms 2017: an early look at the state of telehealth, A KLAS-CHIME benchmarking report; 2017.
[12] Wicklund E. CMS makes a 'landmark change' in RPM, telehealth reimbursement. MHealthintelligence July 20, 2018. Available from: https://mhealthintelligence.com/news/cms-makes-a-landmark-change-in-rpm-telehealth-reimbursement.
[13] Department of Health and Human Services. Medicare program; CY2018 updates to the quality payment program; and quality payment program: extreme and uncontrollable circumstance policy for the transition, <https://s3.amazonaws.com/public-inspection.federalregister.gov/2017-24067.pdf>; 2017.
[14] Goler NC, Armstrong MA, Taillac CJ, Osejo VM. Substance abuse treatment linked with prenatal visits improves perinatal outcomes: a new standard. J Perinatol. 2008;28(9):597—603.
[15] Izzo JA, Bhat R, Blumenthal J, et al. Diagnostic accuracy of a rapid telemedicine encounter in the emergency department. Ann Emerg Med. 2017;70(Suppl. 4):S127—8.
[16] Muller K, Alstadhaug KB, Bekkelund SI. A randomized trial of telemedicine efficacy and safety for nonacute headaches. Neurology. 2017;89:153—62.
[17] Flodgren G, Rachas A, Farmer AJ, Inzitari M, Shepperd S. Interactive telemedicine: effects on professional practice and health care outcomes Cochrane Database Syst Rev 2015;9. Art. No.: CD002098. Available from: https://doi.org/10.1002/14651858.CD002098.pub2.
[18] Lilly CM, McLaunghlin JM, Zhao H, et al. A multicenter study of ICU telemedicine reengineering of adult critical care. Chest. 2014;145:500—7.

[19] Dayal P, Hojman NM, Kissee JL, et al. Impact of telemedicine on severity of illness and outcomes among children transferred from referring emergency departments to a Children's Hospital PICU. Pediatr Crit Care Med. 2016;17:516−21.

[20] Totten AM, Womack DM, Eden KB, McDonagh MS, Griffin JC, Grusing S, Hersh WR. Telehealth: mapping the evidence for patient outcomes from systematic reviews. In: Technical brief no. 26. (Prepared by the Pacific Northwest evidence-based practice center under contract no. 290-2015-00009-I.) AHRQ publication no. 16-EHC034-EF. Rockville, MD: Agency for Healthcare Research and Quality, <www.effectivehealthcare.ahrq.gov/reports/final.cfm>; 2016.

[21] Cascella LM. Virtual risk: an overview of telehealth from a risk management perspective. MedPro Group, <https://www.medpro.com/documents/10502/2820774/Virtual + Risk + - + An + Overview + of + Telehealth.pdf>; n.a. [accessed 15.09.18].

[22] Center for Connected Health Policy. Online prescribing, <http://www.cchpca.org/online-prescribing-0>; n.a. [accessed 24.09.18].

[23] Davidsen BS. New state laws allow telehealth prescriptions for controlled substances; yet, regulatory obstacles still remain. TechHealth Perspectives January 22, 2018. Available from: https://www.techhealthperspectives.com/2018/01/22/new-state-laws-allow-telehealth-prescriptions-for-controlled-substances-yet-regulatory-obstacles-still-remain/.

[24] Resnick JS, Abrouk M, Steuer M, et al. Choice, transparency, coordination, and quality among direct-to-consumer telemedicine websites and apps treating skin disease. JAMA Dermatol. 2016;152:768−75.

[25] Uscher-Pines L, Mulcahy A, Cowling D, et al. Access and quality of care in direct-to-consumer telemedicine. Telemed J E Health. 2016;22:282−7.

[26] O'Connor DM, Jew OD, Perman MJ, et al. Diagnostic accuracy of pediatric teledermatology using parent-submitted photographs: a randomized clinical trial. JAMA Dermatol 2017;153:1243−8.

[27] Kvedar JS. *The internet of healthy things*. Boston, MA: Partners Connected Health; 2015. p. 19−20.

[28] Oreskes N, Conway EM. Merchants of doubt. New York: Bloombury Press; 2010.

# CHAPTER NINE

# Patient Engagement: Our Top Priority

The term patient engagement has so many different connotations that it is almost meaningless. For some, it is all about patient portals and encouraging patients to read lab results and educational materials. For others, it involves sending text messages out that remind patients to take their medication or make an appointment for their next mammogram. Still others consider patients engaged if they are willing to use their mobile device to monitor vital signs like blood pressure (BP) or body weight. No doubt these can all be components of patient engagement, but at its core, patient engagement is a *mind-set* on the part of both providers and patients. Patient portals, text messaging, and mobile BP devices are only tools, what some stakeholders like to call the "plumbing" of patient engagement. At its most fundamental level, patient engagement refers to a person's actions and attitudes and a clinician's actions and attitudes. And that is a far more complex phenomenon—and much harder to achieve.

That mind-set involves active involvement by the patient rather than passive acceptance of whatever the doctor orders. It encompasses an interest in self-care not found in many patients, a willingness to learn, an interest in doing more than just patching up a malfunctioning body with medication or lifestyle modifications; it involves a sense of self-responsibility. And on the part of a clinician, it demands a level of empathy and commitment to each patient's needs that goes beyond the prescription of medical treatment and the digital tools that facilitate that treatment. What we are really talking about is best referred to as patient/clinician engagement. For this kind of connection to happen, it requires a trusting relationship and a partnership that has been far too uncommon in medical practice. The small window of opportunity that exists during each patient encounter limits the establishment of such trusting, respectful relationships. Similarly, the prevailing quick fix mentality that is encouraged by pop culture and mass marketing discourages the public from developing the long-term view of their health and the self-respect needed to devote time and energy to staying healthy. For mobile medicine to be effective, clinicians and patients need to find ways to overcome these barriers.

With this richer definition of patient engagement in mind, a two-pronged issue presents itself: How do we foster the trusting partnership between doctor and patient or nurse and patient? And how can mobile technology enhance that relationship?

In programs in which strong patient/clinician engagement exists: "The relationship between client and physician was described as a healing partnership, a connection made possible through lengthy initial visits with unlimited follow-ups made available

*The Transformative Power of Mobile Medicine.*
DOI: https://doi.org/10.1016/B978-0-12-814923-2.00009-X

for the client. Patients reported a sense of belonging and hope fostered not only by the resources offered by the program, but the caring and supportive services provided by both practitioners and fellow patients. A therapeutic alliance was forged between patients and practitioners who were consistently available and included patient preferences and circumstances in treatment decisions. 'I've found that the support from [a physician] was unbelievable ... (saying) we'll try to do the very best that we can to accommodate and help you out. And that in itself was pretty important for me as a patient to hear. ...' " [1].

## HOW TO ENHANCE PATIENT ENGAGEMENT

Technology enthusiasts once believed that mobile technology alone would enhance patient engagement—an "if you build it they will come" perspective. But statistics suggest that more is involved than simply making these tools available. A 2016 survey from Gardner Consulting found, for example, that 30% of users who were once excited about using a fitness tracker had abandoned them over time. Similarly, a report from the US Government Accountability Office found that 88% of hospitals had installed patient portals by 2015 but only 15% of patients used them [2]. Simply put, engaging patients requires *engaging* technology, and many patients lose interest once the novelty wears off.

Joseph Kvedar, MD, a leading expert on mobile health technology and vice president of Connected Health, Partners HealthCare in Boston, has been struggling with this problem for decades. Along the way, he has come to realize that technology needs to be more personalized to keep patients and consumers involved. To make healthcare technology more compelling, Kvedar has discovered that the issues addressed by digital tools need to be more relevant to a user's near-term concerns and goals. It also helps if these tools have algorithms built in that collect personal data like the person's location, weather, BP readings, and so on. That can be used to motivate patients to act when that information is incorporated into semiindividualized text messages [2]. And lastly, he encourages developers to consider the social aspects of patient engagement, the so-called sentinel effect, that is, the value of bringing the user's peers or health-care provider into the digital loop to help motivate patients.

It is becoming increasingly clear that the social aspects of health are key ingredients in any patient engagement initiative. Patients who do not have a physical means of transportation obviously cannot avail themselves of a hospital or office's medical services. It is hard to imagine a more essential way to engage patients than to provide a way for them to get to your facility, either with a van service or some other form of assistance. Transportation is one of many "social determinants of health" that are receiving new attention as providers come to realize that clinical expertise and mobile technology are not enough, especially for patients with limited financial resources. Some providers are doing more than helping with transportation by addressing clothing, food, and housing needs. Rush University Medical Center, for example, is "writing electronic orders for free food, clothing, housing, and other resources for patients in need. The orders are automatically sent to NowPow, an electronic database of community-based resources developed at the University of Chicago. A NowPow algorithm searches for the best-matched resource and sends the Rush patient a text describing where and how to access the recommended service. Rush has integrated NowPow into its Epic EHR using Fast Healthcare Interoperability Resources (FHIR), HL7's data exchange standard" [2].

Improving clinicians' communication skills and technique can also play a major role in patient engagement. Clinicians can be guilty of several mistakes in this area [3]: We interrupt patients less than 30 seconds into their stories. One study that looked at 29 family physicians practicing in rural Washington, semirural Colorado, and various urban setting in the United States and Canada found that physicians asked patients about their concerns in about 75% of their interviews but patients were only allowed to complete their initial statements about their concerns 28% of the time, with clinicians typically interrupting to redirect the conversation after an average of 23 seconds [4]. Marvel et al. concluded that "Physicians often redirect patients' initial descriptions of their concerns. Once redirected, the descriptions are rarely completed. Consequences of incomplete initial descriptions include late-arising concerns and missed opportunities to gather potentially important patient data. Soliciting the patient's agenda takes little time and can improve interview efficiency and yield increased data."

There is also evidence to suggest that some physicians have trouble responding to the emotional concerns of patients. Surgeons in particular find this challenging according to several studies. Patients often drop clues about their fears and social concerns in the hope that their surgeon will notice these bread crumbs. One study found that patients were sending these signals in 53% of the visits being tracked but surgeons missed the chance to at least acknowledge these concerns 62% of the time. A similar report on orthopedic surgeons found that "patients only fully disclosed 53% of their real concerns about surgery [to the surgeon], compared to disclosure to the research assistant. Most of the patients' expressed concerns were about logistics like the timing of the operation and the health-care facilities, while patients' worries about their ability to cope with the surgery and their recovery or the skills of the surgeons were rarely brought up. Barriers to the surgery, including lack of social support, transportation, finances, and obligations to family and work, were often not raised by the patients" [5]. Apparently patients had sensed that their surgeons were uninterested in these issues or too busy to address them. It should also be noted that female physicians appear to be better communicators than male physicians. Female surgeons spend more time making small talk with their patients early in the visit, and female obstetricians ask fewer biomedical questions than their male counterparts and draw out more information from their patients [5]. Of course, communication is a two-way street, which implies that patients also have to meet clinicians halfway. They have to be willing to listen—and to change—and have a reasonable degree of cognitive skills.

There is evidence to suggest that providing physicians with communications skills training may help improve their ability to interact with patients, increase their ability to empathize, and, in turn, improve patient satisfaction and engagement [6] That evidence is based on a study of the effects of a training course spearheaded by Adrienne Boissy, MD, MA, Chief Experience Officer of Cleveland Clinic Health System, and her colleagues. The training program consists of an 8-hour experiential communications training course that emphasized relationship-centered health-care communication.

Relationship building is only part of the patient engagement equation, however. Medical information can be quite complicated and explaining certain concepts to lay persons with no background in science or statistics can prove challenging. There are ways to get across these concepts to a lay audience. Such explanations are invaluable in fostering patient engagement and trust, especially in situations in which the evidence supporting a particular treatment protocol is limited. Patients sometimes think in black and white terms: "Doc, give it to me straight: This drug will cure my condition or it won't. Which is it?"

Unfortunately, medicine does not always have black and white answers to such questions, thus the need to explain the role of probability and statistical uncertainty. It is especially important when patients read news reports that state a new treatment reduced the incidence of a disorder by an impressive 40% or that a certain food or environmental contaminant will double the risk of a cancer. Consumers are often misled by such statistics because they do not understand the difference between relative and absolute risk. A report that says red dye 2 will double the risk of getting pancreatic cancer may scare Americans and convince them the cancer is almost certain if they eat foods containing the dye. But since the absolute risk of pancreatic cancer is about 1%, the dye only increases the likelihood of developing the cancer from 1% to 2%. Similarly, a newspaper report that features a large clinical trial that found a nutritional supplement improved the memory of Alzheimer's patients may sound impressive. It may even point out that the study was a randomized controlled trial (RCT) and generated statistically significant results. But digging a little deeper may reveal that said supplement only improved memory by 3%, hardly an increase most caregivers would even notice in their spouses. (Statistical significance indicates that a study's results probably did not occur by chance but does not mean the results are clinically significant.) Explaining these issues with simple illustrations or pictographs showing the differences in risk will go a long way toward engaging patients. The beauty of mobile technology is that it lets clinicians give patients quick access to a variety of plain English resources that explain risk and probability.

In addition to relationship building, good communication skills, and explaining complex concepts in easy-to-understand language, the value of shared decision-making cannot be underestimated. It, too, plays an important role in engaging patients and getting them more active in their own care. And one of the best ways to promote shared decision-making is for clinicians to share their patient notes, using a program like OpenNotes. More details on OpenNotes can be found in Chapter 2, Box 2.1.

## DOES PATIENT ENGAGEMENT IMPROVE CLINICAL OUTCOMES?

While improving communication is an essential part of patient engagement, the larger question is will better communication improve clinical outcomes or prove cost-effective. There is evidence to suggest that patient-centered care, which can include better patient engagement, has a modest effect on patients who have experienced an acute myocardial infarction (AMI). Among more than 1800 US veterans hospitalized for an AMI, patient-centered care lowered the hazard of death over a 1-year period (hazard ratio 0.992). The quality of care provided to these patients was measured by a survey that evaluated inpatient care, including courtesy, access, and care coordination, whether they received adequate information about their illness and medical care, attention to patient preferences, emotional support, family involvement, physical comfort, and preparation for their transition to outpatient care [7].

There is also evidence to suggest that empathetic clinicians see better outcomes. Investigators from the Department of Psychiatry and Human Behavior at Jefferson Medical College in Philadelphia have found that diabetic patients whose physicians register high scores on a test that measures empathy have better control of their hemoglobin A1c levels than the patients of physicians with low-empathy scores [8]. An independent research team that looked at the relationship of empathy to HIV care found that HIV-positive patients who were cared for by clinicians with high- and mid-level empathy scores reported the highest medication self-efficacy. And those cared for by clinician with higher empathy scores were more willing to reveal psychosocial and biomedical information [9].

On a similar note, researchers have found that clinicians who are rated as better communicators by patients see better adherence to medication regimes. Specifically, clinicians for the Department of Medicine and New York University School of Medicine did a cross-sectional study of more than 400 low-income African-American patients with hypertension, asking them to rate their providers' communication style by means of a questionnaire. Fifty-five percent of patients said that they were non-compliant with their medication and 51% said that their clinicians' communication was noncollaborative. A multivariate analysis revealed, however, that a communication style rated as collaborative was associated with better medication compliance [10].

Despite these positive findings, it would be a mistake to conclude that a better patient/clinician relationship will have a *major* impact on clinical outcomes. The evidence does not support that conclusion. A systematic review and meta-analysis that evaluated 13 RCTs found a small overall effect size ($d = 0.11$), which was statistically significant ($P = .2$) [11]. (Cohen's $d$ is the standardized mean difference between patient groups that underwent some type of intervention to improve the patient doctor relationship and the patient groups that did not.) Several caveats should be kept in mind when considering these results. The analysis did not include observational studies; it did not include studies that measured intermediate variables like patient satisfaction, adherence to treatment, or patients' understanding of medical advice—all of which are important components of patient engagement. Finally, the small effect size, $d = 0.11$, needs to put into perspective. Aspirin is known to reduce the incidence of myocardial infarction over a 5-year period yet its effect size is only 0.06, while the effect size of smoking on mortality of males over 8 years is only 0.08. Because so many intertwined factors influence the effect of any one intervention, such small numbers are not surprising.

One of the goals of patient engagement initiatives is to convince patients of the need to become more active in their own care. There is considerable research to indicate that interventions that promote patient activation do impact clinical outcomes. Judith Hibbard, professor emeritus at the University of Oregon, and Jessica Greene, director of research at the George Washington University School of Nursing, reviewed the evidence on this issue, looking at studies that used a well-documented metric called the Patient Activation Measure (PAM). The tool estimates how activated patients are by asking a list of questions that measure a person's ability to manage self-care. The metric then categorizes respondents into one of four levels from least activated to most activated [12]. PAM includes questions on 13 issues, including beliefs, confidence in managing health-related tasks, and self-assessed knowledge. Hibbard et al. point out that "Chronically ill patients with higher activation levels are more likely than those with lower levels to adhere to treatment; perform regular self-monitoring at home; and obtain regular chronic care, such as foot exams for diabetes." That conclusion is supported by at least 15 studies cited in their review. More specifically, several investigations have shown that the improvements in health outcomes include better health-related quality of life, improved clinical markers like low-density lipoprotein and BP, fewer symptoms, fewer hospital admissions, and less use of the emergency department. Patients who start with the lowest levels of activation experienced the most improvement in PAM scores.

## REFERENCES

[1] Higgins T, Larson E, Schnall R. Unraveling the meaning of patient engagement: a concept analysis. Patient Educ Couns 2017;100:30—6.

[2] Van Dyke M. Providers aim to build engagement tools that actually work. Health Data Management 2018. Available from: https://www.healthdatamanagement.com/news/providers-aim-to-building-engagement-tools-that-actually-work.

[3] Chou C. Patient engagement: time to start using evidence-based approaches to patient engagement. NEJM Catalyst 2018. Available from: https://catalyst.nejm.org/evidence-based-patient-provider-communication/.

[4] Marvel MK, Epstein RM, Flowers K, et al. Soliciting the patient's agenda: have we improved? JAMA 1999;281:283—7.

[5] Levinson W, Hudak P, Tricco AC. A systematic review of surgeon—patient communication: strengths and opportunities for improvement. Patient Educ Couns 2013;93:3—17.

[6] Boissy A, Windover AK, Bakar D, et al. Communication skills training for physicians improves patient satisfaction. J Gen Intern Med 2016;31:755—61.

[7] Meterko M, Wright S, Lin H, et al. Mortality among patients with acute myocardial infarction: the influences of patient-centered care and evidence-based medicine. Health Serv Res 2010;45:1188—204.

[8] Hojat M, Louis DZ, Markham FW, et al. Physicians' empathy and clinical outcomes for diabetic patients. Acad Med 2011;86:359—64.

[9] Flickinger TE, Saha S, Roter D, et al. Clinician empathy is associated with differences in patient—clinician communication behaviors and higher medication self-efficacy in HIV care. Patient Educ Couns 2016;99:220—6.

[10] Schoenthaler A, Chaplin WF, Allegrante JP, et al. Provider communication effects medication adherence in hypertensive African Americans. Patient Educ Couns 2009;75:185—91.

[11] Kelley JM, Kradt-Todd G, Schapira L, et al. The influence of the patient—clinician relationship on healthcare outcomes: a systematic review and meta-analysis of randomized controlled trials. PLOS One 2014;9:e94207. Available from: http://journals.plos.org/plosone/article?id = 10.1371/journal.pone.0094207.

[12] Hibbard JH, Greene J. What the evidence shows about patient activation: better health outcomes and care experiences; fewer data on costs. Health Aff 2013;32:207—14.

CHAPTER TEN

# Mobile Security

Is Internet security an oxymoron? A contradiction in terms? It almost seems that way. With an endless barrage of news reports about data breaches at large and small corporations and health-care providers, one might get the impression that security is just a lie we tell ourselves and our patients. A recent study in the *Journal of the American Medical Association*, for example, revealed that between 2010 and 2017, there were 2149 data breaches affecting over 176 million patient records. There were increases in data breaches each year—with the exception of 2015—from 199 in 2010 to 344 in 2017 [1]. The investigation reviewed incidents at health-care provider facilities, insurance plans, and business associates. Although breaches occurred most often at provider organizations (70%) versus only 13% in health plans, the total number of breached records that occurred in health plans was much higher (110.4 vs 37.1 million).

The risk of health-care data breaches is not limited to direct attacks on a facility's computers. The mobile devices that clinicians and patients use to connect to these computers are just as vulnerable. In fact, they may be more vulnerable for a variety of reasons. Surveys suggest that nearly nine out of ten physicians use smartphones or tablets in the workplace [2].

Health-care executives and clinicians on the front lines need to weigh several issues, as they determine what type of mobile device policy should be put in place, and what type of security technology to invest in. Among the decisions to make, should you even allow mobile devices to have access to your computer system; if you do allow them access, should they only be devices vetted and purchased by the organization; or will you allow staff members to use their own device to gain access to patient data—the so-called BYOD or bring your own device movement. Regardless of which direction you go in, there are several basic safeguards to put in place to reduce the risk of a Health Insurance Portability and Accountability Act (HIPAA) violation or data breach.

## THINKING STRATEGICALLY

Before putting these safeguards in place, an organization needs a management strategy. The Department of Health and Human Services (HHS) suggests a five-step plan: decide; assess; identify; develop, document, and implement; and train. Step one, *deciding* whether to even allow mobile devices to receive, transmit, or store personal

*The Transformative Power of Mobile Medicine.*
DOI: https://doi.org/10.1016/B978-0-12-814923-2.00010-6

health information (PHI) needs to be thought through carefully in the light of all the risks associated with that move. Among them, they are much easier to steal than a desktop computer, and they are often lost—not usually a problem with a desktop computer. There is also the risk of malware infection, especially if the device is used on an unsecured Wi-Fi network. And using an unsecured wireless network is a hard temptation to resist for physicians and health-care executives who spend a lot of time in airports, hotel rooms, or at Wi-Fi-equipped cafés. If a staffer's family member gets their hands on the device to surf the web or download the latest music videos, the risk of downloading a virus increases exponentially. And there is also the possibility that the family member will see PHI that they are forbidden by law to view. Suppose for the sake of this discussion that your hospital just admitted a movie celebrity for observation, That would pose a big temptation to a teenage member of the household who may want to snoop into their medical records, which may be accessible on one of your physician's tablets.

*Assess*, step 2, involves an analysis that weighs all the pros and cons and looks for existing security gaps in your current network that can be exploited by someone who gains access through a stolen or lost mobile device. You will also need to *identify* your organization's mobile risk management strategy and put in place safeguards to mitigate the likelihood of a HIPAA violation or data breach.

As you *develop and document* your mobile device management (MDM) plan, you will need to answer several questions:

- Have you taken inventory? You cannot manage a collection of phones, laptops, and tablets unless you start with a complete list of all the devices that have access to your network.
- Is someone assigned the responsibility of managing these devices, making sure they comply with your policies and procedures manual?
- Have you spelled out a BYOD policy, if you decide to allow personal devices on the network?
- Will you allow employees to gain access to the organization's network while at home or traveling?
- Do you have a policy for deactivating mobile devices if an employee leaves the organization?
- Will you allow PHI to be stored on the mobile device?
- What kind of *training* will you provide employees who use a mobile device for work purposes?

## COVERING THE BASICS

Many of the physical, administrative, and technological safeguards required to protect your computer network also apply to mobile devices, with some variations.

Physical safeguards may seem obvious but are often overlooked by clinicians and administrative staff, because they can be inconvenient to implement. They include storing a smartphone, laptop, or tablet in a locked desk drawer, keeping the device within sight at all times, not allowing others to use the device, and putting wire locks on laptops and tablets to secure them to a desk.

In Chapter 1, we discussed encryption. The need for encryption on smartphones, tablets, and laptops is especially important if your organization allows employees to store PHI on the device. Several providers have had to pay heavy HIPAA-related fines because someone in the organization lost an unencrypted mobile device containing sensitive data. The federal Office of Civil Rights (OCR) offers guidelines on how to render PHI unusable, unreadable, and indecipherable to unauthorized users, stating that you have two HIPAA compliant options: either destroy the media on which the PHI is stored or recorded, or encrypt it. Obviously, there is a lot of patient data that cannot be destroyed, so when that is the case, it should be encrypted "at rest" and "in motion." In other words, the encryption software needs to protect PHI stored in the device itself (or on the external media, e.g., a thumb drive or DVD). And the PHI needs to be protected as it is moved from place to place, typically by means of email or text messaging, network transfers, backup tapes, thumb drives, and so on. Valid encryption processes for at rest and in motion PHI are spelled out in more detail on the OCR site [3].

DataMotion and Trend Micro, like many comparable vendors, offer a secure mail service; their purpose is to encrypt messages when they leave a smartphone and through their entire journey across the internet until they arrive in a recipient's inbox. DataMotion uses a thoughtful analogy to explain the risk of sending unsecured email, even when the computer from which you send the message is secure and the recipient's computer is secured. It is like writing a private message on a post card and putting it in the mail box. Yes, you can trust the US Post Office to deliver it, but few of us are naïve enough to believe no one will read it before it reaches its destination. Both vendors offer an encrypted email service for a health-care provider's in-house servers and as a cloud service.

Another option is a virtual private network or VPN, which also encrypts data as it is sent across a Wi-Fi connection, for example. Using a secure browser connection has some advantages as well. In the address section at the top of your browser, you will see an "s" after the "http" to verify that it is relatively secure. The US Department of HHS also recommends turning off Wi-Fi capability, Bluetooth, and location services in the mobile device's settings section when they are not needed. With these services turned on, it may be possible for unauthorized users to gain access to PHI even when you are *not* trying to connect to a network [4].

Strong passwords are just as important on mobile devices as they are on workstations—perhaps more so. The best passwords include at least one upper case and one lower case letter, a number, and a special character, such as ^ or *. Many mobile device makers have found a way to circumvent the problem of stolen passwords and identity theft by building in facial recognition as part of a two-factor authentication process. Some providers, including Partners Healthcare in Massachusetts, also send employees reminders on their mobile device to change their password regularly. The device should also be set up to automatically lock after a short period of time, so unauthorized persons have a more difficult time accessing the data if it is lost or stolen. Similarly, installing an antimalware program on each mobile device that has access to PHI makes sense; many cautious physicians who would not think of using a desktop computer without installing antimalware software do not think twice about using a tablet or smartphone that is completely "naked." (See Box 10.1 for more on mobile antimalware programs).

## BOX 10.1 Installing Antimalware Apps on Mobile Devices

Installing an antimalware program on employees' smartphones, tablets, and laptops not only makes sense, it is also recommended by the Department of HHS. And since they are the agency that can impose a heavy fine if your organization experiences a data breach, it would be hard to justify ignoring this advice. HealthIT.gov does not recommend specific antimalware software, but instead says that "Some mobile devices come with security software installed, but you may need to enable the software. If security software does not come installed on your mobile device, you may need to download it. Research the software before downloading to verify it is from a trusted source." [5].

Organizations, such as AV-Test, an independent IT-security institute, can provide assistance to your search for reliable antimalware software. AV-Test evaluates security apps by exposing them to existing malware to see how well they protect mobile devices, as well as other Windows and Mac machines. Their analysis of mobile security programs for Android phones includes several large and small vendors, including McAfee, Sophos, Symantec, Playcastle, and Avira, rating each on their ability to detect malware in real time, as well as usability and features. High malware-detection scores went to AhnLab, Avira, Trend Micro, Symantec, and Sophos, among others [6].

Finding reliable antimalware apps for iPhones and iPads is much harder. Apple has removed several antimalware apps from its Apple store, and currently, the mobile security apps that are available do not protect against viruses, Trojans, and other malware; however, they help reduce the threat of phishing attacks, have the ability to wipe the phone of contacts, and can offer assistance in locating a lost phone. Apparently, Apple does not see the need for antimalware protection on its phones and tablets, a contention that some security specialists question [7].

There are good antimalware programs available for Apple laptops, however, several of which has also been evaluated by AV-TEST. And contrary to accepted wisdom, Macs can be hacked and can be infected with malware.

Another risk is loading an untrustworthy mobile app onto your device, that is, one that is infected or that will copy your address book or other private information and send it to someone else. In 2012, for example, Google removed several mobile apps from its Android store for Angry Birds, a popular game program, because they contained spyware. And the security firm Sophos discovered a mobile version of Angry birds that contained a Trojan, a rather vicious piece of malware that can allow hackers access to sensitive data [8]. (See Box 10.2 for more on the risk of loading mobile apps onto a phone.)

---

### BOX 10.2 How Safe is that Mobile App?

Health-care professionals, just like the general public, still do not appreciate the risks involved in downloading mobile apps to their phone or tablet. *Apple iOS Security* drives up the point: "While apps provide amazing productivity benefits for users, they also have the potential to negatively impact system security, stability, and user data if they're not handled properly." [9].

It is estimated that at least 16 million mobile devices were infected with malware in 2014. Alcatel-Lucent found that about half of these malware infections occurred on Android phones and tablets because the digital certificates used to authenticate Android apps are less vigorously controlled. "Since Android apps are usually self-signed and can't be traced to the developer, it's easy to hijack Android apps, inject code into them and then re-sign them," according to one *International Business Times* report [10]. (Self-signed means the app developer has not purchased a trust certificate from a certificate authority. Some compare self-signing to having a fake driver's license.) Similarly, another *Forbes* report found 97% of mobile malware is located on Android devices [11]. On the other hand, it is estimated that malware affects less than 1% of other mobile devices, including iPhones, Windows phones, and Blackberries [10].

One of the reasons the statistics are so high for Android phones and tablets is the fact that there are so many of them relative to other brands. Even more relevant to health-care providers trying to avoid compromised PHI is the fact that most of the infections appear to be coming from unregulated third-party app stores, most of which are located in the Middle East and Asia. The Google Play Store appears to be somewhat more trustworthy. Several sites that offer Android mobile apps, including Android159 and EoeMarket, did not fare as well as the Google Play Store. A total of 33% of the apps coming from Android159 were infected according to the *Forbes* report. EoeMarket, an Android apps store popular in China had a 7% malware penetration. Many of the threats that creep into Android devices through infected mobile apps would be eliminated if manufacturers and users regularly upgraded their operating systems when a new one became available. After all, one of the reasons technology companies release new versions of their OS is to plug security holes they have discovered in the previous version.

A recent analysis released by Symantec should also make decision-makers think twice about allowing Android-based mobile devices to connect to their computer network. The company's Internet Security Threat Report found 17% of Android apps contained malware, which translates into about 1 million apps. Symantec also discovered the first mobile crypto-ransomware on Android devices, that is, a software program that scrambles all the information on your device or network and then refuses to decrypt unless you pay a ransom [12]. On a more positive note, the odds of being infected from an Android-based mobile app are relatively low if users stick to those apps available from Google Play Store. While a study released by RiskIQ, a cybersecurity company, is somewhat dated and may not reflect any recent improvements to Google's mobile security policy, it does give one reason for pause. RiskIQ found that in 2011, there were about 11,000 apps in the Google Play Store that contained malware. By 2013, that number had increased to 42,000. The greatest trouble makers were apps that personalized a person's phone, and entertainment and gaming apps [5]. Average cost of a corporate data breach is over $21,000/day. 2016 Ponemon Institute.

## BRING YOUR OWN DEVICE: BRING YOUR OWN DISASTER?

CEOs, IT professionals, and security specialists continue to debate the value and limitations of allowing physicians to bring their own mobile devices into work, the BYOD phenomenon. Many organizations say that it lowers their technology hardware costs, eliminating or reducing the need to buy mobile devices for their clinicians. Many also believe it improves staff productivity. But from a security perspective, BYOD can become a nightmare if not managed correctly.

Some health-care executives take the position that if a physician wants to use his/her own device in a health-care system, he/she will not be allowed to keep patient data on it [13], believing that the risks of allowing PHI on a personally owned tablet or smartphone outweigh the benefits. If you decide to implement the same policy, physicians can still access PHI residing on your hospital or medical practice's in-house servers from their phones and tablets, they just cannot transfer it to their device. Many organizations set things up so that clinicians cannot even do a screen capture of PHI they are viewing on their mobile device—or print it.

One option that allows clinicians to remotely access PHI without storing it on their device is referred to as a "thin client." If you are old enough to remember the days in which computer monitors—or terminals—were all connected to a mainframe computer, you will recall that these terminals were not accompanied by a tower, so they did not have a hard drive, fan, or other moving parts, just a screen to access the data in the mainframe computer. A thin client is similar to those early terminals.

Of course the downside here is that most clinicians will not want a personal mobile device that only serves as a monitor to read information on your network servers. They want to use the device for other purposes too. And many thin clients do offer more than just a screen to view information located in your organization's in-house computers. Although the terminology varies depending on who you talk to, currently a "zero client" or "ultrathin client" has very little storage capabilities, whereas a thin client has more storage and functionality, allowing the mobile device to carry out some basic tasks on its own. If you are interested in exploring this area of technology, collectively called desktop virtualization, there are many consultants who can provide more details.

## MOBILE DEVICE MANAGEMENT SOFTWARE

One option to seriously consider is MDM software. Several reputable vendors are in this space, including AirWatch, Good Technology, Kaspersky, Sophos, Mobileiron, and Symantec. Many of these tools will even let the user access some of his or her favorite apps but still help keep PHI safe.

MDM programs include a variety of security features, depending on the service you purchase. One is called device "provisioning," which is another way of saying the software controls the type of information that the smartphone or tablet will have access to on your organization's main computers, including specific applications, services, and files. It may also include restricting the mobile apps that each staffer can download onto his or her device. In fact, many health-care providers will "white list" and "black list" mobile apps based on their reputations and a review of the security threat.

An MDM platform may also limit a member of your staff based on his or her job description. If they need to handle financial information, for instance, but does not need to see patients' clinical data, provisioning can restrict access to that information, assuming the pertinent files are organized appropriately. Other important MDM features include the ability to use the software to remotely lock the mobile device or wipe it of all its content.

MDM programs usually provide a centralized dashboard for administrators to manage all the devices that have access to data on your in-house servers, allowing them to define and enforce your organization's policies and procedures. In practical terms, that means your IT department or consultant can configure all the phones and tablets that have access to your data. They can also send out software updates to all the devices to make sure they have the latest antimalware patches and the latest operating systems. It is also a good idea to invest in an MDM program that can detect and block mobile devices that have been tampered with, including Apple devices that have been "jail-broken" and Android and Windows phones that are "rooted."

Jailbreaking an Apple device is the process by which a user frees it from the limitations imposed by Apple, which subverts the protections on the device that restrict the user to approved software. "Unlocking" refers to freeing the device from the tele-phone carrier company. Many people use third-party software to do a jailbreak, so that they can gain access to mobile apps that Apple has not approved. However, since Apple carefully vets the apps that it allows in its app store, you no longer have the added security that comes from restricting yourself to the Apple security protocols used during that vetting process. (Rooting refers to a similar jailbreaking process on Android and Windows phones.)

Many MDM services also offer the ability to "containerize" or "sandbox" applica-tions and data on the mobile device. The process of sandboxing involves isolating PHI and other sensitive data from personal data on someone's device.

The advantage of this feature is it would allow your IT department to wipe the sen-sitive data from a lost or stolen device without destroying the owner's photos, personal emails, and other valuable information. Do keep in mind, however, that not all MDM programs offer sandboxing, which means that should the need arise to wipe out sensitive information on the mobile device, the user will lose all of that personal data.

Even if you choose not to put an MDM program in place, there are several other security safeguards that HHS encourages health-care organizations to implement.

One of the most important recommendations is to disable any file-sharing software or capability. File sharing lets individuals who are on the same network—which includes the internet since it is the biggest network—to connect to each other and trade files. That opens up the possibility of unauthorized persons gaining access to PHI on your device without you knowing about it. It can also allow them to place mal-ware on your system. Someone on your staff may find it convenient to use a peer-to-peer (P2P) network on their own smartphone to share music or photos with a friend, for instance. That is not a very smart idea for a clinician with patient records on their laptop, tablet, or phone—or for anyone else for that matter. Fans of P2P programs may try to downplay the dangers, but they are real. In addition, some of these pro-grams run in the background all the time, not just when the file-sharing program win-dow is open. OnGuardOnline.gov brings out that "Some P2P programs open automatically every time you turn on your computer." [14]. Unfortunately, there is no single way to disable all the available file-sharing applications in one easy step. It varies depending on the operating system. On an Apple laptop, for instance, it is possi-ble to turn off file sharing in the system preferences window using the "Sharing" icon.

If anyone on your staff is going to be using public Wi-Fi networks, it is also a good idea to enable the firewall and its stealth mode feature if they are on an Apple laptop. That will reduce the odds of attackers even seeing their computer when a staff member is sitting across the room in the local coffee shop. To enable this feature, open the Preferences section, locate the Security icon, click on the firewall option, and enable the firewall. (You first need to click the lock icon to unlock this feature and insert your administrator password.) When the firewall is enabled, you can then enable the stealth mode feature in the firewall options section. On Windows mobile devices, it is also possible to create a measure of "invisibility" while in public places through the Control Panel. The procedure will be slightly different depending on what version of Windows the device is running, but to illustrate the steps, let's use Windows 7. Once the Control Panel is open, click on the Network and Sharing Center, then "Choose homegroup and sharing options." Then the Change advanced sharing settings. The mobile device will be less vulnerable to outsiders if you click on the following buttons marked:

- Turn off network discovery;
- Turn off file and printer sharing;
- Turn off public folder sharing.

It is also wise to disable media streaming while on a public network. Obviously, you will want to turn this feature back on if you are in a protected private network and need access to video or audio streaming [15]. By the way, after all these security features have been selected, the user has to hit the "save changes" button to enable them. That may seem too obvious to mention, but many novices do forget that step.

Another area of concern, especially for anyone bringing a personal mobile device into the workplace, is app downloads. Typically, if you have an MDM program on your hospital or practice computer network, the administrator will vet apps and restrict access to those suspected or known to contain viruses or other malware. But if you are not using MDM, employees need to be very cautious about choosing apps to install on their devices. Some mobile apps will compromise the data on your device or copy your address book or other private data to an external source without your knowledge.

Like any other piece of technology, smartphones, tablets, and laptops eventually wear out. Discarding such devices without deleting all the health information is a serious mistake and a breach of HIPAA regulations. Three acceptable options exist:

- Clearing (using software or hardware products to overwrite media with nonsensitive data);
- Purging (degaussing, i.e., exposing the media to a strong magnetic field in order to disrupt the recorded magnetic domains);
- Destroying (disintegrating, pulverizing, melting, incinerating, or shredding the media).

The National Institute of Standards and Technology offers a detailed guide on how to sanitize data from computers called *Guidelines for Media Sanitization* [16].

Staff education is an indispensable part of health-care security. With that in mind, the Department of HHS offers several educational tools, including posters, brochures, postcards, and a PowerPoint presentation to help keep mobile security front of mind. The materials are located on the HealthIT.gov website [17]. Commercial vendors also have a few helpful tutorials that offer practical advice on keeping mobile devices secure, including Verizon [18].

## THE VIRTUES OF VIRTUAL PRIVATE NETWORKS

A VPN is a wise decision for a health-care provider trying to protect PHI. One of the advantages of setting up a VPN is that it bolsters security for mobile device users when they travel, even if it is to a local bagel shop that has Wi-Fi. A VPN has been likened to a secret tunnel that allows users to send private messages and files across a very large public network, usually the internet. It can connect a mobile user to a practice's or hospital's in-house computers, for instance, or link several offices together, using technology that offers a relative degree of privacy from prying eyes.

Once upon a time, large companies would create a large *actual* private network rather than a virtual one by leasing lines from a telecommunications vendor.

This created a physical connection between a home office and a satellite office because it ran cables between the two locations, which is still an option for large health-care organizations, but it is an expensive one. In essence, it can link two local area networks (LANs), namely, the computer system in your main hospital to a LAN in a second location. Connecting the two LANs creates a wide area network or WAN.

For better and worse, the world now has its own WAN—the internet.

It allows local computer networks to connect at much lower cost, but it does not offer security safeguards, so you risk unauthorized persons gaining access to PHI. VPNs provide that security. VPNs come in two varieties: remote-access VPNs and site-to-site VPNs. Site-to-site VPNs typically connect two or more fixed locations over the internet, whereas a remote-access VPN, also called a virtual private dial-up network, will allow remotely located staffers to connect to the main office through an internet service provider. Since this chapter deals with mobile security, we will concentrate on the latter.

To make sense of how these remote-access VPNs function, it helps to visualize them and understand a few of their main components. As Fig. 10.1 shows, the system requires a network access server, also called a media gateway, which is located in your hospital or main medical office. Your remote users—a physician using a tablet, for instance—installs software on his device. This "client" software connects him to the internet, but any data he/she transmits via the VPN is encapsulated in a secure tunnel. The client software and server also provide the necessary encryption to keep the transmission isolated from the rest of the traffic coursing through the internet.

Depending on the VPN system you choose to use and the type of mobile devices your staff has, you may already have the client software built into the device.

The iPhone 6, for instance, has the software available from its Settings screen.

That software would then connect to a network access server that is located at your main headquarters. The security provided by a VPN system involves a complex system of encryption, hiding packets of data within other packets of data, and a variety of security protocols, including Internet protocol security (IPsec), point to point

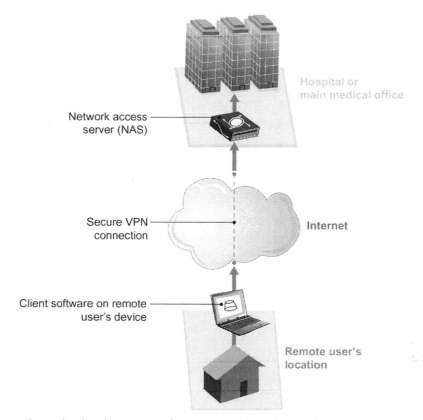

**Figure 10.1** The path taken by patient information as it moves through a virtual private network.

protocol (PPP), Secure Sockets Layer (SSL), and others. Suffice it to say, these technical tools reduce the risk of unauthorized persons gaining access to PHI.

Circling back to the recommendations from the Department of HHS on using mobile devices, in a tutorial on wireless communication, the government poses the rhetorical question: "How should you access health information using your smartphone, tablet or laptop when you are in a public space? Use a virtual private network or VPN..." [19] If your organization does experience a data breach and an OCR investigator comes visiting to determine what happened, having a VPN in place is one less opportunity for blame to be placed at your doorstep.

## THE DIFFERENCE BETWEEN HTTP AND HTTPS

The same HHS video that recommends using a VPN to secure PHI also advises mobile device users to look for a secure browser connection when connecting to the internet. (That advice also holds true when you are using desktop computers inside your facility.) The web page address that appears at the top of each web page is called a URL or uniform resource locator. When the URL looks like this: https://www. hipaa.com/hipaa-protected-health-information-what-doesphi—including that "s" after http means you are viewing a more secure page, and that privacy is achieved by means of a set of rules—a "protocol" in IT parlance—called SSL. Knowing a few basics about SSL is worth your time as a decision-maker hiring a security consultant or employee.

If you work in health care, you know that it has its own specialized language.

Information technology is no different, but just as frustrating for outsiders to decipher. In *Certified Information Systems Security Professional (CISSP) Training Kit*, a training manual to prepare IT professionals to pass the test to become a CISSP, the author offers a rather confusing explanation of SSL—at least for laypersons: "SSL uses a digital certificate to authenticate the web-based server to the client and then performs secure symmetric session key distribution."[20].

That sentence is bewildering on so many levels: the terms client and server will confuse computer novices. A restaurant analogy might help. The client is the customer, and the server is your waiter. The server provides the meal and the customer consumes it. In the IT world, that analogy applies to various situations. The server can be a specialized computer that looks much like a desktop computer tower, except with specialized software and hardware components. It may reside in the practice's home office or hospital building—or in the cloud—and feeds files and services to its customers or clients. The client can be a desktop computer or mobile device that "consumes" the information, taking advantage of the data residing on that specialized computer, either through a wired connection or wireless network. In the quote cited previously, we have a web server, which might be a computer located at Wal-Mart's headquarters and which houses the website's content—pictures of clothing, video clips, an ordering apparatus, and so on. The client can be the Internet Explorer or Safari web browser on your laptop. When you request to see content on the Wal-Mart website, the web server serves up web pages by sending them over the internet to the browser application on your laptop.

Over the years, this client/web server relationship has become rather unsafe, with malware existing on all sorts of web pages. It used to be web surfers were warned to avoid esoteric or unconventional websites for fear they were infected sites, such as Marty's Medical Miracles or Fanny's Fantasies. But these days, even reputable organizations, such as Reuters, Yahoo, and YouTube, have been victimized.

Antimalware software helps to catch many of these problems. And vendors, such as Symantec, offer a "safe browsing" feature that helps detect dangerous sites within a Google search results list. But things still fall through the cracks. SSL is one more weapon in this arsenal of protective services. As the aforementioned quote indicates, it makes use of a digital certificate to authenticate the web server. The owner of a website buys one or more of these certificates from a company—called a certificate authority. Basically, they are buying a very long string of computer code that acts as a lock. It creates an encrypted channel between the client and the web browser on a physician's tablet, for instance—and the server—the login page for a website, such as UpToDate. If you "looked behind the curtain" at the login page for UpToDate—a well-respected clinical reference database—you would notice the statement "The identity of this website has been verified by Symantec Class 3 secure server CA-GA. . .. The connection is encrypted using. . ..." The encryption makes use of a digital key; it is called symmetric encryption because it uses a private key to allow the sender to encrypt the patient data; the same key is used by the recipient to decrypt the data.

You will notice that we refer to SSL as *one more weapon* in the arsenal. Using a SSL-certified website alone does not guarantee that the PHI you send across the internet is impossible to steal. But when combined with all the other safeguards discussed here, it creates a multilayered approach that reduces the likelihood of a data breach. Security specialists like to use the term defense in depth to describe the approach. No single measure will create an impenetrable fortress, but stacking layer upon layer of protections is a lot like using several security measures to keep burglars out of your home. If you add bolt locks, door knob locks, security cameras, guard dogs, and a security alarm system in your home, these measures may not prevent a professional thief from breaking in; but if he sees a much-less-protected house down the street with equally valuable treasure, it is likely he will take the path of least resistance.

## Don't Ignore Dangers Inherent in Social Engineering

No discussion of mobile security would be complete without mentioning social engineering threats, such as phishing. Research suggests that mobile device users are even more susceptible to this trickery than other internet users. The 2017 Data Breach Investigations Report from Verizon Enterprise Solutions found that over 90% of data breaches were the result of phishing attacks. The report pointed out that "While only 7 percent of users fall for phishing attempts. . . those gullible guys and gals tend to be repeat offenders: The company estimates that in a typical organization, 15 percent of users who are successfully phished will be phished at least one more time within the same year." [21].

Social engineering essentially taps into many of the normal human personality traits that allow a society to function, traits such as the desire to help out persons in need, the quest for recognition or financial gain, everyone's natural curiosity about their neighbors' affairs, just to name a few. Hackers rely on these tendencies to convince potential victims to open infected emails or websites. A report from Trend Micro likewise suggests that more than 90% of the cyber-attacks begin with such spear phishing emails [22].

Spear phishing refers to the targeted nature of the emails sent to potential victims. They may call you by name, mention your job title, or mention other personal information that email recipients assume can only originate with friends or business associates, or companies that you already have a relationship with. If a hacker has already infected one person's machine and gains access to their address book, he or she can then send phishing emails to those on that list. Since the intended new victim sees a friend's address, they often assume the message is legitimate.

There are so many ingenious ways to create a convincing phishing email that the best approach to prevent being duped is to assume that almost every message that arrives in your inbox is a scam until proven otherwise: guilty until proven innocent. The most important piece of advice you can give staffers is, do not click on hyperlinks embedded in an email, unless you are absolutely certain it is from a legitimate source. Unfortunately, many people do not believe that they would ever fall for such trickery. "I am too smart to be fooled by social engineering tricks." One way to convince them otherwise is by running a fake phishing scam.

Tom Cochran, formerly in charge of White House digital technology, was able to convince his coworkers at Atlanta Media that they were easy prey by sending out a fake phishing email to all the employees at the firm. Within 2 hours, he had his proof: "Almost half of the company opened the email, and 58% of those employees clicked the faux malicious link." [23]. These statistics were far more convincing to staffers than a memo mandating that they follow certain precautionary steps. In Cochran's view, "Placing someone in a cyber-attack drill is the safest and most effective tactic to build the company's collective security intelligence."

Research on the effectiveness of security education comes from the 2014 US State of Cybercrime Survey by PricewaterhouseCoopers (PwC), which said that 42% of respondents found security education and awareness for new employees helped reduce the risk of a potential attack. The same PwC report found companies that did not provide security training for new employees lost about $683,000 a year, while companies with training averaged about $162,000 [24].

Several security specialists believe that training employees to spot a phishing scam before it is too late has a measurable impact. One Fortune 50 company that used fake phishing emails to test their staffers' security skills followed up with a message that made them aware of their mistake if they took the bait.

They were sent an immediate training message and also enrolled in a training program to help them avoid such scams in the future. Nearly 35% of employees who received the initial email scam failed the test but in a subsequent test, that number dropped below 6%. The Wombat Security Technologies report that discussed the case pointed out that this approach to security awareness had resulted in an 84% drop in susceptibility [25],

Truly effective staff education must go beyond phishing tests, however. One of the reasons so many training programs fail to change employees' security awareness is that they do not harness all the tricks and techniques that major marketing specialists have been using for decades to sell detergent, toothpaste, and soda. Coca-Cola, for example, has been very successful selling brown sugar water to millions of Americans through the use of brilliant commercials that equate soda with fun times, romance, and family togetherness—despite the fact that a single-serving bottle contains the equivalent of 22 packets of sugar, and the overwhelming evidence is that the beverage contributes to America's obesity epidemic [26]. If Madison Avenue can pull off that feat, why can't the health-care industry hire the same spin doctors to promote a worthwhile initiative, such as security hygiene? Granted, campaigns of this nature are expensive. But so are multimillion-dollar federal fines, class action lawsuits, and all the other expenses that often result from data breaches.

There is no way to overemphasize the need to educate health-care staff on hackers' tricks. A company called Knowbe4 has an excellent graphic that illustrates several of the mistakes email users make when exposed to phishing scams. Email users have to scrutinize every component of their emails to look for clues. That includes the From line, the To line, the Date, the Subject, and the link in the body of the text. Granted, this kind of scrutiny will initially slow down employees' productivity, but once it becomes second nature, things will speed up again.

Among the questions the email recipient needs to ask himself/herself,

- Is the sender's email address from a suspicious domain?
- Is it an unusual email with a link or an attachment from a person I do not usually communicate with?
- Are there misspellings in the email?
- Is the message a reply to something I never asked for?
- Is the message from someone or organization that I do have dealings with but the email address is slightly different from the correct address—even by one character?
- When you place your cursor over the link in the email main text, is the address different than what it says in the link?

For an excellent tutorial on phishing, accompanied by visual examples of phishing scams, consult the KnowBe4 website.

## REFERENCES

[1] McCoy TH, Perlis RH. Temporal trends and characteristics of reportable health data breaches, 2010−2017. JAMA. 2018;320:1282−4.
[2] Ventola CE. Mobile devices and apps for health care professionals: uses and benefits,. Pharm Ther. 2014;39(5):356−64. Available from: http://www.ncbi.nlm.nih.gov/pmc/articles/PMC4029126/.

[3] HHS Office of Civil Rights. Guidance to render unsecured protected health information unusable, unreadable, or indecipherable to unauthorized individuals, <http://www.hhs.gov/ocr/privacy/hipaa/administrative/breachnotificationrule/brguidance.html>; 2013.

[4] Healthit.gov. Tips to protect and secure health information, <http://www.healthit.gov/providers-professionals/10-use-adequate-security-send-or-receive-health-information-over-public-wi-f>.

[5] HealthIT.gov. Install and enable security software, <https://archive.healthit.gov/providers-professionals/6-install-and-enable-security-software> n.d.

[6] AV TEST. The best antivirus software for Android, <https://www.av-test.org/en/antivirus/mobile-devices/android/>; 2015.

[7] TrendMicro. Revisiting iOS security as Apple cracks down on antimalware apps, <http://www.trendmicro.com/vinfo/us/security/news/mobile-safety/revisiting-ios-security-as-applecracks-down-on-antimalware-apps>; 2015.

[8] Cerrato P. How your own laptop or smartphone can wreak havoc at work. Medscape Bus Med. 2013. Available from: http://www.medscape.com/viewarticle/779829.

[9] Apple. iOS security white paper, <https://www.apple.com/business/docs/iOS_Security_Guide.pdf>, 2015.

[10] Russon M. 16 million mobile devices infected by malware in 2014 with hacking attempts on the rise, International Business Times, <http://www.ibtimes.co.uk/16-million-mobile-devicesinfected-by-malware-2014-hacking-attempts-rise-1488367>; 2015.

[11] Kelly G. Report: 97% of mobile malware is on Android, This is the easy way you stay safe, <http://www.forbes.com/sites/gordonkelly/2014/03/24/report-97-of-mobile-malware-is-onandroid-this-is-the-easy-way-you-stay-safe/>; 2014.

[12] Miners Z. Report: malware-infected Android apps spike in the Google Play store, PCWORLD, <http://www.pcworld.com/article/2099421/report-malwareinfected-androidapps-spike-in-the-google-play-store.html>; 2014.

[13] Cerrato P. Why BYOD doesn't always work in healthcare. InformationWeek DARKReading 2012; Available from: http://www.darkreading.com/risk-management/why-byod-doesnt-always-work-inhealthcare/d/d-id/1103076.

[14] OnGuardOnline.gov. P2P file-sharing risks, <http://www.onguardonline.gov/p2p>; 2011.

[15] Microsoft. Privacy and security when streaming your media: frequently asked questions, <http://windows.microsoft.com/en-us/windows7/privacy-and-security-when-streaming-yourmedia-frequently-asked-questions>. n.d.

[16] National Institute of Standards and Technology. Guidelines for media sanitization, <http://nvlpubs.nist.gov/nistpubs/SpecialPublications/NIST.SP.800-88r1.pdf>; 2014.

[17] HealthIT.gov. Mobile device privacy and security: downloadable materials, <http://www.healthit.gov/providers-professionals/downloadable-materials>.

[18] Verizon Wireless. 8 Common-sense tips to keep your smartphone secure, <http://www.verizonwireless.com/mobile-living/network-and-plans/security-app-tips-to-keep-yoursmartphone-secure/>.

[19] HealthIT.gov. Can you protect patients' health information when using a public Wi-Fi network? Mobile Health Security and Accessing a Public Wi-Fi Nework, <https://www.youtube.com/watch?v = VIUXVJmXL7E&feature = youtu.be2012 >.

[20] Miller DR. CISSP training kit. Redmond, WA: Microsoft Press; 2014. p. 483.

[21] Verizon. Data breach investigations report. 11th ed., <https://www.verizonenterprise.com/resources/reports/rp_DBIR_2018_Report_en_xg.pdf>; 2018 [accessed 30.09.18].

[22] Savvas A. 91% of cyberattacks begin with spear phishing email. TechWorld, <http://www.techworld.com/news/security/91-of-cyberattacks-begin-with-spear-phishing-email-3413574/>; 2012.

[23] Cochran T. Why I phished my own company. Harvard Business Review, <https://hbr.org/2013/06/why-i-phished-my-own-company/>; 2013.

[24] Rashid FY. Is security awareness training really worth it? InformationWeek, <http://www.darkreading.com/operations/careers-and-people/is-security-awareness-training-really-worthit/d/d-id/1317573>; 2014.

[25] Rashid FY. Security awareness training debate: does it make a difference? Security Week, <http://www.securityweek.com/security-awareness-training-debate-does-it-make-difference>; 2013.

[26] Harvard T.H. Chan School of Public Health. Sugary Drinks and Obesity Fact Sheet, <http://www.hsph.harvard.edu/nutritionsource/sugary-drinks-fact-sheet/>; 2018.

## FURTHER READING

Tynan D. Report: 1 in 5 Android apps is malware, Yahoo Tech, <https://www.yahoo.com/tech/report-one-in-five-android-apps-is-malware-117202610899.html>; 2015.

# CHAPTER ELEVEN

# Designing Mobile Health Apps

A successful mobile health app is composed of several ingredients and is based on a deep understanding of how patients and clinicians think and act. That understanding comes from a thorough needs assessment, empirically derived design principles, a healthy dose of emotional intelligence, and a creative spirit that does not rely too heavily on market research and other "tried and true" techniques that don't always guarantee success. As Steve Jobs once explained, commenting on the limitations of market research: "Customers don't know what they want until we've shown them." Equally important, designers must learn the same lesson that clinicians are slowly learning as we enter the age of personalized medicine: One size does not fit all.

In *Realizing the Promise of Precision Medicine* [1], we discussed the shortcomings of population-based medicine, which relies heavily on large clinical trials and bases its treatment decisions on what works best for the *average* patient. The same shortcoming applies to mobile health apps, telemedicine, and related mHealth programs that assume there is such a thing as the average user. Deloitte, the large consulting firm, realizing the fallacy of this thinking, offers this advice: "Personalize the consumer's experience. mHealth offers tools — consumer engagement strategies, retail capabilities based upon mobile platforms and data analytics, digitization of an individual's wellness and health care needs, and more — that can enable competitive differentiation by creating personalized solutions that help drive consumer loyalty" [2]. That personalization needs to take into account a user's age, gender, income level, and technology preferences. It likewise must consider the local or regional infrastructure in which the mHealth initiative will reside. How dependable are the local networks, what are the typical download speeds and bandwidth metrics? A mobile health app or telemedicine program seeking to reach patients in an affluent urban setting does not face the same challenges as a program reaching rural patients in areas that still don't have fiber optic cable distribution. Similarly, developers have to decide which part of the mobile market they want to reach. Does it seek to meet clinicians' needs for payment management or clinical decision support? Is the app intended to keep healthy persons well, offer them advice on managing an illness, provide access to experts who can help treat their condition? And any initiative that attempts to engage patients with chronic disease should factor government regulations and third-party reimbursement into the equation.

Deloitte's analysis of the mobile health market offers some insights on how to approach the design process. For instance, it points out that users born between 1982 and 1994, so-called Millennials, are about twice as likely to download a health

*The Transformative Power of Mobile Medicine.*
DOI: https://doi.org/10.1016/B978-0-12-814923-2.00018-0
**195**

tracking app (19% vs 10% for the general public). Similarly, 25% of Millennials have used smartphones and tablet apps to manage and track their fitness and improve their health with exercise or nutrition, compared to 17% of the general public [2]. The same analysis divides the potential audience for mobile health apps into six segments. Those that are "online and onboard," which is composed of 18% Millennials, 19% Generation X, 15% baby boomers, and 14% seniors. Their total piece of the market is 17%. The second group includes the "content and compliant," who trust their health-care providers and follow their advice; they make up 22% of the market. But by far the largest segment that needs to be reached are "casual and cautious." More than one out of three Americans fall into this category. Apparently, they just don't care; they're not engaged and see no need for health-related mobile apps. The analysis goes on to categorize 14% of the public as "sick and savvy," 9% as "out and about," and 4% who are actively seeking health options.

Finally, the Deloitte analysis provides a way for developers and designers to see mobile health opportunities by dividing the market into four complexity "buckets." The bucket that one chooses to work in will influence the planning, testing, and implementation of any mHealth project. Level 1, the simplest one, concentrates on the development of a single user and includes apps and wearable sensors that "record data, support and encourage the wearer, and encourage the user, who may decide to communicate the data to others." Examples include Fitbit-type devices and weight loss apps that offer tips and set goals for an individual user. Level 2 focuses on the social aspects of mHealth and includes gamification and competition-based apps that might let users share their statistics with friends and coworkers to encourage better performance. Level 3 involves integrated mHealth; it "links apps and devices with the formal health care system, typically via an electronic health record (EHR); and exchanges data between a consumer and health care provider with real-time monitoring and care coordination." Lastly, the most complex mHealth approach calls for collection and analysis of complex health data to improve population health and facilitate predictive analytics. This type of mHealth initiative aims to improve management of a specific disease through risk analysis, the prediction of epidemics, and the like.

## WHAT DO PATIENTS AND CLINICIANS NEED?

Choosing a specific segment of the mHealth market on which to focus one's development energies is a difficult decision. A needs assessment is one of the best first steps, but it should not be the only tool used to direct one's path. If, for example, a needs assessment reveals that your potential audience wants a mHealth product that you find intellectually and emotionally lifeless, choosing to spearhead such a project may prove disastrous. Even when all your market research suggests a lucrative niche in mobile health, getting behind such a project that you are not really enthusiastic about or one that you are convinced offers nothing of real benefit to the public is ill-advised.

That is not to suggest that there is no value in a needs assessment. While many mHealth initiatives start with a passionate entrepreneur convinced he or she can change the world, one's passion is not the equivalent to the public's interests and needs. There has to be a balance between passion and practicality.

During the early stages of app development, it is important to do a gap analysis to determine not only what information the user may be lacking but whether or not a convenience gap or a time management gap exists. Uncovering such gaps requires intense observation, as well as an understanding of how your intended audience performs its daily professional or personal activities. Unfortunately, that approach runs counter to the development model that many entrepreneurs have found successful in other industries. Many mobile technology innovators live by the motto "Move fast and break things." In the world of healthcare, about the only thing you are going to break is the bank. Paul Yock, MD, a cardiologist and professor of bioengineering at Stanford University's School of Medicine, rightly points out that there are many intertwined gatekeepers and customers in healthcare who do not exist in other arenas [3]. Dr. Yock explains:

> Digital health products need to appeal not just to individual consumers but to a complicated landscape of stakeholders — from doctors and patients to regulators and insurers — all of whom have a say in whether a new technology is adopted. Products, especially those considered medical devices, may take years of jumping through complex clinical and regulatory hoops before they reach the market, and can't always easily be iterated once they do.

This approach requires a deep dive into how clinicians, hospital systems, private and public health insurers, and patients think and act. Gone are the days when an innovative company could just "throw things at the wall" and see what sticks. The penetrating needs assessment required to launch a successful mobile health app is as arduous as the needs assessments conducted to launch a continuing medical education program. Typically, these programs require a team of clinicians, medical writers, marketers, and continuing medical education (CME) experts to compose a grant application, which is then presented to corporate or academic sponsors. One essential component of the grant is a needs assessment document that typically combs the medical research literature using PubMed to gain an understanding of the grant's theme. If, for example, the grant addresses the question what is the best approach to immunotherapy for liver cancer?, it will include a summary of the pathophysiology of liver cancer, the pharmacology of currently used drugs for the disease, the latest clinical trials on relevant drugs, a list of FDA-approved medications, and surveys of clinicians that demonstrate a lack of knowledge about the disease and its management. That is followed by a reasoned argument for why a new CME initiative will help fill the void.

A similar methodology is an essential part of the predevelopment phase of a mobile health app project. If for the sake of discussion, one is trying to determine whether a new app to monitor asthma is warranted, questions about the "pathophysiology" of existing asthma mobile health apps have to be addressed, as well as a point-by-point analysis of each competing asthma app already on the market, whether they are being covered by third-party insurers, how clinicians view the accuracy and usability of the apps, what FDA regulations might apply to the new app, whether there is an international market for the app, and the relevant governmental regulations for each country. One of the criticisms we hear over and over again from physicians is that the medical apps reaching the market do not include their input at an early stage of development. One survey, for example, revealed that fewer than a third of 63 mobile apps intended to serve patients with colorectal diseases had been built with the help of medical professionals input on development and content [4].

The Stanford Byers Center for Biodesign has perfected a design process that utilizes the needs assessment approach described earlier by Paul Yock, MD. For example, the center has developed a mobile platform called IRhythm, which can be linked to a mobile device. Its purpose is to help diagnose suspected arrhythmias in patients who are not hospitalized. During the predevelopment stage of the process, the team took a closer look at how portable Holter monitors are used and discovered that these reusable devices required the patient to be attached to wires and skin electrodes for 24−48 hours. They also realized that this type of set-up prevented patients from using the device in the shower or while exercising. Other shortcomings included the fact that the patient had to return the Holter monitor to the hospital so that the physician could see the collected ECG data.

Once again, the emphasis was placed on intense observation. Those observations helped the design team realize that a new product should be a one-time disposable device and be available in the emergency department (ED) and in primary care settings. Their observations also made them aware of the patient's point of view: "They needed discretion, comfort, and most importantly to get a diagnosis the first time rather than having to make repeat trips to the hospital, which is what often happened with the Holter monitor" [5].

Additional insights gleaned from Stanford's needs assessment were summed up in an interview with Uday Kumar, MD, with the biodesign center:

*The third important realization was around what diagnostic information we needed and how to present it to different physician stakeholders. The data had to cover a diagnostic period of 1−2 weeks. For non-specialists, we needed to provide a clear top-line finding — whether the patient had an arrhythmia or not — that was immediately actionable in terms of referral to a specialist for treatment. But we also had to make sure more comprehensive data were available for heart specialists who needed to dig deeper to guide their treatment. Without that, specialists would often order repeat testing, which was time-consuming and costly.*

*Along these lines, the fourth insight was that it was imperative to make the entire solution cost-effective for payers. In this case, it meant not developing the highest tech solution possible. For example, wireless connectivity and real-time data transmission were starting to take-off when we were developing our solution. Had we incorporated these capabilities into our device, it would have been too expensive and too inaccessible for the majority of patients. Instead, we kept it simple so that the greatest number of patients possible could benefit from the solution.*

## UNDERSTAND THE REGULATORY ENVIRONMENT

The FDA has published extensive guidelines to help developers craft their app so that it does not conflict with government policies. The agency continues to refine its approach to mobile health apps, but currently it sees three broad categories to keep in mind during the design process. "Most mobile apps that are intended to treat, diagnose, cure, mitigate, or prevent disease or other conditions [are considered] as medical devices under federal statute" [6]. At the other end of the spectrum are wellness apps and those that receive, store, transmit, and offer more general health information; these apps are *not* considered medical devices by FDA. And lastly, there are those apps that fall in the middle, for which FDA says it will "exercise enforcement discretion."

The apps are not considered medical devices and therefore will not require FDA clearance include the following categories:

- Mobile apps that are intended to provide access to electronic "copies" (e.g., e-books, audio books) of medical textbooks or other reference materials with generic text search capabilities.
- Mobile apps that are intended for health-care providers to use as educational tools for medical training or to reinforce training previously received.
- Mobile apps that are intended for general patient education and facilitate patient access to commonly used reference information.
- Mobile apps that automate general office operations in a health-care setting and are not intended for use in the diagnosis of disease or other conditions, or in the cure, mitigation, treatment, or prevention of disease.
- Mobile apps that are generic aids or general purpose products. These apps are not considered devices because they are not intended for use in the diagnosis of disease or other conditions, or in the cure, mitigation, treatment, or prevention of disease [7].

The second group, for which the agency promises to use enforcement discretion because they do not pose a serious risk of harm to the public, includes the following:

- Mobile apps that help patients with diagnosed psychiatric conditions (e.g., posttraumatic stress disorder, depression, anxiety, obsessive compulsive disorder) maintain their behavioral coping skills by providing a "Skill of the Day" behavioral technique or audio messages that the user can access when experiencing increased anxiety;

- Mobile apps that provide periodic educational information, reminders, or motivational guidance to smokers trying to quit, patients recovering from addiction, or pregnant women;
- Mobile apps that use GPS location information to alert asthmatics of environmental conditions that may cause asthma symptoms or alert an addiction patient (substance abusers) when near a preidentified, high-risk location;
- Mobile apps that use video and video games to motivate patients to do their physical therapy exercises at home;
- Mobile apps that prompt a user to enter which herb and drug they would like to take concurrently and provide information about whether interactions have been seen in the literature and a summary of what type of interaction was reported;
- Mobile apps that help asthmatics track inhaler usage, asthma episodes experienced, location of user at the time of an attack, or environmental triggers of asthma attacks;
- Mobile apps that prompt the user to manually enter symptomatic, behavioral or environmental information, the specifics of which are predefined by a health-care provider, and store the information for later review;
- Mobile apps that use patient characteristics such as age, sex, and behavioral risk factors to provide patient-specific screening, counseling, and preventive recommendations from well-known and established authorities;
- Mobile apps that use a checklist of common signs and symptoms to provide a list of possible medical conditions and advice on when to consult a health-care provider;
- Mobile apps that guide a user through a questionnaire of signs and symptoms to provide a recommendation for the type of health-care facility most appropriate to their needs;
- Mobile apps that record the clinical conversation a clinician has with a patient and sends it (or a link) to the patient to access after the visit;
- Mobile apps that are intended to allow a user to initiate a prespecified nurse call or emergency call using broadband or cellular phone technology;
- Mobile apps that enable a patient or caregiver to create and send an alert or general emergency notification to first responders;
- Mobile apps that keep track of medications and provide user-configured reminders for improved medication adherence;
- Mobile apps that provide patients a portal into their own health information, such as access to information captured during a previous clinical visit or historical trending and comparison of vital signs (e.g., body temperature, heart rate, blood pressure, or respiratory rate);

- Mobile apps that aggregate and display trends in personal health incidents (e.g., hospitalization rates or alert notification rates);
- Mobile apps that allow a user to collect (electronically or manually entered) blood pressure data and share this data through e-mail, track and trend it, or upload it to a personal or electronic health record;
- Mobile apps that provide oral health reminders or tracking tools for users with gum disease;
- Mobile apps that provide prediabetes patients with guidance or tools to help them develop better eating habits or increase physical activity;
- Mobile apps that allow a user to collect, log, track, and trend data, such as blood glucose, blood pressure, heart rate, weight, or other data from a device to eventually share with a heath-care provider or upload it to an online (cloud) database, personal or electronic health record.

(This partial list does not include numerous other examples that the agency provides on its web site.)

FDA plans to focus most of its attention on mobile apps it considers medical devices. The subcategories include the following:

- Mobile apps that transform a mobile platform into a regulated medical device and therefore are mobile medical apps: These mobile apps use a mobile platform's built-in features such as light, vibrations, camera, or other similar sources to perform medical device functions (e.g., mobile medical apps that are used by a licensed practitioner to diagnose or treat a disease).
- Mobile apps that connect to an existing device type for purposes of controlling its operation, function, or energy source and therefore are mobile medical apps: These mobile apps are those that control the operation or function (e.g., changes settings) of an implantable or body worn medical device.
- Mobile apps that are used in active patient monitoring or analyzing patient-specific medical device data from a connected device and therefore are mobile medical apps.

## ALLEYE: LEARNING FROM FAILURE AND SUCCESS

A grasp of the regulatory environment needs to be coupled with a detailed needs assessment and imaginative thinking. But imagination and creativity cannot be based solely on gut instinct. Some entrepreneurs engage in a type of magical thinking that assumes "if you build it, they will come." Considering the amount of time, resources, and capital required to launch a successful mobile health app, that mindset courts disaster. The antidote for such speculative thinking is *empirically derived design principles*.

Kenny Lienhard and Christine Legner, members of the faculty of business and economics, Department of Information Systems in Lausanne, Switzerland, have developed a series of design principles based on such an empirical approach [4]. Lienhard and Legner set out to build a mobile app that helps elderly persons identify age-related macular degeneration and monitors the disease once it surfaces. The need for such an app is derived from the fact that most treatable age-related macular degeneration is detected too late to be optimally treated.

Creating such a sustainable medical app depends on trusting collaboration between technologists and clinicians, a partnership that too often does not exist. By way of example, fewer than a third of mobile apps that focus on patients with colorectal diseases enlisted medical professionals' advice on development and content, as we discussed earlier in this chapter. Similarly, an analysis of consumer-facing mobile apps designed to assess the risk of melanoma had a low sensitivity rating of 20%. (Sensitivity is a measure of the number of true positive test results, compared to false negative results.) To resolve this common disconnect between IT and clinical experts, Leinhard et al conducted a 30-month experiment that enlisted the help of an interdisciplinary team, and involved 2 clinical studies and 124 patients. The project generated four generic design principles that can be applied across other medical specialties.

The team did their due diligence by first performing a literature search to understand the gaps in this area, which revealed that there are many health apps available to the public that are not based on empirical evidence [8].

The research created more than 50 prototypes of the AllEye app. Patients' usability scores and oral feedback demonstrated that the app was well accepted. Using a well-documented metric called the System Usability Scale (SUS), the researchers continuously refined the app to eventually achieve a SUS of 85, well above the cut-off point of 68. They derived four design principles from their investigation, none of which will come as earth-shattering revelations. But critics who complain that these principles are too obvious miss the point. The study provided the much-needed evidence to demonstrate these principles are in fact worth applying and not just the musings of passionate entrepreneurs.

- "Mobile medical apps should consist of four functional components that guide a patient: instruction, setup, clinical measurement, and analysis and feedback.
- The user interface should be adapted to cope with patients' physical and cognitive restrictions.
- A mobile medical app should build on a robust medical knowledge base, ensuring an evidence-based approach to mobile app design.
- Mobile medical apps should facilitate both patients' and physicians' routines."

# REFERENCES

[1] Cerrato P, Halamka J. Realizing the promise of precision medicine. New York: Elsevier; 2018. Available from: https://www.elsevier.com/books/realizing-the-promise-of-precision-medicine/cerrato/978-0-12-811635-7.

[2] Deloitte Center for Health Solutions. The four dimensions of effective mHealth: people, places, payment, and purpose, <https://www2.deloitte.com/us/en/pages/life-sciences-and-health-care/articles/center-for-health-solutions-four-dimensions-effective-mhealth.html>; 2014.

[3] Yock P. Why do digital health startups keep failing? Fast Company October 17, 2018. <https://www.fastcompany.com/90251795/why-do-digital-health-startups-keep-failing>.

[4] Lienhard KR, Legner C. Principles in the design of mobile medical apps: guidance for those who care. In: Leimeister JM, Brenner W, Hrsg. Proceedings der 13. Internationalen Tagung Wirtschaftsinformatik (WI), St. Gallen, S.; 2017. p. 1066—80.

[5] Stanford Byers Center for Biodesign. Technologies: they needed discretion, comfort, and most importantly to get a diagnosis the first time rather than having to make repeat trips to the hospital, which is what often happened with the Holter monitor, <http://biodesign.stanford.edu/our-impact/technologies/irhythm.html>; [accessed 06.11.18].

[6] Shuren J, Patel B, Gottlieb S. FDA regulation of mobile medical apps. JAMA 2018;320:337—8.

[7] FDA. Mobile medical applications: guidance for industry and food and drug administration staff, <https://www.fda.gov/downloads/MedicalDevices/DeviceRegulationandGuidance/GuidanceDocuments/UCM263366.pdf>; 2015 [accessed 07.11.18].

[8] Majeed-Ariss R, Baildam E, Campbell M, Chieng A, Fallon D, Hall A, et al. Apps and adolescents: a systematic review of adolescents' use of mobile phone and tablet apps that support personal management of their chronic or long-term physical conditions. J Med Internet Res. 2015;17:e287.

# INDEX

Made in the USA
Lexington, KY
06 December 2019